TWILIGHT OF HISTORY

TWILIGHT OF HISTORY

Shlomo Sand

Translated by David Fernbach

VERSO

London • New York

First published in English by Verso 2017
Translation © David Fernbach 2017
First published as *Crépuscule de l'histoire*
© Editions Flammarion 2015

1 3 5 7 9 10 8 6 4 2

Verso
UK: 6 Meard Street, London W1F 0EG
US: 20 Jay Street, Suite 1010, Brooklyn, NY 11201
versobooks.com

Verso is the imprint of New Left Books

ISBN-13: 978-1-78663-022-3
ISBN-13: 978-1-78663-025-4 (US EBK)
ISBN-13: 978-1-78663-024-7 (UK EBK)

British Library Cataloguing in Publication Data
A catalogue record for this book is available from the British Library

Library of Congress Cataloging-in-Publication Data
A catalog record for this book is available from the Library of Congress

Typeset in Adobe Garamond Pro by Hewer Text UK Ltd, Edinburgh
Printed in the UK by CPI Mackays

In memory of E. P. Thompson and Howard Zinn

Contents

Acknowledgements

My sincere thanks go to all those friends who helped me in various ways to write this book. Their encouragement and comments helped me overcome serious moments of uncertainty.

I owe a particular debt to my close friend Michel Bilis, who translated this book from Hebrew into French, without which it would have been less accessible: in the absence of his contribution, it is uncertain whether the book could have been published. Professor Israel Gershoni and Richard Desserme, by their advice and comments, also helped improve the formulation of its complicated meanderings, in both construction and presentation.

Hearty thanks also to Yael Averbuch, Yehonatan Alsheh, Yoseph Barnea, Alexander Eterman, Catherine and Michel Felix, Julien Lacassagne, Yuval Laor, Yardena Libovsky, Eliyho Metz, Anna Sergeyenkova and Assad Zoabi. Each of these in their own way unstintingly helped the completion of this project.

I am grateful to the whole team at Verso (especially to David Fernbach), whose energy and experience made the publication of this book possible in English.

The help given me by my wife Varda has been inestimable and my debt to her is considerable; she stimulated me and gave me the courage to face the complex problems that the book involved.

It goes without saying that those anomalies and mistakes unavoidably present are my sole responsibility, and that all collaborators are innocent.

Tel Aviv and Nice, 2015

PREFACE

Studying History to Free Ourselves from It

History is still a disguised theology. Similarly, the reverence that the uneducated display towards the caste of scholars is a legacy of the reverence that surrounded the clergy. What was formerly given to the Church is given today to Science, if to a lesser degree.
Friedrich Nietzsche, *On the Use and Abuse of History for Life* (1874)

History is the most dangerous product that the chemistry of the mind has developed. Its properties are well known. It makes people dream; it intoxicates them and generates false remembrances; exaggerates their responses; keeps open old wounds; torments them in their rest; leads them to deliriums of grandeur or persecution; and makes nations bitter, proud, intolerable and vain.
Paul Valéry, *Regards sur le monde actuel* (1931)

As a way of starting this book, I would like to share with its readers two episodes in my life that, though they may appear of slight importance, were decisive in the development of my relation to the historian's craft. The first of these, a lecture by Isaiah Berlin, goes back to my youth, at the very beginning of my university studies; the second, a meeting with François Furet, took place when I was already an accredited agent of the past.

Reading History 'Backwards'

In 1973, Isaiah Berlin, the great British historian of ideas, visited Israel. Surprisingly, he had chosen to give a lecture on the enigmatic French thinker Georges Sorel. I was then just starting to study history at the University of Tel Aviv. I already knew Berlin's famous essay on historical necessity, but Sorel was completely new to me. The Oxford professor made no mystery of the reason he had chosen to discuss the author of *Reflections on Violence*, who was almost unknown in Israel. The early 1970s had seen the peak of a wave of violent student demonstrations, greatly troubling this liberal philosopher who deemed it propitious to use an example from the past as an alarm signal. According to him, just as the theorist of revolutionary syndicalism in the early years of the century had gone on to express sympathy and support for fascist violence, so the young 'New Left' risked drifting in due course towards a dangerous right-wing radicalism.[1]

Being already at this point in my life a 'former leftist', certainly still young but already weary and disillusioned, I absolutely wanted to know what was this danger that was threatening me, and how I could guard myself against it. I immediately enrolled in a lecture course on the far right in Europe, and worked on an essay with the title 'Sorel: an Intellectual Father of Fascism'. Not having at this time the least knowledge of French, I resorted to translations, and especially the wealth of English commentaries devoted to the French theorist of violence. I had reason to be

---

1   Isaiah Berlin, 'Georges Sorel', in *Against the Current: Essays in the History of Ideas*, London: Hogarth Press, 1979, 296–332. I mentioned this episode in my book *The Words and the Land: Israeli Intellectuals and the Nationalist Myth*, Los Angeles: Semiotext(e) 2011, but it is so essential to my relationship with history that it seems necessary to repeat it here.

satisfied: not only did I get high marks, but I also assuaged my curiosity in relation to Sorel. And as an added bonus, I knew now that I would never become a fascist!

Not long after, in the mid-1970s, when I was preparing to register for a doctoral programme in Paris, the writings of Antonio Gramsci had begun appearing in French, and, ironically as it might seem, they were among the very first texts I read in the language of Voltaire and Rousseau. I soon came to realize that the thinker from Turin, a Marxist of great originality, had viewed Sorel as the most serious theorist of socialism since Marx. Moreover, it appeared that Gramsci was not the only Italian intellectual to draw from this Frenchman philosophical arguments with which to oppose fascism. I found myself in great confusion and, on the advice of my supervisor, the late Georges Haupt, decided to study more closely this controversial and embarrassing figure from the early twentieth century.

I then rapidly discovered that, despite all his avatars (Sorel was a conservative in the 1880s, a Marxist and a *dreyfusard* in the 1890s, and a revolutionary syndicalist at the start of the new century; he flirted vaguely with the far right around 1910, but took an anti-nationalist stand in the First World War and championed the Bolshevik Revolution in 1917), Sorel's turbulent political thought did not contain an ounce of fascism, and his theoretical violence was more than naive compared with that of many of his followers, both left and right, or even his later detractors.[2]

The fact that Italian fascist intellectuals sought ideological legitimation in his writings is certainly not completely anodyne.

---

2   I could cite, for example, Jean-Paul Sartre's 1961 preface to Frantz Fanon, *The Wretched of the Earth*, New York: Grove Press, 1966, where he refers to 'Sorel's fascist utterances' (12–13). This text, quite aside from Sartre's irresponsible relation to violence and terror, also reveals his ignorance of French intellectual history. As we know, the existentialist philosopher preferred fashionable cafés to dusty libraries. If he was saved by his genius, this was not the case for the majority of his spiritual heirs. Raymond Aron ('Mon petit camarade', *L'Express*, 19 April 1980) wrote of this preface that 'it could figure in an anthology of fascist literature'.

Sorel's presence in Italian culture before the First World War much resembles the status of Michel Foucault in American culture in the 1970s. The Italians found in Sorel sufficient popular and enigmatic formulations to support their political shifts and contortions in the service of the fascist state. But this did not prevent a prestigious liberal anti-fascist, such as Piero Gobetti, being at the same time also a devoted follower of the unclassifiable French thinker.[3] For the first time, then, I learned to read intellectual history in reverse, rather than following the progression of time; in other words, not from Rousseau to Robespierre, from Marx to Lenin, from Sorel to Mussolini, but on the contrary from Robespierre to Rousseau, from Lenin to Marx, from Mussolini to Sorel, and from Zionism to the Bible.[4] I also learned that the word 'influence' explains nothing, either as noun or as verb. New and original meanings always have to be stubbornly teased out and conferred.

In the early 1990s, now a history teacher at the University of Tel Aviv, I returned to Paris for a sabbatical term. Jacques Julliard, my former professor, invited me to meet François Furet, ex-president of the École des hautes études en sciences sociales (EHESS), who was preparing a major book on Communism in the twentieth century, for which purpose he needed certain texts by and on Sorel. I was very happy at the idea of a meeting with the famous historian, who in the 1980s had helped me obtain my first temporary post as a history teacher at the EHESS.

In the course of the meeting, I attempted to explain to Furet that the problematic Sorel had not been a French proto-fascist, particularly on account of his permanent aversion to nationalism; he was horrified by populist leaders who inflamed crowds,

---

3   I refer to my article 'Legend, myth and fascism', *European Legacy* 5/3, 1998, 53–66.

4   I subsequently came across Marc Bloch's injunction to 'read history backwards' in connection with agrarian rather than intellectual history. See his *Les caractères originaux de l'histoire rurale française* [1931], Paris: Armand Colin, 1964, vol. 1, xii.

and did not end his life as a champion of Mussolini. I added that Sorel's 'historical materialism' was not genuinely Marxist, but closer in a certain sense to the anti-Jacobin positions expressed by Furet himself in his stimulating book *Interpreting the French Revolution*. I also remember having emphasized that beneath his revolutionary mantle Sorel remained more of a liberal or even conservative thinker, constantly caught in his own contradictions, who, however, despite everything, managed to surpass many of his contemporaries in his analyses of the presence of myths and the political imaginary.

At the end of our discussion, I spelled out again that the anti-Semitic remarks that figure in some of Sorel's later writings, however unpleasant and particularly stupid they might be, in no way formed part of his world view, which was actually anti-racist; he had indeed supported Dreyfus.[5] I do not remember precisely today either the questions that François Furet asked or the details of my own answers. The conversation continued cordially, and at his request I provided him with a short bibliography of those texts by Sorel that, in my humble opinion, deserved to be read, as well as some interesting studies of his thought.

Imagine my amazement, then, when Furet's book *The Passing of an Illusion* appeared![6] Out of all the material I had recommended to him and provided him with, Furet had chosen to quote only one marginal right-wing journalist, a certain Jean Variot, who happened to have served as media spokesman for the versatile Sorel in his conservative period of the 1910s.[7] In a ridiculous text, published ten years after Sorel's death, Variot, a failed pro-fascist writer, claimed to 'restore' word for word the conversations he had had with the thinker, even in the street, in which

---

5   See my article 'Sorel, les juifs et l'antisémitisme', *Cahiers Georges Sorel* 2/2, 1984, 7–36.

6   François Furet, *The Passing of an Illusion: The Idea of Communism in the Twentieth Century*, Chicago: The University of Chicago Press, 1999.

7   Ibid., 520.

the latter supposedly expressed his admiration for Mussolini.[8] Nowhere else can the least confirmation of this witness be found – quite the contrary. In precisely the same period, Sorel expressed in his correspondence his aversion for the conduct of this nationalist and demagogue during the war, and he lambasted the fascist movement and its partisans. This was at the same time, moreover, that another of his correspondents, the moderate liberal philosopher Benedetto Croce, expressed his disagreement with Sorel and initially supported Mussolini's seizure of power, as did many other Italian liberals of his generation.

In the 1950s, the period of the Cold War, various 'anti-totalitarian' theorists already stigmatized Sorel as a logical link between the two revolutionary movements of the twentieth century, Communism and fascism. This current of ideas made a copious and effective effort to equate two movements (and even three, as this misguided demonstration included Nazism as well), which, despite some resemblances at the political level, were radically different in ideological and socioeconomic terms.

Forty years later, when anti-totalitarianism had become the fashion in Paris (at a time when totalitarianism had already long been on the wane in the Soviet Union),[9] Furet, for the needs of the cause, instrumentalized Sorel as a 'supporter of Mussolini', with the declared aim of bringing to light the roots of the twentieth century's revolutionary passion. It was logical, from his point of view, to link Communism and fascism in the same

---

8   Jean Variot, *Propos de Georges Sorel*, Paris: Gallimard, 1935. This journalist 'forgot' to include in his book a 'prophetic' pearl apparently dating from before the war: an enthusiastic Sorel foresaw a brilliant future for Mussolini, then a radical anti-war socialist. This 'conversation' appeared in his obituary 'Le père Sorel', *L'Éclair*, 11 September 1922. Sorel, now dead, was unable to react to this stupidity, and recall the disgust that political 'revolutionaries' such as Benito Mussolini, or his French counterpart Gustave Hervé, had aroused in him.

9   Serious analysts of totalitarianism of the 1950s in the English-speaking world, such as Zbigniew Brzezinski, for example, by the 1970s had abandoned their theoretical warnings about totalitarianism in the USSR, at the very moment when fashionable French intellectuals were suddenly discovering the totalitarian danger.

chapter of his book, not to mention Nazism. This meant a new recourse to Sorel, since, according to Furet, 'there is a mystery of evil in the dynamic of twentieth-century political ideas'.[10] In order to clarify and authenticate the existence of this 'mystery', it was necessary to infringe a basic rule which any first-year student of history learns to respect: not to base oneself on secondhand evidence when this is unambiguously contradicted by the direct original sources. Is not the modern method of historical research entirely founded on this basic distinction?

Aside from the great interest they shared in intellectual history, and their common liberal sensibility, there were profound differences between Isaiah Berlin and François Furet in their style and strategy of representing the past. Thus, although Berlin attacked Sorel for overtly political reasons, he took the time to study him and, in writing his essay, perceived a certain discrepancy between his initial ideological assumption and the political comparison he deduced from it, even though, at the time of writing his essay, he was unaware that Sorel had never expressed the least support for fascism (most of his critical references to Mussolini only came to light later). Furet, on the other hand, paid no great attention to Sorel and was content with a scanty secondhand literature; above all, however, and what seems to me more serious, is that at the time he was writing his book, the letters of the despised thinker had already been published almost in full.

Isaiah Berlin's critique of the vociferous leftism of the 1960s may well have been correct, although, contrary to his expectations, the phenomenon ended up not on the far right but, for many of those involved, in conservatism, in conformism and, above all, in political stupidity. Certain aspects of Furet's 'anti-totalitarian' doctrine deserve attention, even if, in my view, the

---

10   François Furet, 'La passion révolutionnaire au XXe siècle', in Alain Besançon et al., *Écrire l'histoire du XXe siècle: La politique et la raison*, Paris: EHESS/Gallimard/Seuil, 1994, 39.

explanation of Stalin's crimes should be sought more in an analysis of sociopolitical processes than in the destructive revolutionary passion of certain ideologies of the first half of the twentieth century.

It is time, perhaps, at this stage, to explain to the reader my own political sensibility – knowing that this has contributed to defining my way of writing history, and continues to inspire it still today. As a man of the left, I would have 'preferred' in the 1930s, and the early 1940s, to live in Fascist Italy rather than in the Soviet Union. This is for the quite prosaic reason that my chances of survival would have been greater under the Italian regime. But as the descendant of persecuted Jews, if I had retroactively to choose a place of refuge, this would have been the USSR under Stalin rather than 'Aryan' Nazi Germany or the *État français* of Vichy. This was precisely the choice that my parents made, under force of circumstances, but it enabled them to remain alive in contrast to their own parents, or again to other relatives who had emigrated to France before the war. It is also to this choice that I owe my own birth.

The French Gallo-Catholics of the early 1940s – from Philippe Pétain, Pierre Laval and Charles Maurras to René Bousquet and Paul Touvier – lacked any revolutionary passion; they too felt a strong aversion to Maximilien Robespierre, and they were not really 'totalitarian'. This, however, did not prevent them from extending their support to a work of 'evil' specific of its kind.[11] On the other hand, those who sacrificed themselves in the struggle against the Vichy regime were inspired, among other things, by a nonconformist revolutionary ideology, which is why the young Furet, like many others, joined them at the end of the war. In the last analysis, the great political crimes of modern times

---

11   The 'fascist revolutionaries' were marginal at Vichy, mere caricatures without any real power. It is impossible to carry out a 'national revolution' in a country whose capital is occupied by a foreign army. We may add the case of the Francoists in Spain, who were also conservatives without any desire to change the world. They massacred a far greater number of opponents than did the Italian Fascists.

(colonialism, fascism, Nazism, Stalinism and Maoism) were committed by conservatives greedy for power and by typical conformists, just as much as by radicals suffering from messianic folly.[12] The cunning of a modern and deadly reason 'made use' of them indifferently.

Using the Rearview Mirror

Let me return, however, to the above two encounters, with Isaiah Berlin and François Furet. I learned more from these on the ideological excesses that sometimes affect techniques of transcribing the past than I did from any university course. The doubts about historical constructions that had vexed me throughout my studies were directly and strongly corroborated by two eminent scholars, whose writings had always aroused my curiosity even when I felt in disagreement with them. Certainly, not all historians assert their arguments in so cut-and-dried a way; they generally resort to a more considered style when it comes to producing 'proofs', but the heavy shadow of ideology filters through every window opened on the past. This often appears as a formless and silent magma, which requires an interpreter, necessarily subjective, to make it speak. On the one hand, professional historians in the modern world produce their work in the context of state or private institutions on which they depend, while on the other hand, the writing of history always carries with it an autobiographical dimension that is not just negligible.

We all know that the choice of research project follows from a conception of the world, as well as from political tastes draped in aesthetic preferences and with an anchorage well beyond mere intellectual curiosity. Ideological motivations or affinities become

12   Did the young Furet join the French Communist Party and remain in it for ten years out of revolutionary passion or political conformism? Perhaps for both reasons. I believe this last possibility offers a key to understanding the attraction of Stalinism for elite intellectuals, and subsequently of ultra-leftism.

perceptible sometimes on the margins of historical writing, sometimes at the heart of the subject treated.

For my own part, I turned to the study of history out of a keen interest in Marx. I then chose to devote my doctoral thesis to Georges Sorel, as I wanted to analyse the characteristics of Marxism and particularly the beginnings of its theoretical crises. Other people turn to the 'Middle Ages' because of interest in the origins of their culture, to territorially distant spaces to satisfy a need for exoticism, or to 'Antiquity' after seeing an entertaining film about this era – even perhaps to escape a depressing present. There are thus countless motivations, 'great' and 'small', that influence the character of the future historian. The extent of past time offers a boundless choice of possible subjects; and despite the shocks of scepticism in the discipline of history today, some are still trying to reinvent the wheel of time, believing it each time more 'truthful'.

Do ideologies and political sensibilities have an impact on the elaboration of the past and our shaping of it? Is it possible to leave them aside, or at least to minimize them? Have they not constituted the essential motor of historical research and writing, as well as the financing of its teaching, throughout the last two centuries and throughout the world?

Must we admit the impossibility, present and future, of a morally neutral history, in other words, a 'scientific history'? Or is there rather a definite political ethic at the root of the discipline that deals with human time, and throughout its development? Has not the greater part of historical writing for a long while held the place of a modern theology designed to maintain and transmit national foundation myths, whether consciously or not?

Responses to these questions cannot be uniform, still less peremptory. They deserve to be re-examined, and they only can be if they are placed in their historical context – on the understanding that knowledge of this context is not sufficient to resolve the set of problems. Besides, the concept of 'political', which has undergone many transformations since its use by Aristotle, must also be the object of a renewed historicization.

A few years ago I was struck by a chance remark of Pierre Bourdieu, made in a radio interview and subsequently published: 'The paradox is that historians, for example . . . often show an extraordinary naivety in their use of categories . . . It is the very categories with which the historic object is constructed that should be the object of a historical analysis.'[13] My initial spontaneous response was to reject this point of view, which I saw as sarcastic. I was annoyed by the fact that the famous sociologist did not apply the reproach of 'naivety' above all to his own colleagues, but later on I reached the conclusion that he was basically correct. One of the characteristic weaknesses of historians is their inability to think through the categories that they think with. A similar lacuna is also found in other fields of study, but it is almost intrinsic to the discursive practices of the discipline of history: the elaboration of coherent narratives, which extend over time and are steeped in so many waters, must draw on solid and convincing concepts. Epistemological perplexity and scepticism may appear as a fatal danger, and this is precisely what has happened in recent years to the world's oldest 'profession'.

Negligence and lack of rigour on the part of historiography are not limited to minor terms. Such key concepts as 'Antiquity', 'Middle Ages', 'peoples', 'nations', 'revolutions', 'crises', 'classes', 'democracy', 'liberalism' and even 'state' assume different and even contradictory meanings in various texts.

Historians did not invent these concepts. They generally extract them from documents of the period being studied, or one immediately after it, and subsequently apply them to the analysis of processes and situations pertaining to other times and places without paying attention to the anachronisms involved. And, if

---

13   Pierre Bourdieu and Roger Chartier, *The Sociologist and the Historian*, Cambridge: Polity, 2015, 11.

they should invent a new concept, something that pertains to the specific domain of philosophy, this is a response to ideological motives or clearly political needs. Just as often, and uncritically, 'sources' take the place of 'proofs', and many are thus convinced that what they retrace with the aid of their 'scientific' terminology actually corresponds to a past reality that was impatiently waiting to be pieced together with precision by the historian.[14]

The ambition of the present book is to serve as a provisional summary of my relationship with history over more than forty years. It consists in a sense of working notebooks, its four chapters relating four decisive encounters, each a key moment in my relationship with the discipline at different stages in my life. This means that the narrative does not correspond chronologically to the customary linear historical time. There is certainly a beginning, a middle and an end, but, as Jean-Luc Godard once suggested, they need not always appear in this order. The 'action' unfolds and is pieced together according to an axis of personal biography established as a function of successive significant times. The 'I' that appears in this text deliberately breaks with the marks of pretentious objectivism that are still found in the majority of works of 'scientific' history.

The first 'encounter' took place at the University of Tel Aviv, while I was still a student. Despite my great enthusiasm for research into the past, my first uncertainties appeared concerning the relationships between space and time, and between East and West. The second encounter happened within the walls of the EHESS, where I experienced a long (too long?) fascination with cultural history, before finding the strength to challenge its assumptions and implications. The third important time was

---

14   On the inconsistent use of the term 'fascism', for example, see my article 'L'idéologie fasciste en France', *Esprit* 80–81, 1983, 149–60. *Geschichtliche Grundbegriffe*, the titanic work of Reinhart Koselleck and his colleagues, has unfortunately not been taken as a guide for historical writing, and his conclusions have had no resonance in the empirical writings of historians. See also Reinhart Koselleck, *Le futur passé: Contribution à la sémantique des temps historiques*, Paris: Éditions de l'EHESS, 1990.

after my return to Tel Aviv as a qualified professional: this was
the moment of my first critical reflections on the place of history
as a 'science' and its national-political use since its establishment
in the nineteenth century. The fourth and last encounter tackles
the significance of the turns that the discipline has undergone in
the present period, and questions the loss of confidence in the
power of words to represent 'things'. I openly express here the
growing sense of unease that I feel towards the profession.[15]

Each of these stages was somewhat like a step on a staircase,
where I did not always know which direction I was taking – up or
down; advance or regression in my professional competence. The
trajectory I have undergone, from the materialist certainty of my
beginnings to my present doubtful relativism, actually constitutes a
long journey of perplexity and uncertainty. Knowledge is supposed
to make you more wise, but generally it also makes you age, by
breaking your illusions, inviting you to conform to realities as they
are, and blunting the critical spirit – all the more so if the profession
you practise has also served as a social and cultural escalator.

Conscious of this situation, I have sought not to resemble *les
bourgeois* of Jacques Brel's song (or the 'mandarins' of the university), those young people who mock the bourgeoisie before
comfortably establishing themselves in their place at a more mature
age. The young often have their eyes misted by enthusiasm and
lack of experience, but the view of maturity is disturbed by the
effect of the laurel crowns awarded, or else by tiredness and defeat.

I have the sense today of inhabiting a sociocultural world that
is fragile in terms of values, fundamentally different from that I
was born into and grew up in. The fact that the world is changing certainly strikes me as quite 'natural'. The fact that the
changes are not taking the direction I would have liked to see
certainly disappoints me, but remains logical in my eyes. Does

15   I recognize that the main weakness of this book lies in the fact that it deals
only with debates on Western history, the sole field with which I can claim a little
familiarity. I hope in future to expand this compass for purposes of comparison.

this world have sufficient strength to prevent new catastrophes? I am not at all sure, and this is precisely the problem. I have long since abandoned belief in an ineluctable historical progress; yet uncertainty about the quality of the world we are leaving behind us has pressed me to look into the future with growing perplexity. It has also led me to view the past with far less certainty.

I sometimes have the impression of riding in a vehicle without brakes that is running faster and faster; the windscreen is covered with a layer of dust that completely obstructs my vision. The wiper blades have long since been stolen – by Stalin, Mao, Castro and others. Among the disappointed of my generation, many think that we can continue to drive by looking in the rearview mirror: devotion to collective memory, memory of family, religion, 'ethnicity' or nation, has gained popularity in the last two decades. But to drive in this way, I am persuaded, means heading straight for catastrophe. I still believe that we have to invent a new type of windscreen wiper; or rather, as a student said to me one day, break the windscreen and go forward into the fresh air with our eyes wide open. The rearview mirror, history or memory, is only a secondary tool, and entirely dependent on the gaze we project ahead, into the future. To continue to drive, we have to break this dependence on rearview mirrors, or in other words study history above all to learn how to free ourselves from it.

I hope that the accounts of the past I have presented to my students have occasionally been of interest. I am certain that some of them have found them boring, but the most difficult thing, as I see it, is to know how far they have been true. The reduction of future perspectives seems to project dark and extending shadows over an unstable and evanescent past, and it increasingly appears that we have never managed to decipher them adequately.

N.B.

When students in medicine finish their course and obtain their doctorate, they are made to take the Hippocratic oath. Historians

diverge as to whether the Greek physician of the fourth century
BCE really was its author; it is possible that the famous oath had a
different origin. But this matters little: this oath made the tour of
the Mediterranean and passed into Islamic medical culture, eventually reaching Renaissance Europe. What is important for us,
here and now, is to remember today the first commitment sworn
in this oath: 'First, do no harm.'

History department graduates are not held to swear an oath
of any kind. Theirs is a 'neutral science' that deals with the
dead, not a medicine with the vocation to save lives, and so
there is no need to make any ethical commitment. If bad practice of medicine can kill, it is agreed that a mistaken or deceptive treatment of history apparently injures no one. Yet Eric
Hobsbawm, in the preface to one of his last books, could write,
'I used to think that the profession of history, unlike that of,
say, nuclear physics, could at least do no harm. Now I know it
can. Our studies can turn into bomb factories like the work-
shops in which the IRA has learned to transform chemical
fertilizer into an explosive.'[16]

I only recently came to understand the truth contained in this
eminent historian's assertion. I grew up in a culture where the
Bible was taught as the first history book, rather than a theological legend. We all know how important the first stories we learn
are in forming our consciousness of the past, imprinting striking
memories for the rest of our life. As seven-year-old school pupils,
we already knew for certain that we were the descendants of King
David's warriors, if not of the king himself.[17] As adults, we enthusiastically went off to fight for our 'ancient land', without

---

16   Eric Hobsbawm, *On History*, London: Abacus, 1997, 7.

17   There was a (brief) moment as a child when this idea pleased me. And why
not? The New Testament saw Jesus Christ, despite his virgin birth, as the linear
descendant of David. Similarly, in Jewish tradition, Rabbi Juda HaNassi (the Prince),
who started the compilation of the Mishna, was seen as the legitimate scion of the
red-haired king. All Zionism did was cleverly translate theology into a national
'mythistory'.

questioning for a moment the long 'history' that legitimized the pursuit of our advance in this space. Those of us who survived raised new generations who still study the Bible as a historical account through to school-leaving age, and continue to believe themselves the descendants of ancient Hebrews settled between Jericho and Hebron, Bethlehem and Jerusalem. The students who reach university after their military service still carry with them this mythological baggage, which the humanities and social-science faculties do not deem it useful to unburden them of. In the best of cases they pay no attention to it, but more often they support and validate it as a sure starting point for any debate and reflection on the national past.

I draw attention to this pedagogic legacy, which I will mention from time to time later in this book (in the 'N.B.'s that end each chapter), given the privilege I have had of working as a historian in Israel. Knowledge of European history, French in particular, helped me a great deal, but it seems to me above all that the fact of living in an atmosphere where, as distinct from other contemporary Western cultures, national history is still a living mythology, has brought me a more than negligible advantage. The situation of research into historical time in Israeli universities is similar in many respects to that prevalent a century or more ago in France, England, Germany, Italy or the United States.

When you find yourself so close to Jerusalem, the 'eternal city', or to Hebron, the 'city of the patriarchs', it is easier to understand and examine with a critical gaze the past of Western historiography, and particularly the inherent connection that has almost always existed between 'scientificity' and nationalism. In the place where I live, a space of continuing colonization that has needed historical justification from its very beginning, the construction of the nation and the fixing of the borders of the 'homeland' are still not decided. Thus the fire is still warm that fuels the past, ancient as well as modern, transforming it into a patriotic narrative, inflaming minds and warming hearths.

I wrote my previous books in order to secularize somewhat the gaze of national mythology on this land where I have spent the greater part of my life, and which is very dear to me. I have written the present one in order to secularize myself, to unburden myself of my last professional illusions.

CHAPTER I

Undoing the Myth of Origins

The history of Greece and Rome is already our own history, since the origins of the modern mind and modern politics are already present there.

Ernest Lavisse, 'Enseignement secondaire: instructions, programmes et règlements', 1890

Historical time is a relatively recent and highly artificial invention of Western civilization. It is a cultural, not a philosophical notion . . . Narrativism can explain time and it is not explained by it.

F. R. Ankersmit, 'Six Theses on Narrativist Philosophy of History', in G. Roberts (ed.), *The History and Narrative Reader*

In the early 1970s, I enrolled at the department of general history of the University of Tel Aviv. It did not take me long to realize that, despite its 'general' claim, this department, far from dealing with world history, had taken study of Europe and the West as its exclusive context. Asia and Africa were not viewed as integral parts of general history, and there was no department specifically dedicated to the historical study of these continents.[1] Indeed, my own perception of time was outrageously Eurocentric at this time, and so it was hardly surprising that those around me should also see this as self-evident. Despite the fact that decolonization was now almost complete, the non-Western world was still perceived as lacking a genuine history.

At the start of my studies, I had to enrol for general lecture courses divided according to the familiar canonical division: 'Antiquity', 'Middle Ages', 'Modern times' and 'Contemporary history'. In piecing together the past, as we know, time plays the principal role. It has its own logic and direction; there is what happens before and what happens after. Later, I learned that it is also necessary to distinguish economic, political and cultural time, which each follow a particular rhythm. First of all, however, I learned that time had to be decomposed piece by piece and stratum by stratum in order to render it comprehensible and meaningful. I remember having long been amused by the fact that the counting of years and centuries in Western time (the Gregorian calendar) starts from the date of circumcision of an individual born from an encounter between a virgin and the Holy Spirit. Nor did the systems of Jewish or Muslim dating strike me as particularly encouraging. The Jewish counting of years begins precisely with the creation of the world (one year before the birth of the first man), or 5,773 years before the writing of the present book. The Islamic calendar, though slightly more 'rational', is no less arbitrary than its two predecessors: the starting point of its chronology is set by the date of the Hegira, the moment when Muhammad and his followers fled from Medina to Mecca, in 622 of the Christian era.[2]

---

1   The exception being a distinct department for teaching the history of the Middle East, founded in close collaboration with the intelligence services of the 'Tsahal' (Israeli Defence Forces).

2   It is interesting to note that the term used in Arabic to define history, *taariakh*, appears in modern Hebrew in the form of *taarikh* (date).

For a while, I preferred Chinese dating with its animal names to any of these three calendars: the Year of the Pig, the Year of the Dragon, the Year of the Dog and so on. But I did not learn to use this calendar myself, and had to submit to the prevailing partition of time – while being aware that in such a chronology dates are like empty shelves in a cupboard.[3] The Christian dating, embarrassing or even ridiculous ('before Jesus Christ', 'after Jesus Christ') did not prevent me from joyfully attacking the mysteries of long duration, even while new questions arose with the appearance of each response.

The Marxist background that I had accumulated before becoming a student – thanks in particular to the reading of Frederick Engels and Karl Kautsky, far more than of Karl Marx – helped me greatly in absorbing and digesting the teaching of my professors, some of whom were Marxists, others specialists in social questions, and others again political historians in the style of the English-speaking world. This background even helped at the time to legitimize in my eyes the fact of tackling history on the basis of these standardized concepts: 'Antiquity', 'Middle Ages' and 'Modern times'. Was not history in the view of Marx and Marxism a dialectical linkage in time of successive modes of production? The economy of the ancient world was based on slavery; the contradictions of this mode of production generated the feudal system based on serfdom and farm leases. The development of the productive forces brought about the crumbling of these relations of production, the rise of capitalism and then industrialism. This last mode of production, based on the exploitation of wage labour, necessarily fuels a class struggle that prepares the advent of a classless socialist society. The foundation of

---

3   Claude Lévi-Strauss, however, was not wrong in maintaining that 'Dates may not be the whole of history, nor what is most interesting about it, but they are its *sine qua non*, for history's entire originality and distinctive nature lie in apprehending the relation between *before* and *after*'; original emphasis. *The Savage Mind*, Chicago: University of Chicago Press, 1966, 258.

this conception of time was progress, the justification of which, by teaching and research, formed the object of the discipline of history.

The Marxist teleology considerably stimulated both my approach to sociopolitical struggles and my undying love of history, but it also anchored in me the idea of a linear, rigid and self-evident time, which it was out of the question to challenge. Academic historiography only supported this fundamental approach, if sometimes in a less determinist form than with Marxism. 'Antiquity' necessarily preceded the 'Middle Ages', themselves prior to the modern and contemporary eras. Thus history appeared to me as a rather undynamic archaeology, made up of different geological layers piled one upon the other up to the surface, the outer layer of which is our present time, without our having any real understanding of how the transition from one layer to another has taken place. To take another image, history could be compared with a process of biological evolution: human society develops along an axis of linear advance through to the greatest complexity, which precisely corresponds to the historian's own epoch.

This global classification certainly offered a palette of nuances. Some professors, just like some texts, painted the 'Middle Ages' as less gloomy and regressive than others; the boundaries of this historical period, moreover, were poorly defined and gave rise to legitimate controversies. Sadly, neither my professors nor the history books I read at the time cast doubt on the meaning of the axis of time or the decisive changes that it brought. Everyone agreed that history, on its march from 'Antiquity', had crossed a long intermediate period called the 'Middle Ages' and refreshed itself in the 'Renaissance', before expanding in the age of 'Enlightenment' to reach at the end of a brilliant career the modern Western era, ourselves, the 'elect'. This linear paradigm was, of course, completely pervaded by the arrogant superiority of modernity towards everything that preceded it, necessarily inferior and backward.

Is Europe a Continent?

Hidden behind the linear conception of time is the representation of a space endowed with a similarly long duration. Historical narrative, sure of itself, draws on the legacy of geographical terminology. The continent of 'Europe' has effectively provided the arena where the forward march of history has taken place. The fact that this 'Europe' does not actually coincide with a continent (the Urals are not an ocean) has in no way damaged the consensus and its customary rhetoric: Athens, Sparta and Rome were part of Europe in the past, just as Paris, Berlin and London belong to it today. Antiquity thus began on the chosen continent, with its Indo-European roots and a history that has unfurled for more than three thousand years, if not without a few somersaults.

It is a consummate irony that the term 'Europe' originated precisely in Semitic languages. For the Phoenicians it meant the land where the sun went down; it was thus originally a specific geographical concept for mariners. In later Greek dialects, 'Europe' suggested the combination of words 'wide face'. In Greek mythology, Europa was the daughter (or possibly granddaughter) of Agenor, king of Tyre. Passionately captivated by her, Zeus took on the appearance of a bull, so that with his usual divine cunning he could kidnap her and take her off to the island of Crete. The myth thus indicates the 'Asiatic' origin of Europe, or at least of its cultural 'roots', even if for a long time this was not a matter of concern for anyone.

Herodotus, in his time, explained that the world was divided into three continents: Asia, Europe, and Libya or Africa. This did not mean, however, that there was any correspondence between the name of a continent and the collective identity of its population. We should not forget that Troy, one of the major pillars of Hellenic identity, was situated on the eastern shore of the Dardanelles, and it seems that the *Iliad* was written either in Anatolia or on one of its coastal islands. Originally, the Greeks used the term 'European' to denote the inhabitants of the western part of Asia Minor, mainly those of the Aegean islands. Gradually the term was applied to the inhabitants of central Greece, and especially to those of its northern regions.

The struggle against the Persian Empire, it should be emphasized, was waged by proud Hellenes, not by Europeans; in other words, it was bearers of Greek culture with their different dialects, and not denizens of another continent, who struggled against the 'barbarian' invaders.[4] Although a few isolated expressions seem to have appeared with the arrival of Islam in the Mediterranean, it was only much later, at the beginning of the Renaissance, that 'Europe' became more distinctly a geopolitical receptacle culturally opposed to Asia and Africa. As everyone knows, this word would go on to have a formidable destiny, which would involve, among other things, the creation of a false consciousness of time among 'Europeans'.

My first doubts concerning the traditional order of historical time arose precisely Apropos the geographical problematic. The attempts of Marxists and their allies to explain the birth of feudal society from the contradictions and disintegration of ancient slave society led me into deep uncertainty.[5] Why did new relations of production slowly form on the distant territorial margins of the Roman Empire, and not at its developed centre? Why was it not Athens and Rome, and their immediate periphery, that became the field of action of the new dominant class, as was indeed the case with London, Paris and Berlin when they transformed themselves from 'feudal' cities into centres of capitalism? Why did a world marked by agrarian societies of an unprecedented kind emerge

---

4   See on this subject Gerard Delanty, *Inventing Europe: Idea, Identity, Reality*, New York: St Martin's Press, 1995, 18–19.

5   Perry Anderson, in *Passages from Antiquity to Feudalism*, London: New Left Books, 1974, was the last major Marxist historian to attempt, with panache but, in my view, without any greater success (essentially using the concept of 'synthesis'), an explanation of 'European history' as a linear succession.

precisely in the leafy forests of northern Europe? Was Greek civilization, including the shores of Asia Minor and Crete, the real 'Antiquity' of Europe? Did it prefigure the dawn of the future West, as the majority of historians never cease to maintain? It took me a long road and many years to bring my questioning into a bit of order, and formulate hypotheses that I found more satisfying.

In the early 1970s, theories of alienation, inspired in part by the writings of the young Marx but also by the essays of Herbert Marcuse, enjoyed widespread currency in left-wing circles, in Israel as well as in Europe. In parallel with the birth on both sides of the Atlantic of a cultural history that would go on to prosper as the Western world moved into a post-industrial phase (in which production was increasingly conducted by way of signs and symbols), 'alienated man' found himself placed at the centre of attention for critical left intellectuals.

I did not have this good fortune: one of my most talented professors – Igal Wagner, a subtle scholar who kept away from beaten tracks – clung firmly to the Marxian *homo faber* despite fashionable ideas to the contrary. He regularly reminded us of the 'beginning', in other words the transition from biological evolution to cultural evolution. Human beings, like any living creatures, necessarily have to satisfy their primary needs, to eat and drink. As Marx and Engels wrote, 'The first historical act is thus the production of the means to satisfy these needs . . . the satisfaction of the first need, the action of satisfying and the instrument of satisfaction which has been acquired, leads to new needs.'[6]

Igal Wagner always added to this that, contrary to what one might think, the difference between the first humans and other animals did not lie in work (look at the ants), nor in the use of tools (for example, certain apes), but precisely in the ability to

---

6   Karl Marx and Friedrich Engels, *The German Ideology*, in *Marx Engels Collected Works*, vol. 5, London: Lawrence and Wishart, 1976, 42.

make tools, or, as Henri Bergson nicely spelled out, 'tools to make tools'.[7]

Humans, without our knowing why they opted for a different trajectory from other living beings, sketched out tools in their minds and, by the light of these images formed in their consciousness, fashioned them by accomplishing a series of physical actions. This particular and original praxis of mediation between humans and nature generated *Homo sapiens*, in a lapse of time that was short on the cosmic scale but rapid in the direct and continuous line from the African stone axe to the Swiss particle accelerator – albeit that human emotions did not immediately adapt to the rapid rhythm of technological change.

This initial intellectual and material revolution subsequently formed part of another remarkable cultural achievement. All evidence suggests that spoken language appeared right from the start as a social phenomenon, and yet (an assertion that seems purely hypothetical) the transmission to successive generations of knowledge of innovations in production could not in the course of time remain confined to mere gestures of imitation, or expressions of warning, panic or affection as are found among other animals. The transmission of experience and technical know-how aiming to reproduce and perfect tools needed, particularly between generations, a type of social communication that was still more sophisticated: language, originally just the expression of emotions or the direct designation of objects and events, grew more abstract and arbitrary until it became clearly symbolic.

---

7   Bergson maintains in his major work, 'If we could rid ourselves of all pride, if, to define our species, we kept strictly to what the historic and the prehistoric periods show us to be the constant characteristic of man and of intelligence, we should say not *Homo sapiens*, but *Homo faber*. In short, intelligence, considered in what seems to be its original feature, is the faculty of manufacturing artificial objects, especially tools to make tools, and of indefinitely varying the manufacture' (Henri Bergson, *Creative Evolution* [1907], Mineola, NY: Dover, 1998, 139).

It is well known how this phenomenon is quite specific to the human species. In these phases of evolution, the precious knowledge born from experience began to be stored not only in the genes or the human body but 'outside' the individual, in a collective social memory of which symbolic language was one of the very first vectors. Any collective intervention, and any knowledge of nature, was from now on mediated by words: from the first nouns through to abstract terms.

My favourite professor, Igal Wagner, set himself the task of examining the beginnings of societies and civilizations, especially their reactions and modes of collective organization in response to the challenges of their environment; he always focused on deciphering the perfecting of forms of human labour on the basis of the needs of human collectivities, given the territorial space in which these intervene. In fact, a high level of production always means the formation of a developed centre of power, and a fixed and stable centre of power also implies the existence of a city. Founding a city, however, requires the production of a food surplus that makes it possible to meet the needs not only of its direct producers, but also of the sovereign and the apparatus of power in his service – which, from a certain stage, also includes the masters of written speech who work to his devotion.

At this time, the Frankfurt School was the object of increased interest, and we all learned to revere Max Horkheimer, Theodor Adorno and, of course, Walter Benjamin. My own professor, however, drew our attention to another scholar who had belonged to this famous German research institute in the late 1920s and early 1930s, Karl A. Wittfogel, who, however, enjoyed less celebrity than his philosophical colleagues. Rather than concerning himself with alienation, the blending of Marxism and psychology or the relationship between politics and aesthetics, or indeed the connection between the superstructure and 'false consciousness', Wittfogel asked his readers to pay attention to the 'Asiatic mode of production'. This term already appeared in Marx's writings, but it had subsequently become totally marginal, as it did not fit into the classic succession of the history of social classes as laid down by the Marxist vulgate.[8]

In 1957, having moved to the United States and become an anti-communist (even a McCarthyist), Wittfogel completed his best-known book, *Oriental Despotism.*[9] In this stimulating essay he combines a number of Marxist postulates with theses from Weber in order to tackle the question of differences of development in preindustrial class societies. Wittfogel's main focus is on ancient China, formed on the basis of an agriculture based on irrigation rather than sedimentation, just like the great ancient civilizations of Mesopotamia, Egypt and northern India (and later, in pre-Columbian America, the Aztec and Inca kingdoms). Even if we do not accept the political conclusions Wittfogel draws, in particular that of a linear continuity between oriental despotism and the Communist regimes of modern times, the fact remains that his research makes a contribution of rare quality to the understanding of ancient history.[10]

Reading Wittfogel, and the interpretations and debates that he aroused, provided the beginnings of a response to a number of questions of method and geography that had troubled me over my early years of study. It seemed to me more logical to construct an alternative narrative than to adopt that current with the

---

8   See, for example, the Preface to *A Contribution to the Critique of Political Economy* (1859): 'In broad outline, the Asiatic, ancient, feudal and modern bourgeois modes of production may be designated as epochs marking progress in the economic development of society' (Karl Marx, *Early Writings*, Harmondsworth: Penguin, 1975, 426).

9   Karl Wittfogel, *Oriental Despotism: A Comparative Study of Total Power*, New York: Vintage, 1981.

10   See on this theory Pierre Vidal-Naquet, 'Histoire et idéologie: Karl Wittfogel et le concept de *mode de production asiatique*', *Annales: Économie, sociétés, civilisations*, 19/3, 1964, 531–49. Also the critical remarks of Lawrence Krader, *The Asiatic Mode of Production*, Assen: Van Gorcum, 1975, 115–17.

majority of historians.[11] I am well aware that many readers will reject the periodization I am now going to propose. Others will certainly point out, perhaps correctly, defects of method, generalizations that are not always well founded, inexactitudes, arguments based on insufficient knowledge, not to mention, of course, an attack on the sacrosanct chronology of the historical profession.

It is a well-known fact that only children and imbeciles have the right to ask 'why' and to raise major questions. All those who depart from their narrow field of specialization and venture to propose an alternative metanarrative must know that specialists in the domains they touch on will mount an implacable guard around their stock-in-trade, and mercilessly pillory the intruder. As a general rule today, any narrative that suggests a macrohistorical approach is more liable than ever to be suspected of philosophy of history, and as such is rejected by the 'erudite' of the discipline.

It is far from me to believe that the very techno-material chronology I adopted, at a relatively precocious stage in my university studies in Tel Aviv, cannot be improved on. As I see it, this is not an 'authentic' and perfect reconstitution of a real historic past, rather a kind of ideal type in the Weberian sense of the term – an approach I shall clarify in a later chapter. Being still persuaded that, despite its inadequacies, the different time line I propose here remains within the bounds of possibility, I submit it to the judgement of the reader. Much time has passed since I first reflected on it, and yet it seems to me still today no less plausible than the narratives based on Eurocentric continuity on which almost all Western historiography is built like a fortress.

---

11   We should note the publication in the late nineteenth century of the pioneering essay by Léon Metchnikoff, *La civilisation et les grands fleuves historiques*, Paris: Hachette, 1889. This work signalled the historical particularity and anteriority of the hydraulic civilizations. The geographer and anarchist Élysée Reclus, a friend of Metchnikoff, wrote a fine preface to the book.

From Riverbanks to Seashores

It all began when I asked myself why the long-enduring early civilizations first emerged neither around the Mediterranean, nor in Europe or North America, where climate and natural conditions seem today most favourable to cereal cultivation. Why was it precisely in Mesopotamia, between the Euphrates and the Tigris, that a developed civilization, that of the Sumerian kingdom, appeared already in the fourth millennium before the Christian era, at a time when in the Mediterranean basin and Europe people still lived from gathering, hunting and perhaps a bit of fishing and primitive agriculture? How was it that precisely in ancient Egypt, along the banks of the Nile, we find at the start of the third millennium BCE an organized kingdom capable of maintaining a great fertile and prosperous agricultural space and going on to build monumental pyramids? How, in the twenty-second century BCE, did a powerful empire emerge in China around the Yellow River, endowed with a complex administration and a developed and refined literary culture?

It is well known that these great kingdoms arose in regions that were relatively dry and with poor-quality soil. The specificity of these arid zones, however, lies in the presence of great rivers that cross them and irrigate their land. Should we see the lively commercial shipping on these rivers, or perhaps the particularity and variety of wild vegetation used for domestic consumption, as the secret of the early appearance of these civilizations, as some historians have occasionally proposed?[12] I find neither the commercial thesis nor the eco-biological one really satisfactory.

The debate over Wittfogel's original working hypotheses makes it possible to decipher the enigma. The Neolithic

---

12   See, for example, Fernand Braudel, *La Méditerranée: L'espace et l'histoire*, Paris: Flammarion, 2009, 86–7, and Jared M. Diamond, *Guns, Germs and Steel: The Fates of Human Societies*, New York: Norton, 1997, 134–9.

revolution, it seems, was able to consolidate itself, extend and give rise to a stable agriculture and lasting development thanks to the alluvium carried by the great rivers and their tributaries. With a bit of historical imagination, we may suppose that the first workers of the land, who began to sow and domesticate wild plants, were not in a position to know why the soil became impoverished and dry in a relatively short space of time. They did not yet understand the elements needed for soil fertility – potassium, nitrogen, calcium and phosphorous. These first farmers, accordingly, had either to move their habitat in order to cultivate new fertile land, to follow wild crops, or to settle on land regularly fertilized by natural alluvium.

The first permanent settlements thus arose close to small rivers that brought down silt: Jericho in Canaan, in the eighth millennium BCE, and Çatal Höyük in Anatolia, in the seventh millennium. The early civilizations of antiquity emerged on the banks of great rivers, but these did not flow across spaces full of rich soil and abundant vegetation. It was not without reason that the oldest creation epic, *Enuma Elish*, discovered at Nineveh in Mesopotamia, begins and ends with a violent battle for control of the waters.[13]

The historian Herodotus, a son of Asia Minor who visited Mesopotamia in the fifth century BCE, gave a useful account of this:

> The rainfall of Assyria is slight and provides enough moisture only to burst the seed and start the root growing, but to swell the grain and bring it to maturity artificial irrigation is used, not, as in Egypt, by the natural flooding of the river, but by

---

13   This epic describes two entities that created the world and engendered all the gods: Apsû (sweet water) and Tiamat (salt water, less kind). Marduk kills Tiamat and tears her into two pieces, thus creating the sky and the earth, then he installs a curtain so that the waters from above do not flood the earth. See J. Bottéro and S. N. Kramer (eds), *Lorsque les dieux faisaient l'homme: Mythologie mésopotamienne*, Paris: Gallimard, 1989, 602–79.

hand-worked swipes. Like Egypt, the whole country is inter-
sected by dykes . . . As a grain-bearing country Assyria is the
richest in the world.[14]

It goes without saying that human organization on such vast
expanses, if it is to control nature, cannot be based on voluntarism and equality. The absence of elementary communication
between tens or hundreds of thousands of farmers, lacking any
education and speaking different languages or dialects, logically
imposed the slow constitution of a centralized and even despotic
coordinating power. The governmental and military 'bureaucra-
cies' of these kingdoms established, with the aid of a hierarchical
administrative apparatus and immense bodies of slaves, arrangements for the regulation of water and soil. Their main mission
was the construction of sophisticated dams and canals to prevent
flooding and the destruction of crops, and the maintenance of
these over long periods of time.

Thus the function of these first great kingdoms was not just
military defence; they were also closely involved in the process of
production. Moreover, the direct involvement of state bodies in
the hydraulic division of labour gave these a particular legitimacy
and status in history: their supremacy over the mass of simple
farmers, who were totally subjugated, structured their absolute
power. A number of scholars, from ancient Greece through to
Montesquieu and Max Weber, subsequently pondered over the
origins and causes of this 'oriental despotism'.

The ruling elites – members of the monarchical apparatus,
military leaders, functionaries and priests – also made it possible,
thanks to a large production surplus, to store food reserves for
years of drought, while developing an opulent culture of a high
level that combined monumental architecture with the art of

---

14 Herodotus, *The Histories*, London: Penguin, 2003, 85. This 'first historian'
described at length the prodigies of irrigation in Mesopotamia and Egypt. See on this
subject Karl W. Butzer, *Early Hydraulic Civilization in Egypt: A Study in Cultural
Ecology*, Chicago: University of Chicago Press, 1976.

magnificent mural painting, the formulation of codes and the drafting of laws. A hesitant semi-monotheism began to appear, along with an advanced geometry. The 'oriental hydraulic brain', in the expanses of India, China, Mesopotamia and north-eastern Africa, invented the wheel, cement, matches, paper, the compass and the sextant, as well as discovering the principles of steam power, gunpowder and printing. The majority of these remarkable technical and scientific inventions were not actually applied on a large scale (the exceptions being the wheel and cement), in the absence of a developed division of labour with advanced specialization and technological competence capable of providing a productive base for their reception, application and deployment. Thus in ancient Egypt steam was used for a system to open temple doors, while in China gunpowder was used mainly for fireworks.

The ancient civilizations must be credited with the first invention of writing, which is very likely explicable in terms of the level of communication required by the bureaucratic apparatus for its technical and centralizing intervention on works to be carried out in continually expanding spaces. Information on the regulation of waters and the number of slaves needed in each region, likewise calculation of the tax to levy on the production surplus of the peasants, was preserved and engraved on tablets, rolls of skin, bones, tortoise shells, pieces of wood and bamboo, shells, and even with the help of knots in a network of threads.

As we know, the first cuneiform writing was born in the ancient Sumerian kingdom. Though there is some controversy on this point, it seems that it also appeared independently in other hydraulic societies: pharaonic Egypt (hieroglyphics), imperial China (*hanzi*) and the Inca Empire (*quipu*). Originally used to convey instructions from the monarchical power as well as economic information, cuneiform writing was soon used for transcribing religious myths, correspondence between leading figures, and the chronicles of royal dynasties. Writing was a tremendous intellectual discovery, and a revolutionary phase in the formation of collective memory. It also marks the end of 'prehistory' and the beginning of history, since we construct and piece together our accounts of this from the creation of writing.[15]

At their margins, the kingdoms of Mesopotamia and Egypt bordered on different geographic zones in the south-eastern Mediterranean: Canaan, Phoenicia and Asia Minor were alternately under the power of Egypt and of successive Mesopotamian kingdoms. Some of their scientific and technical knowledge, and subsequently of their cultural wealth, thus permeated these 'peripheries' bit by bit.

The Mediterranean periphery – from Canaan to Asia Minor, Crete and Greece, round to Sicily, southern Italy, Spain and North Africa – has a different climate from that of the hydraulic societies. The amount of rainfall is moderate and confined to a single season, but it made possible the development of an agriculture based chiefly on soil formation. The necessary condition for the development of agricultural production is a basic knowledge of the caprices of the land – in other words, understanding the elementary need to let it rest and to enrich it with natural fertilizer. Beyond the other achievements of hydraulic societies, this was a major and decisive discovery in the development of humanity.

In the biblical myth, when God gave the Torah to Moses in the Sinai desert, after the Ten Commandments and other instructions about slaves and women he suddenly felt it necessary to add an 'exotic' agricultural precept, which did not find a place in the majesty of established worship, but whose sacred character would from then have to be imperatively respected:

---

15   It seems that in parallel with writing (c.3000 BCE), money also originated in Mesopotamia, initially in the form of a quantity of barley, before silver was substituted rather later. Coin only appeared in the seventh century BCE in Asia Minor. The 'monetary revolution' in hydraulic societies also involved credit: 'banks' of cereals made their appearance at many places in the Fertile Crescent and became an integral part of agricultural trade.

'For six years you may sow your land and gather its produce; but in the seventh year you shall let it lie fallow and leave it alone' (Exodus 23:10–11). This later literary and mythological illustration of the obligation of fallowing provides us with an initial insight into the way that agricultural knowledge spread in the peripheral margins of Canaan, in parallel with the development of monotheism.

The Mediterranean societies began to form and consolidate when the various hydraulic civilizations had already reached a high level of development: the chronological gap was more than a millennium. Besides knowledge of the principles of regular fertilization of the soil, cultivation of the Mediterranean lands also demanded use of the light plough, another technological achievement imported from Mesopotamia.[16] Starting from the second millennium BCE, there arose in Canaan and to its north small city kingdoms (more like large villages, in fact) that attest to the progress of agricultural production, as well as the ability, particularly in Phoenicia, to build small craft and even ships. It seems to have been the presence of forests close to the coast and the absence of a sufficient expanse of cultivable land that contributed to make the Phoenicians pioneers of maritime trade. Endowed with means of navigation that were increasingly developed, the population that arrived from the sea continued to rapidly spread the technologies of agricultural work around the northern and western shores of the Mediterranean: first of all in Crete and on other islands, then in Greece, in Sicily and the long peninsula known today

---

16   It is worth noting that biblical mythology contains a fascinating verse on the main character in the story of the flood: 'He named him Noah, saying, "This boy will bring us relief from our work, and from the hard labour that has come upon us because of the Lord's curse upon the ground" ' (Genesis 5:29). And the text goes on to say that, thanks to Noah, Jehovah decided, 'Never again will I curse the ground because of man' (Genesis 8:21). That is why Rachi (Rabbi Salomon de Troyes), the eminent Bible exegetist, attributed to the Mesopotamian Noah the lifting of the divine curse on the aridity of the land, as well as the invention of the plough (Midrash Tanhuma 1, 11).

under the name of Italy, in Iberia and particularly the fertile regions of North Africa (Carthage). The process of development of civilization, from the south-east towards the west, confirms these hypotheses about the origins and context of its emergence.

We should remember that around the Mediterranean use was made of a light wheelless plough (*aratrum*, in Latin), made entirely of wood, whose ploughshare was simply a stake, easily drawn by an ox or a man. The furrow this dug was not deep (scarcely more than ten centimetres), serving to preserve the scarce rainwater close to the upper layer of soil. Mediterranean agricultural technology had hardly evolved by the end of the first millennium BCE, when political institutions, the developed literary culture and the refined art of ceramics reached their peak. The peasants of ancient Canaan and those of the declining Roman Empire sowed and ploughed in almost the same fashion, even if the Pax Romana, at its apogee, made possible a level of agricultural production and trade that was particularly developed and secure.[17] The magnificent inventions of Archimedes, in the third century BCE, were not produced in the sphere of agricultural work and were scarcely applied to it (with the possible exception of the hydraulic screw for irrigation); they were used above all in navigation and the art of war, where they brought advances.

At the time of the Crusades, in the thirteenth century CE, the European invaders were surprised to see, on the south-east shores of the Mediterranean, peasants using wheelless ploughs. At the end of the eighteenth century, Napoleon's soldiers were similarly surprised by the technical 'backwardness' of the Egyptian fellahin. They found it hard to understand that these farmers did not

---

17   An attempt aiming to explain the stagnation of working technologies in the Mediterranean economy in terms of mentalities, rather than modes of cultivating the soil, appears in a famous article by Moses I. Finley, 'Technical Innovation and Economic Progress in the Ancient World', *Economic History Review*, 18/1, 1965, 29–45.

need much power to plough. This is why Mediterranean civilization did not discover the advantages of using a yoke on the chine
of the ox or harnessing the horse with bridle and bit. The technological development of metalwork, other than the production
of sickles and hammers, was chiefly oriented to the instruments
of combat and circulation, rather than perfecting the development of tools for production.

As distinct from the collective slavery prevalent in hydraulic
societies, the Mediterranean world was characterized, alongside
an agriculture of small independent peasants, by the accepted
and widespread recourse to private slavery, not only in domestic
service but also for agricultural production and in mines (with
the possible exception of Sparta, where a kind of state slavery
existed). This type of slavery was more widespread in the Roman
Empire than in the Canaanite city kingdoms (Israel, Judea,
Moab) or the Greek cities, though in Athens the number of
slaves was relatively large.

The exploitation of slaves formed one of the pillars of the
division of labour, the stratification of social classes, and the
creation of centres of administration and culture. On the
Mediterranean littoral, with the exception of Rome, production was carried out mainly by free peasants, but the abundance
of leisure time for the ruling classes was everywhere made possible thanks to a slave economy that prospered alongside free
labour. Without slavery there would probably have been no
Plato (the owner of just five slaves) or Aristotle (a fervent champion of slavery), and certainly no Cicero or Julius Caesar. The
slow expansion of monotheism around the Mediterranean
shores, from Jahwehism to the formation of Christianity, only
validated and supported these practices of human exploitation
that made possible the flourishing and splendour of the 'high'
culture of the Graeco-Roman world.

The diffusion among the Mediterranean populations of
production techniques deriving from the hydraulic societies was
thus accompanied by an intensive intellectual transmission. The

still rudimentary literary culture that came from Egypt and Mesopotamia beat a path across the Sinai desert to the coast of Phoenicia, where it underwent a remarkable metamorphosis, in all likelihood thanks to the vigour of maritime trade. This led to the invention of the first alphabet and the beginning of its wide spread across adjacent shores,[18] which is why the books of the Bible provide an unmatched ancestral testimony of the transition from a semi-monotheism, Egyptian or Persian, to an abstract and more developed monotheism in the land of Canaan. The Mediterranean 'pillaging' of the cultures of antiquity, apart from its abundant mythologies, also includes the foundations of geometry, astronomy, and the legislative codes that state power needed.

The Mediterranean civilization, beyond its diversity and the multiplicity of its cultural and linguistic sources, was united by an effective network of communication, with the various cities lying around the inland sea 'like frogs around a wide pond', as Plato put it. This situation subsequently gave rise to the imposing Hellenic 'globalization', whose advent and then expansion at the time of Alexander the Great, king of Macedon, would bring about the end of the hegemony of the hydraulic kingdoms over the shores of the south-east Mediterranean, and thus prepare the ground for a still more extensive globalization, that of the powerful Roman Empire.[19]

---

18   On cultural penetration, from language to myths, see the standard work by Walter Burkert, *Babylon, Memphis, Persepolis: Eastern Contexts of Greek Culture*, Cambridge, MA: Harvard University Press, 2004.

19   Egypt was conquered by the Persian kingdom in the sixth century BCE, without the hydraulic system being modified (see Herodotus, *The Histories*, Book 2 (99), 132). Symbolically, the transition of Egypt into the Mediterranean orbit was expressed by the shift in the capital city of the Pharaohs, who had not been interested in the sea: the coastal city of Alexandria became the capital of the kingdom in the fourth century BCE, retaining this position until the arrival of Islam. The developed hydraulic system would survive in Mesopotamia until the Mongol conquest of the thirteenth century. The Mongol horsemen, who had no understanding of local agriculture, destroyed it systematically, which led to the extinction of Baghdad as a centre of power and the site of the Islamic 'renaissance'.

The publication of *Black Athena* by a British historian, nearly thirty years ago, was a scandal for the historical profession.[20] Martin Bernal launched a frontal attack on the fundamental conception of nineteenth-century European historiography, which saw the refined Greek civilization as the direct and authentic product of an Indo-European inheritance. Bernal maintained that despite substantial evidence left by ancient Greece itself, starting with its mythology, which displayed borrowings from Egyptian and Phoenician elements buried in the formation of Hellenism (perhaps by way of the Hyksos tribes that arrived in the Aegean), the writing of history and 'pan-Western' narcissism tended to view Greece as an authentically 'European' creation. Thus, since the Greek and then Latin languages were not Semitic but Indo-European, it followed that these cultures and even the 'races' that bore them were by definition Aryan and had come from central Europe. In other words, the ancestors of modern Westerners were 'whites', whose ancient aristocratic origin went back to northern India.

It was the Renaissance that retrospectively invented not only a European 'Antiquity' – a matter I shall return to below – but also the ideal of 'white' Greek beauty. The racist and more erudite nineteenth century took over this initial myth and confirmed it. It did not much bother the scholars of the nineteenth century and even the twentieth that the Greek and Roman marble statues, originally in varied colours and very often gilded, had been bleached by the action of time: the 'bleached' Greek culture was adopted as a pure and exclusive legacy of the European genius.[21]

Bernal's book unleashed a wave of anger; several articles

20   Martin Bernal, *Black Athena: The Afro-Asiatic Roots of Classical Civilization Volume One: The Fabrication of Ancient Greece 1785–1985*, New Brunswick, NJ: Rutgers University Press, 1987.

21   See on this subject Philippe Jockey, *Le mythe de la Grèce blanche*, Paris: Belin, 2013. Twentieth-century Hollywood perfected this 'white European' representation of not only the Graeco-Roman world but the biblical world as well.

were published to contradict his views and point out his inadequacies, some of which he subsequently acknowledged. The lobbies of the academy saw a busy Eurocentric pressure to fine-tune these attacks, and it was particularly in the field of traditional classical studies that the rumbling of discontent was loudest. To recognize that the roots of development of this discipline in the nineteenth century had been steeped in racism and anti-Semitism seemed intolerable to its upholders, and was radically rejected. The challenging title of Bernal's book (chosen not by its author but by the publisher) was resented as a provocation and aroused the anger of specialists virtually en bloc. To claim that Athena, the Greek goddess of wisdom and war, was identical to Neith, the celebrated goddess of the Egyptians, was hard to accept, despite Plato's own account of this.[22] And to imagine that she was in all likelihood a black woman was excessive and terrifying.

But that was not all. It was also hard to digest that in Greek mythology, Adonis (containing the Semitic word *adon*) was in fact a belated version of the Mesopotamian Tammuz (Dumuzi), though in the end this had to be admitted, however unenthusiastically. Herodotus himself was already inclined to credit the Egyptian priests when he wrote, 'They also told me that the Egyptians first brought into use the names of the twelve gods, which the Greeks took over from them, and were the first to assign altars and images, and temples to the gods, and to carve figures in stone.'[23]

And yet the stimulating hypothesis of the fundamentally eclectic character of Greek culture, as of all other cultures, and the idea that the creative imagination could have been aroused

---

22   Plato, *Timaeus* (21e), in *Timaeus and Critias*, London: Penguin, 2008, 34.

23   Herodotus, *The Histories*, Book 2 (4), 96–7. Elsewhere he adds, 'There is plenty of evidence [that] the Greeks took the name Heracles from the Egyptians', and not the other way round ([44], 113). Herodotus goes on to show that the name filtered through the Phoenicians before reaching the Greeks ([44], 113–14 and [50], 116).

and crystallized there on the basis of Semitic and African sources, embarrassed the fundamentalist guardians of the temple of classical culture. Was Egypt really one of the progenitors of Athenian culture? Was there not on Bernal's part an attempt to muddy the sources of the entire Hellenic legacy, and by doing so indirectly question the exceptional character of 'Western culture' as a whole?

It is true that no one dared explicitly contradict Bernal on the Phoenician origin of the Greek alphabet, nor on the fact that the grammatical roots of a quarter of the Hellenic vocabulary (counting all dialects together) have a Semitic origin. However, the assertion that a third of the words in these dialects come from Pharaonic Egypt was perceived as adventurous or exaggerated. Finally, his reference to the famous legend of Cadmus of Tyre, founder of Thebes, the city of Oedipus located in the very heart of Greece, to demonstrate the Phoenician presence there, was particularly contested.[24]

In the great polemic around Bernal's essay, there is one point that particularly merits attention: the Egyptian presence in Greek culture was denied or minimized with a fervour which was only paralleled by the natural conception of the latter as immanent precursor of Western civilization. In other words, we can observe a Eurocentric need, even if not always conscious, to create a continuous and complete European story breaking sharply with its eastern wing, and arising rather from an intimate historiographical dialogue with Western civilization. Almost no one raised the basic question: in what sense is Greece really the antiquity of European society?

It would certainly be foolish to deny the basic fact that Europe

---

24   Herodotus discusses right at the start of his work the relationship between Phoenicians and Greeks. According to his evidence, the Phoenicians brought goods from Egypt and Assyria to the shores of Greece. See *The Histories*, Book One (1), 3. It is interesting that many centuries later Ibn Khaldun likewise wrote, 'The intellectual sciences are said to have come to the Greeks from the Persians' (*The Muqaddimah*, London: Routledge, 1967, 373).

would later draw copiously from Mediterranean civilization, both Judaeo-Christian and Graeco-Roman. Terms, concepts, beliefs and juridical elements formed a substantial envelope for the birth of authentically new contents. Nonetheless, this intrinsic European culture was never 'Judaeo-Christian'; it was rather ecclesiastical Christian, in various versions, pervaded by a tremendous theological execration towards Judaism, which itself was formed along a Jerusalem–Babylon axis before gradually infiltrating into Europe. European culture was never Greek (neither pagan nor Orthodox); it rather remained closed towards and for a long time suspicious of the legacy transmitted by the intermediary of Byzantium. Nor again was it Roman: neither in its social class structure nor in its mentality, despite the fact that the Church and its clerics later resorted to a form of dialect Latin, preserved fragments of the Code of Theodosius, and adopted the pleasures of wine.

True, the year 843 saw the foundation of the *sacrum romanum imperium*, about which Voltaire, in his aversion for both European barbarism and Christian hypocrisy, wrote, 'This agglomeration, which was called, and still calls itself, the Holy Roman Empire, was neither holy, nor Roman, nor an empire.'[25] It was a new and different cultural mosaic in terms of its societies, its sensibilities and its identities, whose heartlands were formed subsequently and most often far from the shores and effervescence of the ancient centres of the 'inner sea'.

It is possible, in my view, to see the opulent Mediterranean civilization as a sort of important 'medieval' epoch, which at the end of the day played a role of mediator between the antiquity of western Asia and the later advent of the European north-west. Just as the technology and culture of the great riverine

---

25   Voltaire, *An Essay on Universal History, the Manners, and Spirit of Nations, from the Reign of Charlemaign to the Age of Lewis XIV*, London: J. Nourse, 1759, chapter 70.

civilizations flowed towards the shores of the Mediterranean, so in turn Mediterranean technology and culture flowed into the veins of a Europe still stuck in the infantile phase of its economy and creativity. The conquests of its shores by Egypt and the Mesopotamian kingdoms accelerated the birth of a specific new culture, and the Roman conquests similarly stimulated the birth of the young European culture, or even provided the necessary condition for this.

The diagram below is intended to spell out my position, by situating these three agrarian structures along axes of time and space. Each configuration is tangential to its neighbour and partially superimposed on it, being indirectly responsible for its appearance, without the later structure constituting in any way an immanent or dialectical product arising from the orbit of its predecessor. What we have here is not a concatenation or continuity of societies, but a trickling and an original acclimatization of fragments of material and intellectual culture that come to fertilize new spaces.

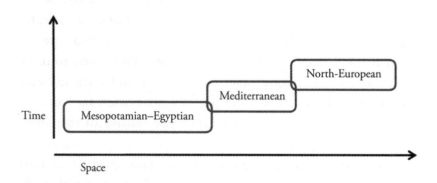

We should be equally aware that, in zones with a climate similar to that of the Mediterranean shores, but totally outside the orbit of diffusion of the agricultural knowledge of hydraulic societies (California, Chile, south-east Australia, for example), there was no continuous development of agriculture in the period of antiquity. The same was true of those expanses with rich soil and luxuriant vegetation, such as the central forested regions of North

America, when they did not come up against an older adjacent agricultural technology, such as had existed on the shores of the Mediterranean, and where there was no rise of a dynamic agrarian culture, as in northern Europe.[26]

And the European 'Genius'?

The Mediterranean civilization, which had taken its first hesitant steps some two thousand years before the Christian era, reached full maturity in the fourth-century Roman Empire. At that point, the development of this civilization was halted, and it slowly began to lose its hegemony. The invasions of 'barbarians' from northern Europe in the fifth century, then the Arab Islamic conquests arriving from the south in the seventh century, slowly eroded the rich and diversified maritime unity that had been achieved. Yet it would be wrong to believe that this was completely destroyed: shipping trade was certainly reduced, but it was never interrupted. The Byzantine Empire to the east of the 'inner sea', and Andalusia to the west, remained until the thirteenth century vectors – belated, but very active – of a Mediterranean cultural legacy that was in the process of mutation. These two regions, despite their vibrant commercial activity, also offered living evidence of a long-term stagnation of the technological and economic capacities of Mediterranean agriculture.

The hydraulic societies, like those of the Mediterranean, were based on specific conditions of agricultural production, which experienced prosperity and increase up to a certain level of complexity that they were unable to surpass. Both types had recourse to a basic and relatively simple technology that did not demand any further perfecting – its object always being nature. Neither the vigour of maritime trade nor the

26 Lacking sufficient data on agrarian development and cultural elements drawn from the ancient hydraulic civilization developed around the Yellow River, which went on to permeate the Korean peninsular and later Japan, I abstain from writing about this subject.

power of intellectual creation was in a position to modify a certain ceiling of development of production. The agricultural civilization of northern Europe, on the other hand, which got under way more belatedly, would be the first and only one in which the means of labour continued to be perfected until they brought about a type of society marked by a division of labour and a ramification of specializations that overflowed the limits of agricultural production and its characteristic mode of life.

What was the secret of this specific dynamism in north-west Europe, in relation to other agrarian civilizations? Should it be sought in the energetic character of the Indo-European white race, as many people believed in the nineteenth century? Or was it rather due to an innate sense of initiative and competition, with which this same 'white' race was deeply impregnated? Was it thanks to Christianity, initially Catholic and then Protestant, which instilled values of excellence in the Europeans, as some have been inclined to believe? Or was there perhaps an effect of the philosophical legacy of Plato or the scientific doctrine of Aristotle? In other words, was it the rationalism of 'Antiquity' that in a particular form shaped the European legacy, without having a similar effect on other cultures? History books from the nineteenth century to today, and even political and philosophical essays, are stuffed with references, implicit or explicit, that emphasize the preference given to culture and values by 'Western civilization, from Greece and Rome', in relation to other cultures that developed on the planet.

The European Goths who invaded the Italian peninsula, conquering Rome and the whole northern coastline of the Mediterranean, even part of North Africa, could not know that their descendants would see themselves as direct and natural scions of Graeco-Roman culture. They did not yet have any real knowledge of the New Testament, and had certainly not read Plato or Aristotle. Their direct legacy was their pagan tribal culture, and the dialects in which they expressed themselves.

Their technological and material development simply continued an ancient tribal phase; it is they far more than Mediterranean antiquity who embody the ancient past of Europe. After having lived from hunting, stock-raising, nomadism and conquest, they settled into a more lasting sedentary and agricultural way of life a long time after the formation of the high civilizations in the south of the 'continent' and on the other shores of the Mediterranean. The causes of this historical 'delay', just like the factors of the technological dynamism to come, should more likely be sought in the nature of the soil and the climatic conditions that, despite their differences and variations, mark the great space between northern Italy and southern Sweden, between Great Britain and western Russia.

The greater part of these northern lands, being rich in sediment, were covered with forests that had fed and fertilized the soil for millennia, through rotting wood and falling leaves. The inhabitants who lived from gathering and hunting found an abundant supply of food. They beat paths, established temporary villages in clearings, domesticated animals, cleared pasture for their flocks, and even used and preserved wild plants. The arrival of the light plough made it possible to cultivate the soil in the more southerly regions.

It needed a fuller and more decisive revolution in production than that undertaken around the Mediterranean to begin and permanently establish the agricultural take-off in the heart of green Europe. From its earliest phase, relatively sophisticated means of production were needed in order to cultivate wet and heavy soil, as compared to those used in other civilizations. This meant having available a technological lever that was previously unknown. The simple light plough, imported from the Mediterranean, was not suited to effective intervention in the greater part of the lands of European agriculture, particularly north of the Alps. It was necessary, in fact, to plough differently in order to obtain an adequate and continuous harvest in the rainy northern regions, where the soil had to be turned deeply, by at least half a metre, so as to drain enough of the sediment and bury it deeper before sowing.

As early as 1931, Marc Bloch had drawn attention to the appearance of the new plough.[27] The American Lynn White completed the description made by Bloch, which he succeeded in developing into a sufficiently detailed and convincing hypothesis.[28] In both cases, the conclusions were not always assured, for the simple reason that we have very few written traces concerning the technological past. It is a well-known fact that far more documents and written evidence were produced about kings, princes, priests and saints than on the life and technical problems of workers on the land, 'people without history'. Only a few snippets of speech and some fragments of tools that escaped total corrosion allow us to piece together, at least approximately, some of the practices that formerly characterized the everyday labour of the majority of men and women.

Though we have no precise dates, it is likely that the plough dedicated to the specific treatment of 'wet' land began to appear and slowly develop between the late seventh century and the tenth. Called *carruca* in Latin, *Pflug* in German and similar terms in Germanic dialects, this was a heavy asymmetric plough, already equipped with one or more fixed wheels and, no less important, a substantial metal blade. Because of its weight and the difficulty of traction, the Mediterranean harness, fixed to the chest of the draught animal, had to be replaced by a new kind of bridle inserted in the horse's mouth or alternatively a yoke solid and wide enough to harness two oxen or more; in this way the power of the plough could be at least quadrupled. Iron shoes appeared at around the same time, greatly assisting the work of oxen, and still more so that of horses, which in due course proved

---

27   Bloch, *Les caractères originaux*, vol. 1, 51–7 and vol. 2, 76–8.
28   Lynn Townsend White Jr, *Medieval Technology and Social Change*, Oxford: Oxford University Press, 1962, 39–57.

more efficient. The power of a horse is similar to that of an ox, but the animal is faster and allows far more flexible movement, as well as having better endurance (not to mention that it makes for an easier homeward journey after a day spent in distant fields). The new energy obtained from animals, in ever wider regions of Europe, endowed the agricultural producer with a domination and power over nature that had previously been neither required nor known in the technologies of other civilizations.

Besides the domestication of cattle and the crops imported from the Mediterranean, the earlier 'southern' achievements in the treatment of iron ore, both for military needs and in connection with transport, were also a necessary condition for the invention of the heavy complex plough and the birth of the new northern agriculture. The casting of metal ploughshares and horseshoes required a technological know-how in the production and fashioning of iron, which originally seems to have appeared around the Mediterranean, but was only little applied there in the sphere of labour, as the need for this hardly made itself felt.

We know that iron mines multiplied and prospered in the Carolingian period, in the late ninth century. The division of labour that slowly established itself generated in the European village a handicraft industry with many branches, closely bound up with the process of producing and extracting foodstuffs. It did not have as its initial and main objective the construction of pyramids and gigantic walls, nor of sumptuous palaces, hanging gardens and great bridges, nor again the improved instruments of warfare that were familiar to other agricultural civilizations. The manufacture of leather belts, and the production of rope, cloth, chains, rings, barrels, wheels and axles became regular trades, along with the sophisticated use of wood. Above all, the craft of the blacksmith and the alloying of metals, including steelmaking, became typical elements of European villages.

Tree trunks, available on a massive scale in most regions of northern Europe, served as the main source of fuel for metal-working. It was not by chance that Smith became one of the most widespread surnames in the English language, and that names derived from the same craft appear likewise in the Germanic world and even in Russia. The small foundries that grew up in the heart of agricultural regions, close to the forests that supplied them with abundant organic fuel, constituted a springboard for the future economic take-off of northern Europe.

At the same time, by way of their collective organization and devotion, monasteries contributed to the spread of agricultural techniques, the clearing of forests, the draining of marshes and the ploughing of new soil for cereal cultivation. The system of three-year rotation, with its cycle of crops, was a practice suited to the fertile soils of Europe, being almost unknown around the Mediterranean (in this three-year cycle, a third of the fields in turn are left uncultivated, while the other two-thirds are sown in spring and autumn). This system brought a diversification of harvests and gave a very substantial boost to food production. Triennial rotation and the heavy plough formed the technical basis for the rise of a new material civilization until the early eighteenth century and the invention of four-field cultivation in England.

The advances in terms of fertilization and natural manuring, followed by the perfecting of watermills and windmills as the means of production developed, made possible a considerable increase both in the productivity and quantity of harvests and in their transformation into foodstuffs. This itself led to a local and then wider trade, which steadily expanded in ever wider circles. It is important to note here that if production and consumption still remained at largely self-sufficient levels, a portion of the new trade would soon involve the instruments of labour themselves, materials and tools, and not simply the fruits of the earth or the surpluses of agricultural production. This system and all its instruments would continue to advance and broaden thanks to the participation of various actors and the division of labour between them.

Through to the tenth century, production not only took a great leap forward, it also enabled a significant demographic advance, as well as the formation of a society of feudal vassalage with its various constituents. Seigneurial society, with its ramified mechanisms of protection and dependence, would initially appear in many respects more fragmented and heterogeneous than other agrarian societies. It drew mainly on armed force and the loyalty of nobles and knights, and rested on a growing exploitation of the labour of peasants reduced to serfdom as a counterpart to the physical security provided. The dominant seigneurial class did not intervene directly in production, in which it displayed no particular interest. Similarly, the Mediterranean slave – most often a prisoner of war with no particular competence, or a descendant of one bought on the market – was no help in tackling the difficult working of the land in Europe. It fell to the shrewd peasant serf to take responsibility for the new modes of subsistence: despite not being a free man, he did dispose of certain rights that made him in practice a kind of 'proprietor' of the means of production. Neither he nor his family could at any price be separated from his precious tools, his cattle, or his land, which demanded a developed initiative and know-how right from the start of the labour process.

It is likely that the creation of the large seigneurial domain and the organization of autonomous village communities were closely bound up with the grassroots solidarity required from the peasants in order to ensure together the maintenance of agricultural equipment. They were obliged to ally in relatively large groups in order to acquire and use costly ploughs, and particularly the large number of animals needed to draw these. Slavery, characterized by a totally different relationship between the producer and his means of production, proved to be increasingly ineffective as a response to the new conditions of production. Yet it did not immediately disappear in the regions of the old Roman conquest. Even after the great change had been effected, slaves remained here and there for domestic tasks, though no longer in production.[29]

At the end of this formative period of specific new modes of production, an urbanization of a new type also appeared in the eleventh century. Rather than being political, administrative and commercial centres, as in the Mediterranean civilization, the towns that arose became active organs in the division of labour of the surrounding agricultural system, which grew ever more developed and ramified. There were not only power elites and a financial and commercial bourgeoisie, but also intermediate layers of handicraft producers who organized themselves into powerful autonomous guilds. These towns were not simply the starting point in the future constitution of absolute monarchies; they also became places of accumulation of culture and technical knowledge, thus contributing to the decisive junction between experimental and theoretical science subsequently known as the 'scientific revolution'. This revolution, as we know, surpassed in its achievements everything that had been attained in the other preindustrial civilizations that developed elsewhere on the planet.

It is necessary all the same to repeat and emphasize one fact: it was neither the Indo-European genius, the 'Judaeo-Christian' legacy nor the remains of Graeco-Roman rationalism that brought the cycle of technological and scientific inventions without which the industrial surge of north-west Europe would not have been possible. As we have mentioned above, these inventions were essentially well known already in the

---

29   We should point out here the absolute difference in the development of the peasantry in the vast stretches of Eastern Europe and particularly in Russia, as compared with Western Europe, despite the use of the term 'serf' in both cases. On all these changes, see Marc Bloch, 'Comment et pourquoi finit l'esclavage antique', in *Mélange historique*, Paris: CNRS Éditions, 2011, 261–85. The Mongol conquests possibly played a key part in the difference between Eastern and Western Europe.

hydraulic civilizations of Asia. Yet they had never been regularly applied there on a large scale, for lack of a developed division of labour and in the absence of ramified specializations and handicrafts on the periphery of agricultural production. Only a developed practical knowledge and years of dexterity in the handling of technologies could bring the treatment of metals (such as the screw, the gearwheel or the spring), the 'Chinese' idea of printing, or the 'Egyptian' discovery of steam power to play a leading role in the technological and social processes of Europe.[30]

It would certainly be exaggerated and erroneous to see the heavy European plough as the exclusive ancestor of the computer, Internet and spacecraft. No one has a single ancestor, neither a person nor the chain of human actions. The factors involved in great technological innovations, their diffusion, their application and the speed of their perfecting, are multiple – a combination of commercial trends, competition, the concentration of capital, colonial conquests and the exploitation of the natural resources there, class struggles, the constitution of centralized political structures, shifting cultural sensibilities and religious beliefs, and a set of interactions and relations of mutual dependence in a wide range of social expressions – as well as many other 'causes' of which we are still unaware.

I persist, despite everything, in sticking to the idea that without this material ancestor, and the dynamism of the division of labour it induced right from its very first steps, it is unlikely that European civilization would by the early eighteenth century have arrived at Jethro Tull's remarkable seed drill, the particularly effective four-field system of crop rotation, the powerful

---

30   It is hard to give a clear response to the question of the degree to which the discoveries of Asian antiquity permeated into the west European space. The bold attempt of John M. Hobson, in *The Eastern Origins of Western Civilization*, (Cambridge: Cambridge University Press, 2004), to grant Eastern technological progress a precedence in almost all domains fails to carry conviction. His assertion that the first industrialization took place in China is hardly consistent (ibid., 51–6).

demographic impulse that followed, and thus the key phase of development of human society: the Industrial Revolution and an end to the agricultural glass ceiling that no society had previously been able to break.[31]

I also permit myself to question the capacity of the 'West', without the initial climatic constraints and the technological responses that these aroused, to have arrived, in the same time-scale and in the same region of the globe, at the railway, artillery, the internal combustion engine, warships, the camera and radio, gas chambers, antibiotics, nuclear weapons and the Internet, as well as the global atmospheric pollution that increasingly covers the Earth's surface and places a great question mark over its continued existence.

The Invention of 'Antiquity'

A thousand years or so passed, from the fifth century to the fifteenth, before learned Europe suddenly began to discover its Graeco-Roman ancestry and its European identity. Ecclesiastical chroniclers had certainly recognized the Mediterranean, or more precisely Palestine, as the point of origin of their Christian history. The conquest of the Mediterranean coastline by Islam had also led to a wider use of the term 'Europe' as a religious entity, and accordingly as a geographical one as well. But it was particularly with the Renaissance – a term that was itself not used until the sixteenth century – that the concept of 'Antiquity' was introduced to denote a period of time, coupled with that of *media aetas* that was already in use. In the seventeenth century, any educated man knew that the fifteenth century had seen a new 'birth' of Europe, after the fatal decline of the Roman Empire and the fall into the dark hole of time for a long and empty medieval period.

---

31   The cultivation of potatoes, imported from the American continent, also contributed to this population growth.

Just as in due course the Jacobin revolutionaries would see themselves as Roman senators and adopt a corresponding posture, and like those nations in the nineteenth and twentieth centuries who continuously scrutinized the past in order to invent for themselves roots in imaginary races, peoples with a long duration and even an eternal essence, so the clerks of the Renaissance and philosophers of the Enlightenment, themselves pre-national intellectuals par excellence, needed prestigious spiritual fathers, witnesses and actors in the high culture of the Mediterranean basin in order to constitute their modern identity and confirm their own consciousness.

The humanists of the sixteenth century were all still Christians, but this did not prevent them from identifying with the idolaters of 'Antiquity', whose arts of thinking, and particularly of writing, they deemed superior to those of the theologians of the church. The more secular philosophers of the eighteenth century would be less hesitant in glorifying their antique 'ancestors' from before the triumph of Christianity.

The movement of the 'Renaissance', as we know, took its first steps in northern Italy, among the distant 'descendants' of the Ostrogoths and Lombards. The new elites of flourishing commercial cities such as Venice, Florence and Genoa (rather than Athens, Rome or Constantinople) furthered the formation of a real cultural melting pot, favourable to the development of refined art and sophisticated literature, emblems of a creative sensibility that would spread further north and focus on other European cities. With Niccolò Machiavelli (1469–1527) in Florence, François Rabelais (1483–1553) in Lyon, Johannes Reuchlin (1455–1522) in Württemberg, Desiderius Erasmus (1466–1536) in Rotterdam, Nicolaus Copernicus (1473–1543) in Polish Prussia and Thomas More (1478–1535) in London, a sceptical and critical intellectual world gradually took shape, with no previous historical precedent. The revolution in printing (lead had previously been used only in cannon) and the spread of printed texts formed the material basis for a trend that would eventually lead to the luminaries of the Enlightenment.

While the church and the universities under its control had always been the masters and guardians of scientific knowledge, a fierce desire to escape the inertia of scholasticism, and above all the stifling restrictions imposed by religious institutions, made itself felt at this time. Nostalgia for Graeco-Roman high culture became an obligatory norm, and soon a combat strategy for shaping minds now freed from ecclesiastical patronage and providing weapons against theology.

European scholars, who had come from the new urban bourgeoisie, aspired to behave like the Romans, those men of antiquity (*alle romana et alla antica*) who had initially appeared to them (not at all misguidedly) as their superiors. They liked to see themselves, and here again not totally without reason, as contemporaries of Plato and Archimedes, Cicero and Horace.[32] This identification, across the ages, with the literati of a classical world in full cultural upswing helped the men of the Renaissance to invent a totally new culture. If in the twentieth century, given the mass distribution of products, any new high culture always has to be innovative and exclusive, this was not the case in the sixteenth century. In this preindustrial age, high culture had on the contrary to seek resemblance: in both sculpture and poetry, it was necessary to imitate as far as possible the works of the Mediterranean past.

In order to complete their imaginary 'bi-temporality', scholars turned to the libraries of monasteries in search of ancient documents that had been long forgotten. They discovered there, indeed, Latin texts that had been many times recopied in the monastic scriptoria and buried for centuries in obscure secondary archives. Pre-Renaissance Europe had been familiar with certain writings of Virgil and Ovid, but those of Cicero and Livy

---

32   *The School of Athens*, Raphael's famous fresco dating from 1510, gives a fine pictorial expression of this intellectual and mental phenomenon.

were only very little read, and selectively at that, in the form of summaries and isolated quotations designed above all to prove the existence of God. The rich Hellenic legacy, for its part, remained almost unknown.

Many Greek texts had been preserved in the Byzantine Empire, while many more, translated into Arabic, were to be found mainly, though not exclusively, in the Iberian peninsula. After the city of Toledo fell into Christian hands, an intense enterprise of translation of this material took place in the twelfth century, from Arabic into Castilian and Latin. The reception of the classical past reached its apogee in the thirteenth century with the conquest of Cordoba and its immense library. It was at this time that Europe was truly brought face to face with the treasures of scholarship and science of Athens and the Graeco-Roman world.[33]

Writings of Plato and Aristotle (such as Plato's *Timaeus* or Aristotle's *Categories* and *On Interpretation*) had been known until then only in a few isolated monasteries, as the real bearers of the science and culture of the Mediterranean past were the Muslims, those of 'Spain' in particular. The Arab philosopher and physician Averroes (1126–1198) had a much greater knowledge of Aristotle than did any European Christian of his generation; he continued the Aristotelian legacy that had been maintained by his predecessors, particularly the 'Syrian' Alpharabius (872–950), the 'Persian' Avicenna (980–1037) and the 'Andalusian' Avempace (1085–1138), among many scholars who lived in the great Islamic space.

The *Almagest*, the manual of astronomy compiled by the eminent Hellenic–Egyptian Ptolemy, had been translated from Greek into Arabic, but not into Latin. This work, and the book of geography by the same author, remained unknown in Europe

---

33   On Helleno-Islamic culture, see the celebrated work by Franz Rosenthal, *The Classical Heritage in Islam* [1964], London: Routledge, 1994; and more recently Dimitri Gutas, *Pensée grecque, culture arabe*, Paris: Aubier, 2005.

until the early thirteenth century. For a thousand years, Christian Europe had been totally insulated from the impressive advances in the sphere of cartography that had been made by Arab geographers (which is why the term 'geography' did not appear in the English language until the mid-sixteenth century).

The scholastic method, which was so important in the subsequent development of Christian thought, reached it through the intermediary of Islam. In the same way, the Platonic concept of the academy was transformed into the Islamic *madrasa* or *nizami-yyah*, before becoming the European university.[34]

Western historians have sometimes found it hard to admit that the rationalist culture and philosophy of the Greek world had been immortalized and preserved for long years, and even undergone more profound scientific development in the fields of astronomy, geography, medicine, mathematics and geometry, thanks to the Muslims (in close and fruitful cooperation with Christians and Arabic Jews, such as Maimonides, for example), than it did by way of the 'direct European heirs' of the Greeks and Romans.[35] The reasons why Arabic philosophy and Helleno-Islamic science came to a halt at a certain historical moment is an important question, but outside the terms of the present debate.

Although the principle of linear periodization – 'Antiquity', 'Middle Ages' and 'Modern times' was invented early on in the Renaissance (in particular by Leonardo Bruni and Flavio

34   See the stimulating book by George Makdisi, *The Rise of Colleges: Institutions of Learning in Islam and the West*, Edinburgh: Edinburgh University Press, 1981. Makdisi points out that the first college, founded in Paris in 1180, was the act of a pilgrim who returned from Jerusalem (ibid., 225). Simone Weil had already written in 1940 (*Écrits historiques et politiques*, Paris: Gallimard, 1960, 362), 'Can we say that we brought culture to the Arabs, given that they preserved the Greek traditions for us during the Middle Ages?'

35   See on this last point Sylvain Gouguenheim (*Aristote au mont Saint-Michel: Les racines grecques de l'Europe chrétienne*, Paris: Seuil, 2008, 198), who argues that Islam brought nothing to the chosen Western civilization, since 'a guiding thread starts from the Greek cities and unites Europeans across the ages'.

Biondo), the definitive formulation of this chronology owes much to Christophe Cellarius, who published in the late seventeenth century a historical trilogy: *Historia antiqua, Historia medii aevi* and *Historia nova*. From then on, many European literati came to see themselves as the direct and authentic heirs of the 'Greek miracle'.[36] As Marcel Detienne, a subtle Hellenist, ironically pointed out, 'The Greeks, *our* Greeks, are not like the others. No need to argue, just academic routine.'[37]

The philosophers and revolutionaries of the eighteenth century thus borrowed abundantly from the cultures of the Mediterranean. The words 'democracy', 'republic' and 'citizenship' were on everyone's lips, and would soon become guides for action. And yet these masters of language were unaware that in so doing they were radically changing the ancient meaning of the words. If Machiavelli, for example, still evoked the scholars of Rome in his conception of the republic, this was not the case with Jean-Jacques Rousseau. Nothing was more foreign to the latter – whose central political principle rested on the idea that all men are born free and equal, and should therefore participate in the choice of who is to exercise sovereignty over them – than the slave culture of Greece and Rome: without slaves, the direct democracy of Athens would have been unable to function.

Similarly, the slow rise of juridical and political liberalism, emerging from the polycentric world of European agricultural society (from Magna Carta to the beginnings of parliamentary representation), led eventually to a so-called liberal society at the cost of a long process punctuated by struggles. Liberalism appeared as the fruit of a particular three-way conflict, between monarchy, nobility and clergy, which had absolutely nothing in

---

36   On this subject see Lawrence Besserman (ed.), *The Challenge of Periodization: Old Paradigms and New Perspectives*, London: Routledge, 1996, 7–10.

37   Marcel Detienne, *Les Grecs et nous*, Paris: Perrin, 2005, 177; original emphasis. Michel Foucault (*Discipline and Punish: The Birth of the Prison*, New York: Vintage, 1995, 223) also waxed ironic on this point: 'We are much less Greek than we believe.'

common with the Judaeo-Christian or Graeco-Roman worlds of the Mediterranean.

In the same vein, and despite the etymological connection, there is not the slightest equivalence between the productive 'proletariat' of the nineteenth century, as evoked first of all by Gracchus Babeuf and then by Marx, and the *proletarii* of ancient Rome; no more does another borrowing that Babeuf also took from Rome, that of 'tribune of the people', attest to an identity between the two concepts. And, at the other end of this list of analogies, the fact that the Germanic sovereigns proclaimed themselves 'caesar', or that the Russian tyrants had themselves crowned as 'tsars', in no way means that we should see Charles the Bold as the successor to Julius Caesar, or Ivan the Terrible as the distant political heir of Caesar Augustus.[38]

Here is another example, less expected but equally plausible, in the imaginary game of parallelisms designed to establish a solid historical 'continuum' of 'white' civilization from 'Antiquity' on. The reappearance in the West of the trade in slaves, and the massive use of their labour in the eighteenth century, did not lead any Eurocentrist, as far as I am aware, to claim that this horrible phenomenon was part of the 'legacy of Graeco-Roman antiquity'. But why not? Thomas Jefferson, for example, one of the authors of the United States Declaration of Independence, was the owner of more than two hundred slaves, both women and men. In his capacity as architect, moreover, he consistently sought to imitate the classical style of 'Antiquity'. He could therefore be considered, along with his fellow founding fathers of the American nation, a direct descendant of the Graeco-Roman 'mother culture'.

---

38   When Shakespeare wrote his plays *Julius Caesar, Anthony and Cleopatra* and *Coriolanus*, in the late sixteenth and early seventeenth centuries, he was more interested in the power struggles of the English kingdom than in the late years of the Roman Republic. His knowledge of 'Antiquity' was drawn uniquely from Plutarch's *Parallel Lives*, which had recently been translated for the first time into English from French.

 In this example as well, the historical continuity is again totally mistaken. It is obvious today that the expansion of slavery in the eighteenth century, the Age of Enlightenment, was a response to the need to save and accumulate an initial capital, which made a large contribution to the Industrial Revolution. Without cheap cotton produced by slaves, this powerful economic takeoff might well not have occurred in the time and place that it did. In the same way, the republican ideals advanced by Jefferson on the separation of state and religion were an indigenous American phenomenon (and very anti-British), rather than part of a classical inheritance that had followed the West from ancient Rome. As far as slavery is concerned, moreover, the return to a form of collective slavery in the Soviet gulag, established under the authority of a 'proletarian tsar', did not derive from nostalgia for the enslavement of classical times, nor was it the legacy of a collective slavery characteristic of hydraulic societies. Here again, it was a response to the needs of the time: the accumulation of an initial 'socialist' capital to lay down the foundations of an accelerated industrialization.

 The eminent French historian Fustel de Coulanges warned in the nineteenth century against the tendency, very fashionable in his day, to make parallels between the Graeco-Roman era and modernity – whether in terms of vocabulary or ideas. In the preface to his pioneering work *The Antique City* he repeatedly emphasized the profound difference, in terms of both values and mentalities, separating his contemporaries from the people of Athens and Rome, whose history, he pointedly suggested, we should study 'as if we were studying ancient India or Arabia'.[39] Unfortunately, this author did not himself resist the temptation he warned against, and for nationalist and in no way European reasons he went on to argue that the creation of France arose directly from the Latin spirit and not from the Germanic

---

39 Numa Denis Fustel de Coulanges, *The Ancient City: A Study of the Religion, Laws, and Institutions of Greece and Rome*, Boston: Dover, 2006, 12.

inheritance.[40] Under the French Republic this idea would become the guideline of all teaching of history, from Ernest Lavisse in the late nineteenth century through to today.

While Fustel de Coulanges swore fidelity to Roman law, ardent attachment to the Greek spirit reached its apogee in Germany. The pan-Hellenic strand in the construction of German identity has already been much studied.[41] From the Age of Enlightenment through to nineteenth-century nationalism, Greece and Rome were seen by the German historical imaginary as the cradle of Europe, and especially of an exceptional Germany that had managed to preserve the classical inheritance better than other nations. In the writings of the Romantics, the culture of the Greek cities deeply pervades the Indo-European tribal spirit, and both become anchor points for shaping the model of the new German 'self'. In parallel with this, Rome served as a 'natural' foundation for the nascent Reich, and here again as an ancient and venerated model that it was appropriate to continue to imitate.[42]

The new French and German historians were not the only ones to appeal to 'Antiquity' as the starting point for the construction of a young national identity. Italians, English, Americans, Dutch and Belgians each spent a great deal of effort in linking their respective national legacies to a supposed Graeco-Roman past. In the nineteenth and twentieth centuries, in fact, 'Antiquity' appeared the main plank on which the national stories of all the

40   See on this subject Claude Nicolet, *La fabrique d'une nation: La France entre Rome et les Germains*, Paris: Perrin, 2003, 209–25.

41   See, for example, Eliza M. Butler, *The Tyranny of Greece over Germany* ([1935], Cambridge: Cambridge University Press, 2012), in which the author seeks to describe the 'influence' of Greece over circles of the German elite. See also the more recent work of Suzanne L. Marchand, *Down from Olympus: Archaeology and Philhellenism in Germany, 1750–1950*, Princeton: Princeton University Press, 2003.

42   See on this point the article by Zvi Yavetz, 'Why Rome?', *American Journal of Philology*, 97/3, 1976, 276–96. We should add that in this same period, and starting from the sixteenth century, several authors, from Ulrich von Hutten to Heinrich von Kleist, celebrated the 'Teutonic inheritance', taking Tacitus's famous text on Germany as their source. On this subject, see Joep Leerssen, *National Thought in Europe*, Amsterdam: Amsterdam University Press, 2006, 42–4.

chosen peoples of Europe were based. And yet the use of identical terminology to invoke an 'influence', a portmanteau term that means both everything and nothing, was not particularly realistic when the problem was to give shape to a continuous and credible narrative: modern Europeans have at different moments drawn selectively from remote history only what they needed, altering this at will and, as always when the question of 'influence' comes up, deliberately or otherwise leaving aside what they saw as superfluous or unsuitable.

The Western European Narrative

The existence of an 'antiquity' prior to the north European 'West', then in the process of raising itself above the limits of purely agricultural production, contributed more than a little to the creation of the philosophy and history of a long-run progress, supported by thinkers as distinct from one another as Turgot, Condorcet and Kant in the eighteenth century; Hegel, Marx, Comte and Lord Acton in the nineteenth. Indeed, this debatable periodization already formed the foundation of Vico's spiral philosophy of *ricorsi*, formulated in the early eighteenth century.

Given the 'dark Middle Ages', history did not in fact progress on a continuous linear trajectory; on the contrary, it experienced successive ups and downs, phases of decline, awakening and renovation. Already in Herodotus, and in the writings of Ibn Khaldun, we find a tendency to identify a cyclical evolution in certain historical processes. Moreover, the notion of decadence taught by the laws of biology, according to Oswald Spengler in the twentieth century, or Arnold Toynbee's idea of cultural and psychological cycles, are both marked by the terrible 'tragedy' suffered by Western culture with the great collapse of Rome.[43]

---

43   Ferdinand Lot, author of *La fin du monde antique et le début du Moyen Âge* ([1927], Paris: Albin Michel, 1989), is probably the historian who most emphasized this 'tragedy' and break.

And this is still how, in our own day, many intellectuals continue to deplore the decline of a classical culture that was reborn only thanks to the European 'eternal genius'.

Marxist historians have not been alone in considering 'Antiquity', meaning Mediterranean slave society, as the first stage in the history of Western progress; almost all contemporary scholars have also shared this point of view. Three eminent examples, representative of a broad and diverse spectrum of ideas, are presented here, deliberately chosen from authors whom I hold in great esteem.

Marc Bloch, for example, one of the leading historians of the twentieth century whom I have already cited more than once, began his methodological work *Apologie pour l'histoire* with the following declaration:

> For, unlike others, our civilization has always been extremely attentive to its past. Everything has inclined it in this direction: both the Christian and the classical heritage. Our first masters, the Greeks and the Romans, were history-writing peoples. Christianity is a religion of historians. Other religious systems have been able to found their beliefs and their rites on a mythology nearly outside human time. For sacred books, the Christians have books of history.[44]

---

44   Marc Bloch, *The Historian's Craft* [1943], New York: Vintage, 1964, 4. Bloch's declaration is all the more surprising given that, at the start of the gospel of St Matthew, the birth of Jesus is presented against the background of Jahwehist chronology: 'A table of the descent of Jesus Christ, son of David, son of Abraham. Abraham was the father of Isaac, Isaac of Jacob . . . Jacob of Joseph, the husband of Mary, who gave birth to Jesus called Messiah. There were thus fourteen generations in all from Abraham to David, fourteen from David until the deportation to Babylon, and fourteen from the deportation until the Messiah' (Matthew 1:1–2, 16–17). The Koran also contains part of the Bible's chronological mythology, and the name of Jesus is even mentioned (more often than that of Muhammad himself), though as a completely historical figure rather than as Son of God.

It is odd to consider the Old Testatment a book of history, and still more so the New Testament. Bloch's generalized assertion is open to serious question. Not only were the Greeks and Latins not 'our first masters', but as little were they 'history-writing peoples': it is enough to recall the very limited number of people able to read and write in ancient agricultural societies. Neither independent peasants nor slaves had any history, other than a folklore and a cyclical agricultural time. It would be more accurate to say that in the Greek and Roman world there were literati, masters of myth and memory, who left behind them historical stories designed for a narrow stratum of aristocratic elites. In the centuries that followed, no similar stories were written anywhere.

It is still more surprising that Marc Bloch showed no interest in the fact that Ibn Khaldun wrote his remarkable historical works in the fourteenth century, at a time when Christian Europe essentially wrote only chronicles of church history and hagiographies. In Mesopotamian, Egyptian, Chinese and Hebrew antiquity, chronicles of the lives of rulers and priests were already written; they were not invented by the Catholic Church, which to my mind did not decisively raise the quality of such works. In Europe, in fact, Christian writers before the Renaissance were not really able to act as historians in any serious and systematic way, as the pagan scholars of 'Antiquity' had done. For the clerics of the church, as for their contemporary rabbis, though the past might be past it remained deeply present in people's consciousness; it never really died.[45]

At the start of its Mediterranean odyssey, the Christian Church certainly preserved in its archives some major historical texts, but in the universities of Europe, all founded under its aegis, history was not recognized as a discipline worthy of teaching and study, as distinct from theology and law; this situation continued

---

45   On the relation of the 'Middle Ages' to history, see Philippe Ariès, *Le temps de l'histoire*, Paris: Seuil, 1986, 13.

beyond the seventeenth century (the first chair of history in France was not established until 1808). Herodotus, Thucydides and Polybius, whom we see as the founding fathers of history, hardly interested the European chroniclers, and were not translated into Latin before the rise of the humanists; the same was true of the majority of other Greek and Roman historical writings. Even Tacitus, being hostile to monotheism, aroused no interest on the part of Christian scholars (he was unknown to Dante), and could be said to have only emerged from anonymity in the early sixteenth century. Flavius Josephus, on the other hand, a Jew who lived in the first century CE, was revered in the Middle Ages, when his hostility to paganism clearly worked in his favour.

It has to be recognized that the writing of history got under way relatively late in Europe. Until an advanced stage of the Renaissance, when 'Antiquity' was erected into a model of cultural and political behaviour, the first historians were careful not to rival their classical forebears, and therefore abstained from 'correcting' them; in other words, they wrote no history of antiquity. Instead they cautiously undertook to write the history of their own age, which until the eighteenth century mainly took the form of accounts designed to serve the education of royal and princely elites. We can reasonably maintain that the relative 'delay' of history writing in Europe stands out all the more when compared with certain achievements in China and the Muslim-Arabic world before the fifteenth century.

'Antiquity' as the beginning of Europe is an idea so deeply linked to the Western historical imaginary that even the greatest critic of Eurocentrism was unable to avoid the trap of this particular axis of time. Edward Said, despite revealing the discriminatory prejudices of the West towards the East, did not manage to rise above this assumption. Thus he does not begin his account with the Renaissance, the Enlightenment, let alone nineteenth-century Europe (which to my mind would be more credible and accurate).[46] To convince us that 'the Orient, and particularly the Near Orient, became known in the West as its great complementary opposite since antiquity',[47] Said, in the typical mode of Western scholarship, begins his representations of orientalism with Aeschlyus's *The Persians* and Euripides' *The Bacchae*.

Edward Said sees Europe, ever since ancient Greece, as a single continuous civilization that constantly displayed pride and contempt towards the East. To construct this essentialist binary division, it is necessary to leave aside completely the picturesque and admiring descriptions of Near East cultures by Herodotus, along with his propensity to show their historical priority and their contribution to establishing the foundations of ancient Greece. In the name of the unity and linearity of European time, it is also necessary to exclude from the structure of the narrative the points of view expressed by Greek and Roman literati on the non-Western inhabitants living to their north and west. From the 'Indo-European' Thracians, who formed the largest reserve of mercenaries and slaves for the Mediterranean basin, to the Gauls described by Julius Caesar, all these populations living in Europe were perceived as barbarian or semi-barbarian, no better (indeed, often worse!) than the 'Eastern' subjects of great Asian monarchies.

It is hard to imagine Caesar falling for a Gallic queen or a princess from the island of Britannia and giving her a child, as he did with the African-Oriental Cleopatra, queen of Egypt. The objection might be made that Cleopatra was also Hellenic. But though this may be true, Julius Caesar only continued a tradition of Mediterranean 'openness' that was well established: long before him, Alexander the Great did not hesitate to take for his wife the daughter of Darius III, king of the Persians, while Titus, who later became Roman emperor, fell madly in love with

---

46   Edward Said, *Orientalism*, New York: Vintage, 1979.
47   Ibid., 58.

Berenice, the Judaean princess who came to Rome from Jerusalem – a city located in Asia, if there is need to spell this out.

It is sadly not just the typical Eurocentrists who have forgotten that Europe was not the Mediterranean civilization, any more than the shores of the Mediterranean were Europe; their opponents also frequently adopt the same mistaken geo-historical paradigm, thus confirming Westerners in their conviction of being the authentic descendants of the inventors of all-powerful Zeus.

We could cite many other authors on this subject, yet none has gone so far as Christian Meier, a historian specializing in 'Antiquity'. In *From Athens to Auschwitz: The Uses of History*, Meier lays into those who claim to situate the start of Europe's specific scientific and cultural leap forward only in the year 1500.[48] According to him, it is completely mistaken to stick to materialist explanations, whether techno-economic or socioeconomic, as the cities of Europe owe their liberty, their security, and their notion of citizenship above all to the Roman legislative inheritance: 'The modern state is based on a rational conception – would it have been possible without Roman law, or Greek philosophy, for that matter, and Greek political thought?'[49] To sum up, 'Antiquity' forms the starting point and sine qua non of the development of a pluralist and rationalist Europe, from the Middle Ages to modern – and even postmodern – times. Europe owes its impressive achievements in the fields of science and culture above all to 'its' Greek philosophers and 'its' Roman legislators.

In this case, why 'from Athens to Auschwitz'? Meier is a sincere, intelligent, and of course anti-Nazi historian, but he is also very German. His admiration for the world of 'Antiquity', and his insistence that its riches constitute the first stage of

---

48   Christian Meier, *From Athens to Auschwitz: The Uses of History*, Cambridge, MA: Harvard University Press, 2005.

49   Ibid., 57.

Europe's magnificent history, make it hard for him to understand the mass extermination that took place at the heart of this same Greek, Roman and Christian Europe. Why did the European trajectory lead to such a terrible tragedy? The response, according to Meier, lies in the very evolution of the rationalism that, although descending from ancient Greece, was terribly perverted when applied to all fields of existence. Drawing on Max Weber's analyses of the connection between European rationalism and the process of bureaucratization (as well as, in a less evident way, Horkheimer and Adorno's theory of instrumental rationalism), Meier sees Hitler, Lenin and Stalin as representatives of a hermetic logic deprived of spirituality and heart, which set out to transform radically and at top speed the destinies of the societies in which they lived.[50]

If Meier had titled his book 'From the Gothic Barbarians to Auschwitz', this would scarcely have altered the determinism and the cultural and spiritual linearity that mark his overall historical approach, but it would at least have made it possible to approach his essay with greater empathy. The ideal of a 'rationalist Athens' serves him as an escape route: consciously or not, he allows himself to avoid confrontation with the deep irrationalism characteristic of an ethno-biologism in which the notion of a German national community was steeped, something unmatched in the other hegemonic national expressions of Western Europe.

It is possible, with a great deal of effort, to detect a certain cruel instrumental rationalism in the extermination of the Amerindians (the needs of white colonization), the crimes of European colonialism in what has since the Cold War been called the 'Third World' (the exploitation of the mines of the Belgian Congo required docile and cheap labour power), the construction of deadly labour camps under Stalin (the primitive accumulation of capital in the Soviet economy) and even the idea of a

---

50   Ibid., 176.

Nazi German *Lebensraum* (to catch up in the race for colonies). However, sending a shaven-headed 'Semitic' child or a 'congenitally degenerate' Sinti infant to a gas chamber does not betoken a want of spirituality or sensitivity on the part of modern bureaucracy; and still less can responsibility be pinned on the legacy of Athenian rationalism, or the distortions this underwent in the course of time. Even if the rational bureaucracy of the modern state made possible a monstrous industrial massacre, even if it was a necessary condition for this, it was still in no way its cause.

The origin of the German phrase *Arbeit macht frei*, placed at the entrance to Auschwitz and other concentration and extermination camps, seems to have referred rather to a tradition of thought in the Protestant world, figuring already in a text of 1873 by the German philologist Lorenz Diefenbach. This formula establishes a direct connection between 'work' and 'freedom', two 'European' notions par excellence, but the link between them has nothing Greek or Roman about it, nor even Judaeo-Christian.

In the developed Mediterranean space, it would have been very hard to associate work with freedom; more commonly, labour was perceived as a curse rather than a blessing: 'You shall gain your bread by the sweat of your brow', was the injunction of the biblical myth to Adam and Eve, cursed and cast out of Paradise (Genesis 3:19). It is not accidental that in ancient Hebrew terminology, as adopted in modern Hebrew, there is an etymological link between *avoda* (work) and *avdout* (slavery), just as between *oved* (worker) and *éved* (slave). The great Aristotle confirmed this Mediterranean way of thinking when he wrote, 'Nor will those who are to be citizens live an agricultural life; for they must have leisure to cultivate their virtue and talents, time for the activities of a citizen.'[51] The Greek philosopher knew very

---

51   Aristotle, *The Politics*, Harmondsworth: Penguin, 1962, Book VII, 9, 273. Herodotus, also a slave-owner, displays the contempt for manual work that was current among the Egyptians and Greeks of his time. See *The Histories*, Book 2 (167), 164; as well as Xenophon, *The Economist*, Book IV (3) (CreateSpace, 2015, 23).

well that freedom is, above all, the privilege of the master who does not work (and is not a woman), and it is also the condition for active participation in the life of the *polis*. Leisure, not having to engage in laborious activity, forms the foundation of human liberty. It is particularly in this respect, and because it was very little applied to the world of production, that the famous Greek rationalism hardly resembles the rationalism of the modern European bourgeoisie.

I am careful, however, not to claim that a Europe deprived of Greece and Rome forms the geo-historical space from which Auschwitz inexorably emerged; in the same way, I would not venture to maintain that the first German Reich led directly or indirectly to the Third Reich. There was nothing ineluctable about the extermination of human beings as an industrial process, and no chain of connections starting from 'Antiquity'. Despite the fact that in no interpretation of history can the connection between cause and context be seen as scientific, and any explanation actually proceeds from the reconstruction of the past and is not its transparent reflection, I persist in thinking that, without the particular combination of a German nationalism with purifying ambitions and a form of socialization of the masses made apathetic by accelerated industrialization, and without the large-scale butchery of the First World War and the devastating economic crisis of the 1930s (as well as many other factors, primary or secondary, which remain hidden from our gaze), the history of the 1940s might have unfolded in a totally different way.

The Invention of Heterogeneous Time

In my humble opinion, if we can detect a certain form of conditioning, always ambiguous, that presides over the development of human communities, this is located neither in the political or cultural field, nor in that of mentalities, but precisely in the modes of development of technology. In this area of material–intellectual activity, long time is the plasma within which other phenomena emerge and coagulate, with greater or lesser delay. I also incline to believe that only in this domain, and not in those of ethics or aesthetics, is it possible to cautiously invoke the notion of 'progress', in relation to achievements of a growing complexity.

It should also be spelled out that, in this *longue durée*, tempo speeds up with the improvement of material instruments. At the same time, the strong concentric resonance this creates in social ensembles and in ideological and political systems, and also in the form of emotional reactions, has had an impact, sometimes a very surprising one, on the speed of advance, the direction taken, and some of the character of its results. One example can help to clarify this point: the discovery of atomic energy followed directly from the progress of science and technology, whereas the atom bomb is purely a cultural product.

When Charles Péguy asserted in 1913 that 'the world has changed less since Jesus Christ than it has changed in the last thirty years',[52] he was not much mistaken, but perhaps he was a little premature: at the time these words were written, the absolute majority of human beings still worked on the land, as their forebears had done for millennia. A hundred years later in the Western world, at the start of the twenty-first century, between 5 and 10 per cent of workers produce food for the remaining 90 per cent who live in towns. In other parts of the world, half of the population has also experienced rapid urbanization. This is indeed an unprecedented situation for humanity.

Marc Bloch used 'plasma' as a metaphor for time in history, and the concept of *longue durée* comes from Fernand Braudel, who made it a key element of his approach to history, already in the introduction to his doctoral thesis of 1949 on the Mediterranean world. In 1958, Braudel published in *Annales*,

---

52   Charles Péguy, *L'argent suivi de l'argent (suite)* [1913], Paris: Gallimard, 1932, 1.

whose editor-in-chief he had since become, his famous article
'History and the Social Sciences: The *Longue Durée*', which
may be seen as an invigorating historiographical manifesto on
the essence of time.[53] He paid no attention to the traditional
sequencing of historical time, being concerned rather to
understand the various rhythms that mark different sorts of
past and establish a prevailing temporal triad that is now very
familiar.

The longest time is an almost immobile one, undergoing only
slow and almost imperceptible changes: this is the time of climate
and geography. It is the time of plants, the time of the soil, and
of the domestication of living things. Yet this has a decisive
importance, being both the foundation and the starting point of
the movement of other times. Though he never explicitly formulated this, Braudel gave us to understand that this long time is
the most scientific. It is a time that embraces a whole system, and
can hardly be partitioned except at the risk of destroying its
internal logic.

There then is economic and social time, which is itself historically slow and sometimes also cyclical. This level of time includes
long-term processes of trade, developments in prices and monetary exchange, economic growth and recession, demographic
upsurge and decline, the formation of societies and social classes.
This intermediate time offers the possibility of quantifying data
and positing stable structures that may be deciphered scientifi-
cally, as is done in anthropology or sociology.

The short time is that of the journalist or chronicler. It is
especially, though not exclusively, the time of politics: it may
also include economic events (crises, for example) and even
natural phenomena (hurricanes). This rapid time has always
constituted the field of action for the political history of events,
which has documented wars, revolutions and so on. According

---

53   See Fernand Braudel, *On History*, Chicago: The University of Chicago Press,
1982, 25–54.

to Braudel, 'the short time span is the most capricious and the most delusive of all'.[54] Traditional history has unfortunately focused on very short-term political events, which like waves on the ocean rise and fall with great rapidity; neither can they be quantified, nor do they provide immanent objects for social science.

These three levels of time: geo-material time, socioeconomic time and individual-event time, together form a total and globalizing history. Unfortunately, Braudel had little to say on the nature of the relationship between them: we do not know where to make the division between political and economic time, and it is sometimes even hard to settle and identify periods between social time and climatic time. Nor is it clear what criteria are required to define sequences and fix the relations between them. Braudel's aspiration to transform time into a kind of moving structure is certainly logical and stimulating, and it corresponded to the structuralist fashion of the day, but unclear zones remain, particularly in terms of methodology. His thesis may allow us to conclude that the division of time into different periods can never be carried out without taking relations between these levels into account. Yet there is still a gradation of importance: short-run time is the least decisive for understanding large-scale historical processes, the currents of the deep, so to speak, as distinct from the superficial foam. A logic of this kind leads us if not to ignore, then at least not to take seriously into consideration, such short-term revolutions and 'capricious' wars as the French Revolution, the First World War, the Bolshevik Revolution, the Second World War, the conflicts of decolonization and so on.

It would not be completely misguided to see 'Braudelian' conceptions of time as a form of turning away from politics and political history, in the best tradition of the *Annales* school

---

54   Ibid., 28.

(a subject I shall return to in the next chapter).[55] And yet it was Braudel who openly and positively contributed to questioning the one-dimensional and homogeneous conceptions of time that were characteristic of traditional historiography. Ever since the birth of the discipline, which coincided with the emergence of the nation-state, historical time had been seen as purely uniform, and too often teleological by its very definition. The questioning of objective time by Einstein's theory of relativity did not arouse any particular echo in the community of historians. But the introduction of a heterogeneous conception, by Braudel and his *Annales* colleagues, had the effect of beginning to decompose historical time, which ceased to be linear and empty – continuously recharged, like a pistol, by 'great' political events.

From now on, time would also be relative and flexible, better suited to a variety of narrative strategies. The metaphysical time of the priests had ceased to resemble the mental time of the peasants; the autonomous and cyclical time of the latter was not identical to the time of the urban bourgeoisie or the workers in modern industry who had begun to live by the rhythm of the clock (originally placed on buildings and in public spaces, before ending up on the wrist). The investigators of the past had to adapt to this new approach, and integrate the pluralist dimension of time into their historical writings.[56] To a certain

---

55   In the same year that Braudel published his article on the long continuum of time, France was experiencing a particularly 'capricious' history: the 'events' in Algeria were reaching a climax, with hundreds of thousands of victims, and de Gaulle returned to power. Braudel had himself spent more than ten years in the tormented French colony, which had inspired his love of the Mediterranean, yet as far as I am aware he never publicly expressed an opinion on the war and its tragic consequences. His uncritical relationship with colonialism appears in a brief review that he wrote on the anti-colonialist historian Charles-André Julien: 'La double faillite "colonial" de la France', *Annales: Économies, sociétés, civilisations*, 4, 1949, 451–56.

56   See on this point E. P. Thompson, 'Time, Work-Discipline, and Industrial Capitalism', *Past and Present*, 38, 1967, 56–97. Debord wrote in the same year, 'The victory of the bourgeoisie was the victory of a *profoundly historical* time – the time corresponding to the economic form of production, which transformed society

degree, the 'decomposition' of time would indirectly contribute to destabilizing historiographical objectivism, as I shall seek to show below.

Historical interpretations and the meaning that they carry are formed on the basis of temporal sequences and varied periodizations that give rise to different narratives.[57] If the revolution in printing is taken as the start of the modern age, this yields an understanding of history completely different from that which sees the Industrial Revolution as the end of the 'Middle Ages' and the most significant temporal milestone in the history of modern life. In the first case, high culture is more decisive, while in the second, the description of mechanized capitalism and its take-off are the major axis in deciphering codes of modernity. If 1789 is seen as the start of the nineteenth century, historiographical representations of revolutions and changes are not the same as if the 'founding' date is taken as 1815 and the end of the Napoleonic Wars. The same is true for the twentieth century: if the Bolshevik Revolution of 1917 and the fall of the Soviet Union in 1989 are taken as the temporal limits of the last century, then this is essentially the century of Communism. It is quite clearly a different picture if the century is seen as starting in the 1870s and ending in the 1970s: democracy, the expansion of imperialism and decolonization are then the major prisms through which historical knowledge is structured and organized.

In principle, therefore, there would be no problem with a doctoral thesis on the advances of social insurance in Germany from the 1920s to the early 1950s, in which the National Socialist period appeared as simply a marginal chapter in the description

permanently, and from top to bottom. So long as agriculture was the chief type of labour, cyclical time retained its deep-down hold over society and tended to nourish those combined forces of tradition'. Guy Debord, *The Society of the Spectacle*, New York: Zone Books, 1995, 104; original emphasis.

57   See Olivier Dumoulin, 'Les guerres des deux périodes', in *Périodes: La construction du temps historique*, Paris: Éditions de l'EHSS, 1991, 145–53.

of the development of the modern welfare state. In real life, I would hope such a sequencing of time would at least affront our moral conceptions, but it might indirectly aid our understanding of the arbitrary character of all historiography. Perhaps it would also help us understand that a certain partitioning of time can be applied to one field of social activity without necessarily leading to parallel divisions in other domains of human existence.[58]

According to Chronos, the god of time in Greek mythology (in fact, of Phoenician and Canaanite origin), time was eternal, continuous and whole. For Saint Augustine, the brilliant North African philosopher of the fourth century, time always proved deceptive and fleeting: 'I confess to you, Lord, that I still do not know what time is, and I further confess to you, Lord, that as I say this I know myself to be conditioned by time.'[59] Walter Benjamin, for his part, was not mistaken in maintaining, shortly before his tragic death, that the erroneous and damaging conception of humanity's automatic progress 'cannot be sundered from the concept of its progression through a homogeneous, empty time'.[60]

For us common mortals who aspire to study and understand history, time is always divided into slices; in other words, it is a constructed and ideological time, even if we use supposedly objective anchor points known as 'decades' or 'centuries' to define it. Scarcely more than two hundred years ago no one thought in these categories of time: the reigns of monarchs were then the main markers by which historical time was set. Periodization is

58   Paul Veyne (*L'Inventaire des différences*, Paris: Seuil, 1976, 48) perfectly summed up the division of historical time in maintaining that 'historical facts are not organized by periods and by peoples, but by notions'. Marc Bloch, on the other hand, still hoped that history, as a science, would be capable in due course of 'accurate periodization' (*The Historian's Craft*, 181).

59   Saint Augustine, *Confessions*, Oxford: Oxford University Press, 2009, Book XI, xxv (32), 239.

60   Walter Benjamin, 'Theses on the Philosophy of History' [1940], *Illuminations*, London: Pimlico, 1999, 252.

less inscribed in the 'essence' of past events than it is the fruit of our creative imagination (or that of institutions), and it is imposed on the boundless flux of time. This is true even if time does unfold in 'decisive' political events (such as wars, the birth of states, or revolutions), which at the end of the day have themselves been fashioned by historiography in the form of historical events inscribed in certain limits. The partitioning and division of time always display a certain artificiality. The historian's intelligence requires him to be conscious, to wear away and undermine the conventional periodization in order to struggle against the general somniferous effect of today's scholarly 'establishment' and its sworn guardians of the past.[61]

It is equally incumbent on the historian to have an external gaze (or at least glimpse) on his or her own time, and on his or her own identity and status as well, while being perfectly aware that this is an impossible task.

The thesis that sees the Graeco-Roman era as prelude to Europe has been, and continues to be, a doubtful appropriation of a time that in fact never belonged to the Europeans, but which over the centuries has become a 'natural' element of their identity. The stranglehold of the West on this symbolic capital (to the detriment of all other civilizations) is not devoid of flattery and self-glorification. The history of Europe has thus been made much longer and richer than it is, and, still more important, it has been erected into a sublime and 'white' mythistory in which philosophy, mathematics, science, theatre, democracy, civil society and the state were born – and much else besides.

However, these phenomena, just like monotheism, have their origin in another civilization. It is important to emphasize yet again: the infiltration, imitation and borrowing by one

---

61   On the embarrassment of a history professor vis-à-vis the arbitrary periodization of his profession, see the perspicacious text by André Ségal, 'Périodisation et didactique: Le "Moyen Âge" comme obstacle à l'intelligence des origines de l'Occident', in *Périodes: La construction du temps historique*, 105–14.

civilization from another, whatever the degree of presence and power of the fragments in question, do not justify the construction of deceptive representations of historical origin, succession and continuity. No more than European Christians before the Renaissance were 'sons of Israel' or the 'true Israel' (despite their believing this in all sincerity), have European scholars since the Renaissance been 'Greeks' or 'Romans' (despite being persuaded that the men of Mediterranean antiquity were their direct ancestors). These erroneous representations of a continuum also serve to confirm the myth of Eurocentric ownership and domination of Mediterranean civilization that is still buried in deep layers of our collective consciousness.

This phenomenon can certainly be generalized to all national historiographies, which have constantly gone astray by stretching out their collective time, almost back to the first human beings. In our day, however, with the first signs of a retreat of traditional nationalism, intellectuals of the 'old continent' feel the need to continually revisit certain common European foundations in order to supplement, even if partially, their local particularism: French, German, British or Italian, the political demands of which are slowly tending to shrink. In the general opinion, this mission is complicated by linguistic problems, as well as, of course, by the history of such different and varied kingdoms and then nations, so opposed to one another within the European space. Thus, even if we go back to the time of Charlemagne, in the early ninth century, the British Isles and some other regions remain outside this new construction of memory.

All that is left, then, is to throw ourselves into the arms of what supposedly unites us: the 'Judaeo-Christian' legacy (we prefer not to just say 'Christian', to avoid certain distant and forgotten events), or again the cultural tradition of the classical world. We should not be surprised that Jacques Le Goff, one of today's most sensitive and productive historians, and a leading figure in the *Annales* school, could boldly and proudly declare that 'medieval Europe emerged directly from the Roman

Empire',[62] thus confirming that the mythology of white continuity has not yet ended its historic role.

N.B.

I spent a large part of my life enclosed in a consciousness of the past marked by long time. When I was very young, despite growing up in a family who escaped from Eastern Europe and before becoming at all aware of the Nazi extermination, I was taught – in a secular school – about 'our ancestor' Abraham and 'our prophet' Moses. This was my first important encounter with history. Thus, thanks to a long time that was remarkable for its imaginary character, I was recognized as belonging to an 'ancient people', going back four thousand years, and who only 'yesterday', in fact two thousand years ago, were exiled from their homeland and compelled to wander across the world until they decided to make an about-turn and voluntarily regained this land. In present-day Israeli language, there is a common expression for something that does not finish. For example, 'The chapter you have just read is boring and interminable, it's as long as *exile*.'

It took me a great deal of time to 'make the continuum of history explode',[63] to finally free myself from the long national time and fall back to a shorter span of time, that on which my real life unfolds. It was not studying history at university that helped me to take this leap into the unknown, into a less national and therefore less mythological time; it was two wars in which I took part, and above all my participation in the conquest of another people, in an intolerable occupation that has not come to an end, and is 'almost as long as *exile*'.

---

62   Jacques Le Goff, *The Birth of Europe*, Oxford: Wiley-Blackwell, 2005, 10.
63   Benjamin, 'Theses on the Philosophy of History', 253.

CHAPTER 2

Escaping from Politics

I have a bad conscience. I believe that we should all have a bad conscience . . . We let things slide, in 1919–20 and after . . . We sold our souls for the sake of a quiet life and our intellectual work . . . We were wrong. After this present war we shall be too old to act, even with our brains. At least we should help the younger ones to avoid the same mistakes.

Letter from Marc Bloch to
Lucien Febvre, 8 November 1939

Contrary to historical objects, lieux de mémoire *have no referent in reality; or, rather, they are their own referent: pure, exclusively self-referential signs . . . what makes them* lieux de mémoire *is precisely that by which they escape from history.*

Pierre Nora, 'Between Memory and
History: *Les Lieux de Mémoire*' (1984)

In 1977, attracted by its aura of prestige, I began studying at the École des hautes études en sciences sociales. The EHESS had acquired the status of an independent establishment two years earlier,[1] but

---

1   It had formerly been the sixth section of the École pratique des hautes études, established in 1947.

almost all the history students from the Western world (the EHESS students came from several countries) already knew the close connection it had with the *Annales* school. I studied there for five years, defended my doctoral thesis, and had the opportunity to teach within its walls before returning to Tel Aviv. Despite the doubts and fears I initially felt, on account of its prestigious reputation, my encounter with the École counts among the most important and beneficial events of my life. Thanks to this French institution, I was able to become a historian living from this craft, and I am also indebted to it that history became the core of my theoretical preoccupations.

It was particularly fruitful and stimulating for me to rub shoulders with the school's teachers, as well as with its French and foreign students. Through my contact with them, some of my initial views of history were transformed and gave way to a more flexible and dynamic approach. The plurality of methods absolutely captivated me, as well as the dialogue with both sociology and anthropology. The social–technical time I had constructed in Tel Aviv became somewhat more flexible by the addition of supplementary layers. From now on, I would cultivate a time which I called 'cultural', but which would also confuse my mind for several years. I shall try in this chapter to explain the nature and significance of this.

The same year that I began my studies, François Furet was appointed head of the École, succeeding Jacques Le Goff, who had himself taken over from Fernand Braudel with the latter's full approval. By 1977, the socioeconomic history of 'long time' was already no longer the master discipline; it had ceded its hegemonic place to what was called the 'new history', alternatively known as cultural history, anthropological history or, most often, the history of mentalities.

'Cultural history' is a portmanteau concept, and seems capable of embracing the greater part of human activities. Formerly used to denote the world of the arts, literature, science and ideas, the term subsequently took a more anthropological turn, to include art, ritual, different forms of social communication,

conceptions of space and time, personal and imaginary representations, even amorous relations. On the other hand, I never
knew, and still do not know exactly, what is meant by the history
of mentalities – even though this expression is emblematic of an
era.[2] Despite many attempts at clarification, which I shall come
back to, there is no precise definition of this discipline. It is a
theoretical and empirical approach that has given rise to dozens
of interpretations, sometimes opposite and even contradictory. If
the term is vague and wide, the current it denotes remained
unambiguously loyal to the *Annales* tradition, at least in its
constant and categorical rejection of the dramatic 'event' history
of political elites as the central object of the study of the past.

What Was the 'New History'?

Georges Haupt, my doctoral supervisor, was the first to help me
understand what the history of mentalities meant. One day, he
offered a lecture on the Communist International. As the majority of students present, including myself, were anti-Communist
leftists, his presentation was punctuated by sarcastic remarks.
After a while, the angry lecturer rebuked us in no uncertain
terms. I did not note down his precise words and cannot reproduce them exactly, but I remember that his reaction was in
substance as follows: we could continue to wax ironic at the
stupidity, naivety or evil of the Communists, but so long as we
failed to understand why, in Auschwitz, party members tried to
obtain cigarettes to pay their dues at the price of superhuman
sacrifice, we would be unable to grasp the power of Communism
in the first half of the twentieth century. I should also point out
that Georges Haupt bore on his forearm the number that had
been tattooed there at Auschwitz, and that he had subsequently
'deserted' Communist Romania in 1958.

---

2   On the question of the use of this term, see Geoffrey E. R. Lloyd, *Demystifying*
Mentalities, Cambridge: Cambridge University Press, 1990.

Contrary to a large number of professors at the school, Haupt, a political historian, remained to his death a left-wing socialist. It was he who taught me that the mental background of the programmes of parties and movements, inasmuch as it is possible to discover this, can be decisive for the understanding of history. Unintentional and unconscious actions, the world of emotions and symbols that is at work behind public positions, beneath ideology – all this sometimes proves particularly significant and useful for deciphering the codes of modern mass politics.

In the beginning, this approach seemed surprising and problematic for me as a student: a young Israeli whose only baggage was an eclectic mixture of British historiography and Marxism. The eminent historian and philosopher of history R. G. Collingwood had asserted, after all, 'All history is the history of thought', going on to maintain that 'the historian is not interested in the fact that men eat and sleep and make love and thus satisfy their natural appetites; but he is interested in the social customs which they create by their thought'.[3] The historian's ability to bring to light the motivations of people in the past necessarily proceeds by way of logical paths and rational meeting points between his or her own consciousness and theirs. It is incumbent on historians to piece together the thoughts of the past even if they are generally in no position to experience the emotions that went with these. For Collingwood, irrationalism appeared as a blind force that generated in man a behaviour impossible for the historian to objectivize, and thus to decipher or clarify. That task had consequently to be left to the psychologists.

It was Georges Haupt who suggested to me the subject of my doctoral thesis (the relationship of Georges Sorel to Marxism), and I am still grateful to him for this today. This work not only

---

3   R. G. Collingwood, *The Idea of History* [1946], Oxford: Oxford University Press, 1994, 215–16.

enabled me to understand better how Marxian socialism, whatever is said of it, was never a science, but also why history has
never been so either, and never will be. The confrontation with
Sorel, the 'irrational' engineer, taught me that the share of myth
that pervades class consciousness is present in one form or
another in all historical consciousness. Which means not only
that any revolutionary politics oriented towards the future is
always steeped in mythology, but also that the same holds for any
historical narrative examining the past, which is equally conditioned by a view of the future, frequently enveloped in an illusion of progress.[4]

When I began my studies, historians active at the École
constantly referred to the 'new history'. This meant, above all,
cultural history, which increasingly relegated structuralist socioeconomic history, previously omnipotent, to the back burner.
After the champions of a scientific and total history, embodied in
the 1950s and 1960s by Fernand Braudel and his followers,
Annales was now in a third generation. This developed various
versions of cultural history, one wing of which can be termed the
history of mentalities, while another rapidly came to be called
the history of everyday life or micro-history.

In 1974, Jacques Le Goff and Pierre Nora published three
substantial volumes under the title Faire de l'histoire[5] – a banner
planted by the profession at the summit of its Everest. In presenting this work, they denied that they represented any orthodoxy
or particular current, spelling out that 'the new history owes
much to Marc Bloch, Lucien Febvre, Fernand Braudel, and those
who follow on from their innovations'.[6] Bloch, Febvre and
Braudel began to be invoked like Marx, Engels and Lenin had

---

4   On this question: Georges Sorel, *Illusions of Progress*, Berkeley: University of
California Press, 1973.

5   Jacques Le Goff and Pierre Nora (eds), *Faire de l'histoire* (3 vols.), Paris:
Gallimard, 1974 (see a selection in English: *Constructing the Past: Essays in Historical
Methodology*, Cambridge: Cambridge University Press, 1985).

6   Ibid., vol. 1, ix.

been in the Marxist tradition. Certainly, the authors of *Faire l'histoire* each took the historiographical path that seemed to them most suitable, but they all continued to swear allegiance to the holy trinity.

This in no way detracts from the remarkable quality of this collection of articles: from quantitative history to the history of climate, from demography to social history, from politics and economics through to Marxism, displaying a wide spectrum of research methods and fields. The structuralist approach of immobile time dear to Braudel and his disciples still figured, but the dominant tendency was clearly the new cultural and anthropological approach. The unconscious, myth, religion, the body, books, cooking, youth, art, language, cinema and festivals were now the favoured themes of the most eminent French historians.

Jacques Le Goff, one of the two co-editors, focused in this collection on presenting the specific problems and theoretical foundations of the history of mentalities. The particular object of this history, according to him, was to reveal and display the everyday, the automatic, that which is not always rational but remains always interpersonal and pertains to research in social psychology. Mental time differs from the rhythm of development of technologies and social relations, in relation to which it always shows a relative delay: taxi drivers sometimes behave like the drivers of horse-drawn cabs, and workers may preserve the mentality of their peasant ancestors.[7]

Four years later, in 1978, Le Goff explained the development of this approach in a complementary volume entitled *La nouvelle histoire*, co-edited with two other colleagues.[8] This time, he entrusted presentation of the history of mentalities to Philippe Ariès, an original historian who had recently won recognition at

---

7   Ibid., vol. 3, 76–94.
8   Jacques Le Goff, Roger Chartier and Jacques Revel (eds), *La nouvelle histoire*, Paris: Retz, 1978.

this time, and who introduced the concept of mentality by the detour of demographic history.[9] The two volumes amount to a representative summa of the emergence and variations of cultural history at that time. We can also see here the forerunners of the great revolution that would overwhelm history departments throughout the Western world.

From the late 1970s to the early twenty-first century, an increasing number of scholars across the world devoted doctoral theses to subjects that could be classified either in the category of cultural history or in that of one of its two younger sisters: the history of mentalities and the history of everyday life. From the establishment of academic historiography in the nineteenth century to the mid-twentieth century, political history (also flanked by two younger sisters: diplomatic and military history) had been the dominant discipline. From the 1950s to the early 1970s, this had to share supremacy with socioeconomic history; subsequently, however, despite sometimes managing to infiltrate the interstices left to it by cultural history, political history would no longer show the same characteristics: grand national political history had made way for the fragments of post-national history.

To a large extent, as I shall come back to below, the hegemonic expansion of cultural history would contribute to many questions that would stalk the profession at the turn of the century and beyond. Yet, the better to discern this phenomenon and the historiographical turns of the last few decades, we must first return to its sources and developments. Many details are already well known and have been often repeated; yet for a long time they played a decisive part in the formation of my historiographical sensibility.[10] I cannot imagine debating history without a permanent dialogue, both conscious and unconscious, with the

9   Ibid., 402–23.
10   A broad panorama of the history of *Annales* has been brilliantly traced in the four volumes edited by Stuart Clark, *The Annales School: Critical Assessments*, London: Routledge, 1999.

writings of the professors of my Paris years, and those of their teachers before them. And I must at the same time warn my readers from the start that by introducing some of these profiles I also seek to make clear my doubts and criticisms, which grew with the passing of time.

For this reason, I shall present a number of markers in twentieth-century cultural history, mainly French, in the form of brief 'flashbacks'; this is a way of examining not only the subjects that historiographical strategies have succeeded in promoting and placing at the centre of historic memory, but also those that have been omitted or 'forgotten' – certainly not by chance.

The Birth of Post-politics

If the development of cultural history has been closely entwined with that of the *Annales* school, we should also bear in mind two scholars outside France who each played a pioneering role. Jacob Burckhardt, in the second half of the nineteenth century, and Johan Huizinga, in the first part of the twentieth, may be seen as founding fathers of the discipline's 'new' orientation.[11] It is not fortuitous, perhaps, that at the peak of the century of nationalism in Europe – in other words, at a time when the writing of history was similar to a national ideology – these two 'cultural' historians came from 'marginal' regions (Switzerland and the Netherlands) rather from such major centres of history production as France, Germany and Great Britain. Not only were these two scholars the fathers of cultural history; they can also be seen in a certain sense as the inventors of total history, a history that boldly seeks to capture the vibrations of the zeitgeist.

---

11   We could also see Herodotus as the first historian of culture. Despite his proclaimed starting point being an account of the Persian wars, his descriptions of the everyday life, customs and beliefs of the Egyptians, Phoenicians and Greeks are remarkable for their anthropological approach. Ibn Khaldun, Voltaire, and even Fustel de Coulanges could also be included in the category of chroniclers of the past who were interested in human practices beyond the traditional acts of politics.

Such 'arrogant' works as Burckhardt's *The Civilization of the Renaissance in Italy* (1860) and Huizinga's *The Autumn of the Middle Ages* (1919) can certainly be criticized in many respects today, yet we should not minimize the renovation and originality that they display when compared with the 'political-science' historiographies that held the high ground at this time.[12] The relative priority that these two atypical historians gave to art, the imaginary, dreams, song, celebration and myth, rather than to descriptions of government, war and diplomacy, signalled their exceptional character. And although the first part of Burckhardt's work deals with the advent of the Renaissance in a precise political context, it is not by chance that it is entitled 'The State as a Work of Art'.

Many of the arguments made in these pioneering writings proved audacious; others subsequently turned out to be unfounded. Much criticism has been levelled at the generalizations of these broad syntheses, their impressionistic and even intuitive writing, and above all the fact that their sources were all drawn from so-called high culture. The authors made no effort to seek out the least evidence from the popular culture of the age that they otherwise brilliantly reconstructed. They also wrote very little on the 'lower' classes of producers, despite these forming the great majority of the population. Burckhardt felt an explicit repugnance towards such people; Huizinga certainly tried to show some interest, but without any greater success. Little attention has been paid to the fact that these two great works held themselves aloof from the rise of nationalism in the history writing of their day, while at the same time they expressed for the first time a kind of panic fear at the idea of any serious reference to contemporary politics.

Huizinga published his major work in 1919. Five years later,

---

12   Jacob Burckhardt, *The Civilization of the Renaissance in Italy*, London: Penguin, 1990; and Johan Huizinga, *The Autumn of the Middle Ages*, Chicago: The University of Chicago Press, 1997.

from the pen of a brilliant French historian by the name of Marc
Bloch, there appeared an essay entitled *The Royal Touch*.[13] This
was the first bold attempt to integrate into historical analysis
certain working hypotheses recently formulated by an embry-
onic anthropology. *Primitive Mentality*, published two years
earlier by the anthropologist Lucien Lévy-Bruhl, clearly reso-
nates in *The Royal Touch*, at least as far as its underlying assumptions are concerned. Marc Bloch focused his attention on expressions of popular belief, and on the place of worship and rituals as
generators of healing and miracles, which the holders of monar-
chic power and authority could deploy.

To install irrational mentality at the heart of the 'Middle Ages'
was original and completely different from the Eurocentric
approach of the pioneers of anthropology, who investigated
'primitive' tribes far afield from Europe without the least historical concern. A curiosity for supernatural beliefs may perhaps
have been kindled in Bloch as an indirect result of his experience
as a soldier in the First World War, and his intellectual and political inability to come to terms with the vehemence and enthusiasm of the masses at the outbreak of war. His article on the
subject of false rumours from the front and the rear may support
such an explanation, without, however, really confirming it.[14]

Four years after the publication of *The Royal Touch*, Lucien
Febvre, a colleague and future associate of Bloch on *Annales*,
published a book on Martin Luther, which took a further step in
the penetration of historical time by psychology and the analysis
of mentalities.[15] In contrast to Bloch, who sought to include a
large number of people in his study, Febvre chose to focus on the
mental and psychological dimension of a single character. By this

---

13   Marc Bloch, *The Royal Touch: Sacred Monarchy and Scrofula in England and
France* [1924], London: Routledge, 2015.

14   Marc Bloch, *Réflexions d'un historien sur les fausses nouvelles de la guerre*
[1921], Paris: Allia, 1999. Several texts by Bloch refer to his impressions of the First
World War.

15   Lucien Febvre, *Martin Luther: A Destiny* [1928], London: J. M. Dent, 1930.

approach, and by studying the reception of Luther's ideas, he aimed to examine the general state of mind of the age. And if it was anthropology that attracted Bloch at this stage, Lucien Febvre's interest seems to have been more directed at the psycho-logical reactions that facilitated and conditioned the dominant ideology in the sixteenth century, in other words, the Christian faith.

How should we explain that in 1920s France historical analy-sis came to place such emphasis on the mental and psychological dimension? It is hard to answer this question with certainty, knowing as we do that in history any relationship between cause and effect remains extremely hypothetical. We can assume that it was not the long path of Cartesian culture that prepared the ground for this. On the other hand, we can recall that, in the late nineteenth century, two cultural centres, Vienna and Paris, both displayed a major interest in the irrational and unconscious. The works of Gustave Le Bon on crowd psychology, or of Georges Sorel on myths, cannot be compared with the intellectual contri-butions of Sigmund Freud, but we should at least bear in mind that in all European capitals the old placid rationalism had expe-rienced a fatal blow in the wake of the First World War, and that it was in Paris that surrealism arose and made its mark.[16]

In 1929, the same year that René Magritte exhibited his work *The Treachery of Images*, in which a painting of a pipe was accom-panied by the witty motto 'Ceci n'est pas une pipe', Marc Bloch and Lucien Febvre founded the journal *Annales d'histoire économ-ique et sociale*, bearing the standard of anti-positivism into the field of historiography. Of course, there is a great gap between the two historians and the surrealist painter. Bloch and Febvre's project should rather be seen in the line of the successful essay published two years earlier by Julien Benda, *The Treason of the*

---

16   In the 1930s, the journal of the Frankfurt School, then published in Paris, likewise showed great interest in introducing psychology to sociological analyses, with the important advantage, in relation to those of *Annales*, of a pioneering recourse to Freudianism.

Intellectuals.[17] I am tempted to cautiously define the common feature of these works as a flight from politics.

We are in 1929, the year of the great economic crisis. The new journal, which appeared just before the Wall Street crash, unambiguously expressed the beginning of a significant change in historical research. Historians would now start to dethrone politics from its position as the permanent queen of historiography. The shocks of finance and economics in the Western world would only confirm this emphasis on the impotence of human society to master its destiny by any intention from above.

Right from the start, the two Strasbourg scholars made the traditional history of political events their number one enemy. They saw the many works that discuss kings, knights, armies, wars and peace treaties as secondary at best, most often superfluous, if not insipid. In their articles, they regularly expressed contempt for high politics, which they saw as a by-product of more profound and essential social processes. They referred to the dominant political historiography as 'positivist', a term that would subsequently become pejorative. They constantly presented the social sciences that were flourishing and prospering around them – sociology, demography, ethnology and economics – as examples to follow. For the historian, it was society as a whole that was the central object, not just its elites. But, in contrast with these adjacent disciplines, the vocation of history was to examine society in time, in its evolution, and not just as an immobile structure. They saw the prevailing discipline of Durkheimian sociology, with its frozen models, as something to be blocked, an object for pillage and competition, and at the end of the day, annexation. Very early on, the ambition of *Annales* was to be a journal for all social sciences – an objective finally achieved.

---

17   Julien Benda, *The Treason of the Intellectuals*, New Brunswick: Transaction Publishers, 2006.

The two founders, however, like the other researchers whose articles they published, never translated their hostility and contempt towards traditional history into a serious and systematic critique of the national-political historiography that still dominated all the systems of research and diffusion of historical knowledge. Despite their background in the 'Great War', they did not trouble themselves with deep reflection on how to modify the principles that underlay the teaching of political history, or the way it was transmitted to generations of new students in the educational system. Moreover, despite a comparative approach and their openness to other national histories, these two fervent patriots, who had supported the war to the bitter end, always believed in the venerable longevity of the French nation – a subject that I shall return to in the next chapter.

During its first forty years, in other words until the late 1960s, what *Annales* published above all was economic and social research. While it gave slight supremacy to social history in the 1930s, the hierarchy was reversed in the 1950s and 1960s, to the advantage of economic history. A special and almost sacred place was granted at the same time to demography, alongside geography: history had to be scientific, and there is no solid science without quantifiable and precisely measurable data. Statistical series were thus fundamental to historical reconstruction; measurable data were clearly privileged in every analysis and interpretation. One particular fact, often lost sight of, should be recalled: despite the journal's two editors having been specialists in the 'Middle Ages' and the early modern era, they stood for a suppression of the rigid separation between past and present. Thus more than 40 per cent of the articles published dealt with contemporary history: 'The banking crisis in Germany', 'Controversy over the role of gold in the world crisis', 'Banking organization in Belgium since the war', 'Agrarian discontent in the American West', and 'Agricultural collectivization in the USSR' are among the many subjects of this type that filled the journal's pages for a whole decade.

We should also observe that the school that was in the process
of foundation did not make the analysis of modes and processes
of economic production its primary focus, privileging instead a
history of prices, commodity circulation and economic geography. We do not find among the contributors to *Annales* critical
analysts of existing economic and political structures, as were
being produced by Frankfurt School scholars such as Friedrich
Pollock, Henryk Grossman or Karl Wittfogel. It is no exaggeration to say that, for the majority of writers in *Annales*, economic
history was always chiefly concerned with the market economy,
cycles of capital and exchange processes, rather than the historical study of human labour, its context and its exploitation. This
is perhaps the reason why we also find, throughout the long
existence of *Annales*, scarcely any profound research on industrialization and its social consequences.

It is perhaps no surprise that this completely new journal
contained no serious articles on the nature of the enormous
political and mental fracture provoked by the 'Great War'. It
would be misguided to expect to find in the many issues of
Annales any analysis of the enthusiastic mobilization of the
community of historians themselves 'for the homeland' – let
alone a voice among historians equivalent to Romain Rolland,
Bertrand Russell or Albert Einstein. However, the fact that a
historical journal, which had begun to appear ten years after the
ratification of the peace treaties, carried no debate on the causes
of the first total war, its development and its dramatic consequences for European societies, is particularly revealing of its
orientation and ideological tendencies.[18] At a time when politics
was ceasing to be the reserved domain of narrow elites and

---

18   Not all historians remained indifferent to the war and its consequences, even
if they had initially supported it enthusiastically. Albert Mathiez, for example, had no
hesitation in denouncing as early as 1926 those clauses in the Versailles treaty that
held Germany solely responsible for launching the war. See J. Friguglietti, *Albert
Mathiez, historien révolutionnaire*, Paris: Société des études robespierristes, 1974, 186
and 226.

becoming a mass affair, something that affects, disturbs and abuses everyone, it was losing its pertinence in the eyes of the new historians.

In the same way, despite the major place and attention paid to the contemporary era, the issues of *Annales* contain very little information about the 'events' of the 1920s and 1930s. Yet the presence in Paris of a large number of refugees had created a singular situation: the Austrian exile Franz Borkenau, who was close to the Frankfurt School, was invited to publish a short article on Fascism and syndicalism in Italy, while Lucie Varga, his partner, also contributed in the form of an impassioned article on the subject of Nazism.[19] Most people would see this as a meagre harvest for a period stretching over eleven years for Italian Fascism and seven years for Nazism. More strikingly, however, there is nothing to be found on the rise of Judaeophobia right across Europe (including France), nothing on collectivization in the Soviet Union and the Ukrainian famine, nothing on the Civil War in Spain and Franco's seizure of power, nothing even on the socioeconomic causes of the strike wave triggered by the victory of the Front populaire in France. This gives the impression that the 'event' politics of the time was not sufficiently historical for *Annales*, and that everything that risked arousing an ideological difference or a debate about values, particularly concerning France, was rejected for publication (we must assume that such articles were at least submitted).

It is worth adding that, despite this focus on the economic and social, we find very little serious reference to class conflict, and still less to its relationship with existing politics and regimes. The two

---

19   Franz Borkenau, 'Fascisme et syndicalisme', *Annales d'histoire économique et sociale*, 6, 1934, 337–49. Lucie Varga, 'La genèse du national-socialisme: Notes d'analyse sociales', *Annales d'histoire économique et sociale*, 48, 1937, 529–46. See also the apologetic article of Peter Schöttler, 'Marc Bloch et Lucien Febvre face à l'Allemagne nazie, in *Genèses: Sciences sociales et histoire*, 21, 1995, 75–95, and the more serious essay by Natalie Zemon Davis, 'Censorship, Silence and Resistance during the German Occupation of France', in Clark, *The Annales School*, vol. 1, 122–37.

'socioeconomic' editors had read very little of Marx, despite both possessing a solid background in German historiography. As moderate and cautious republicans, they preferred not to give this baggage too visible an expression, and stuck to a few non-committal observations. It is no less surprising that, in a pioneering approach that rightly rejected the simplistic determinist and materialist causalities of dogmatic Marxists, and was quite reasonably content with correlative explanations of the interaction of socioeconomic, psychological and ideological processes, the presence of Max Weber is very discreet, if not totally marginal (perhaps due to the fact that analysis of the state apparatus and political power forms a constant central axis in his sociology).[20] If we want to read an original and innovative analysis of assembly-line work in the factories of the time, or understand the development of mentalities in connection with the situation of manual workers in the first half of the twentieth century, we have to refer to Simone Weil's *La condition ouvrière*, and perhaps certain well-selected pages of *Journey to the End of the Night* by Louis-Ferdinand Céline, an anti-Semitic writer, but with a cutting gaze.[21] The cinema-going public could also 'study' Taylorism in the 1930s, not in the pioneering socioeconomic journal but thanks to two genuinely 'sociological' films: René Clair's *À nous la liberté!* of 1931, and Charlie Chaplin's *Modern Times* of 1936.

If anyone should have persisted in looking for a serious political-economic analysis of the relationship between social classes and fascism or Nazism, they would have found it less in

20   This absence is all the more strange, given that in the very first issue of the journal, Maurice Halbwachs had tried in vain to draw attention to the German sociologist. See his article 'Max Weber: Un homme, une oeuvre', *Annales d'histoire économique et sociale*, 1, 1929, 81–9.

21   Simone Weil, *La condition ouvrière* [1937], Paris: Gallimard, 2002; and Louis-Ferdinand Céline, *Journey to the End of the Night* [1932], New York: New Directions, 2006. *Annales* only published an article by Georges Friedmann, a young Marxist still enthusiastic about industrial progress who, however, already expressed reservations about its psychological effects. See 'Fréderic Winslow Taylor: L'optimisme d'un ingénieur', *Annales*, 36, 1935, 584–602.

the only 'Marxist' article by one of the *Annales* contributors than in an essay (perhaps too strong in its commitment) by Daniel Guérin, a left-wing socialist outside the academic world.[22] And if they wanted to read a historically significant critique of the oppressive role of French colonialism, then at the summit of its national 'glory', they could not have been satisfied with the regular reports in *Annales* by Henri Labrouet, a former colonial official, but would have needed to turn instead to André Gide's *Travels in the Congo*, a bold 'anthropological' account.[23]

All these points, and other similarly sensitive subjects, were treated with the utmost caution, if not passed over in silence, in the debates of a journal that billed itself as struggling against 'academic immobilism'. The well-known assertion that contemporary history is always too important to be left to academic historians proves fully justified in the case of the 1930s *Annales*. We should be in no way surprised, accordingly, that in 1933, four years after the foundation of the journal, Lucien Febvre was appointed to a chair at the prestigious Collège de France.[24] Marc Bloch, for his part, had to 'content himself' with a professorship at the Sorbonne, in 1936.

It was a short step, therefore, from the margins to the centre of the university milieu, for a current that presented itself as 'nonconformist' and intransigently critical of the institutional writing of history. We know, however, that the conformism of '1930s nonconformists' was the prevailing fashion in the Paris of the time – not much of a threat to either the political

---

22   Henri Mougin, 'Le destin des classes et les vicissitudes du pouvoir en Allemagne entre les deux révolutions: Un essai d'interprétation', *Annales*, 9, 1937, 570–601; Daniel Guérin, *Fascisme et grand capital: Italie–Allemagne* [1936], Paris: Gallimard, 1945.

23   André Gide, *Travels in the Congo* [1927], New York: HarperCollins, 2000.

24   A year before this appointment, Anatole de Monzie, minister of national education, had commissioned Febvre as editor-in-chief of the prestigious *Encyclopédie française*.

institutions of the Third Republic or its traditional intellectual production.[25]

First Steps in 'Mentality'

Politics, and the whole balance of forces inherent to it, was not the only subject to be evicted from the new historiographical agenda. The history of mentalities, despite its promising beginnings, appeared less pertinent in the 1930s, when the focus was on the shocks and instability of the economy. I can find only one important text, from an author close to *Annales*, that attempts an interesting imbrication of history and mass psychology: Georges Lefebvre's *The Great Fear of 1789*, published in 1932.[26] Marc Bloch, for his part, made a brilliant turn to social history par excellence – a trajectory already announced by his masterpiece *Feudal Society*, published just before the Second World War.[27] *Annales* also abstained almost completely from publishing material on cultural and anthropological history. However, despite the strongly 'economic sociology' orientation given to the journal, Lucien Febvre's personal intellectual trajectory proved to be more varied and interesting, and the unusual breaches he opened up deserve to be placed in a rather larger context.

Four books, written in the years 1938–42, form, in my opinion, the starting point for a new type of approach to history: *Homo Ludens* by Johan Huizinga, Norbert Elias's *The Civilizing Process*, Mikhail Bakhtin's *Rabelais and His World*, and Lucien

25   I am referring here to a certain proximity between the founders of *Annales* and the technocratic theories of the 'neither right nor left' currents of the 1930s. See on this subject, François Dosse, *L'histoire en miettes: Des* Annales *à la 'nouvelle histoire'*, Paris: La Découverte, 1987, 63–4. This standard work is the first to attempt a critical synthesis of the history of this school.

26   Georges Lefebvre, *The Great Fear of 1789*, New York: Schocken, 1989.

27   The chapter 'Modes of Feeling and Thought' contains a stimulating psychological analysis: Marc Bloch, *Feudal Society*, London: Routledge, 2014, 79–94.

Febvre's *The Problem of Unbelief in the Sixteenth Century.*[28] On the eve of the great catastrophe, and even during it, these four fundamental works totally distanced themselves from the twentieth century and cast light on fragments of a remote past, while marvellously sketching the mental and intellectual developments that marked the history of the West.

The fact that these four books turned their back on the politics of their time does not mean that politics did not affect their fate, their positioning, and that of their authors, as well as the development of historiography. Just after the war, the works of two institutional professors, Huizinga and Febvre, whose respective position and fate under the Occupation had been very different, aroused great interest and brought their authors high consideration. The most original work, that of Elias, a German Jewish refugee from Breslau, deprived of employment and stateless, was published in Switzerland in 1939 before disappearing from bookshops and libraries for thirty years. The destiny of Bakhtin's work, himself an exile in his own country, was in a certain sense still more unfortunate. Presented as a thesis in Moscow in 1940, this was never accepted as a doctorate, and published only in 1965.

Homo Ludens is both enjoyable and serious. In his preface of 1938, and after seeing the torchlight marches organized in German cities, Huizinga declared that the term *Homo sapiens* had become inappropriate for the present age. *Homo ludens* seemed to him more appropriate, and Huizinga proposed to examine how culture was reproduced in the form of play. In other words, play is not an element of culture, it precedes it, being to a large degree its very origin after the fundamental

28   Johan Huizinga, *Homo Ludens: A Study of the Play-Element in Culture*, London: Penguin, 2014; Norbert Elias, *The Civilizing Process: Sociogenetic and Psychogenetic Investigations*, Oxford: Blackwell, 2000; Mikhail Bakhtin, *Rabelais and His World*, Bloomington: Indiana University Press, 2009; Lucien Febvre, *The Problem of Unbelief in the Sixteenth Century: The Religion of Rabelais*, Cambridge, MA: Harvard University Press, 1985.

human needs have been satisfied. It is a non-lucrative activity that procures pleasure, and is found in all known societies. In the form of a comparative analysis, Huizinga reviews the meanings of the word 'play' in several languages as well as its evolution and its presence in various sectors of social activity: from law to politics, religion to poetry. The most important element, perhaps, in the original point of view of the Dutch historian, is that ludic activity implies acting in a disciplined way, as it requires both order and freedom, submission to law but also a wide space left to invention and imagination.

Elias's *The Civilizing Process* is a work of a very different kind. It is based on a large volume of textual evidence and has a far more panoramic scope. We certainly find in it quotations from canonical philosophers and thinkers, but also extracts from codes of court customs and texts that were more secret or had fallen into oblivion. The main actors in the historical account, which stretches from the twelfth century to the twentieth, are the knife, the table, the fork, the handkerchief, clothing, and, above all, of course, the evolution in the uses made of them. The models of behaviour and rules of politeness that appeared at the court of the sovereign and then filtered down to the bourgeois class were not the result of chance, but responses to a sociopolitical historical logic. The same goes for the public expression of sexual relations, the concealment of nudity and the appearance of shame. Contrary to his many imitators in the 1970s, the particularity of Elias's pioneering position lies in a subtle depiction of mental reactions, which he does not separate from the evolution of the system of social classes, and which he also connects by a sophisticated analysis with relations of political power. The monopoly of the use of force claimed by the state, for example, forms one of the main factors in blocking and restricting personal violence. Sadly, this interaction between force and culture would be the object of only little subsequent research – with the notable exception of Michel Foucault and Pierre Bourdieu, who continued in a different form the fruitful approach of *The Civilizing Process* (which itself followed several texts of Max Weber).[29]

If we see Huizinga as a historian of culture par excellence, and Elias as an anthropological historian, Bakhtin may seem 'only' a theorist of literature. The original title of his thesis, however, was 'The Work of François Rabelais and Popular Culture in the Middle Ages and under the Renaissance', which fully qualifies its inclusion in the field of cultural history rather than that of the history of literature. If Bakhtin was interested in Rabelais, this was above all to illustrate, through him, what he saw as a form of popular humour in a world in the process of moving towards modernity. It is no longer possible to hear the jokes of peasants, who left behind them no comic legacy. Rabelais, however, took up some of their laughter in the pages of his picturesque work. True, he wrote for intellectuals like himself, but thanks to his fine and sensitive ear he was able to convey the joy of popular carnival, thus attesting to the ambivalence of class relations at the dawn of the modern era. Carnival, a festival held once a year, offered the occasion to let off steam; it was one of the rare moments when the superior plays at inferior and vice versa, in both the social and the physical sense. Carnival, where spectators become actors, where masks express topsy-turvy identities, was a singular cultural microcosm, which unleashed and gave free rein to popular imagination and even joyous sexual debauch. The caricatured and fantastic figures of Rabelais, directly borrowed from the tradition of peasant festivals, aroused great interest in Bakhtin. What interested him was not Rabelais as an intellectual, but precisely the popular culture that had

---

29   This does not mean that Elias is immune to criticism. The state monopoly of the use of force certainly restrained in the West the impact of physical violence on individuals, but it also translated this into national violence abroad, as well as towards dissidents 'within'. Colonialism and colonization, the two world wars and Nazism all show that the modern state, far from ending or moderating impulses, regulates them and orients them into consensual collective acts, as an integral part of this 'civilizing process'. As for public nudity, this has not disappeared but, on the contrary, been abundantly used in a variety of cultural representations both 'high' and 'low'.

been wiped off the map, disappearing without leaving behind any direct trace.

The Rabelais who attracted Lucien Febvre's attention in 1942 was quite different. As against the many commentators who saw the author of *Gargantua* as one of the first atheists of modern times, Febvre set out to show that unbelief was impossible in the sixteenth century. Rabelais was certainly treated as a heretic, particularly by his rivals at the Sorbonne, and if he did not spare his mockery of the church and its servants, he maintained a God particular to himself. Like all his contemporaries who believed in a supreme being, Rabelais remained attached to the New Testament. Febvre's central question relates to how Rabelais's contemporaries, rather than ourselves, read and understood him, for which purpose we have to try to piece together the moral climate of the sixteenth century, particularly with the aid of the tools of collective psychology. Febvre constantly insists that it is important not to resort to anachronistic categories and classifications, those of our own age. Faith and church were still in Rabelais's time the horizon of mental life, and we must be aware, in contrast to certain historians, that Rabelais was still far from the Age of Enlightenment of the eighteenth century.

The main innovation Febvre introduced into his procedure for presenting the spirit of the time lies in his original use of the formula 'mental equipment'. Despite not giving a clear definition of the concept, his descriptions allow us to infer that this equipment corresponds to a system of representations (words, concepts, images, symbols and so on) that express an ensemble of sensibilities, corresponding to the level of social, technical and scientific development of an era. Collective mental changes provide the necessary foundations for deciphering intellectual expressions and their written traces; if these are not revealed and integrated into historical analysis, one will always fall into a sterile ahistoricism. There are certainly in every society different strata, bearers of specific psychological lines, as not all humans of a particular era use the same items of mental equipment; but there remains nonetheless a foundation common to all members of a society, representing what one can call the cultural code of the age.

Febvre applied this fine association of psychology and intellectual biography to another historical work, a book on Marguerite de Navarre, and in the postwar years he dealt with the significance of the history of mentalities in a series of short but very complete articles.[30] However, the specific orientation of research that he inaugurated found no immediate followers after the Second World War; for many years historians turned their gaze to other horizons.

An Almost Scientific Structuralism

Lucien Febvre, who as a historian rejected 'politics', practised it with talent and ingenuity in the world of the university. In contrast to Marc Bloch, he was appointed to the Collège de France and continued his teaching for the whole period of the German Occupation, even managing to preserve his journal (at the price of suppressing Bloch's Jewish surname from the editorial committee and the publication) – all elements that confirm his sagacity, his savoir faire, and a strong conformism.[31] At the

---

30   Lucien Febvre, *Amour sacré, amour profane: Autour de l'Heptaméron* [1944], Paris: Gallimard, 1966. Febvre's articles on the history of mentalities are collected in a stimulating anthology: *La sensibilité dans l'histoire*, Brionne: Montfort, 1987.

31   In the same year, 1941, Martin Heidegger removed from the second edition of *Being and Time* the Jewish name of Edmund Husserl. We can note here that Febvre was no more conformist than the majority of French people. He was not anti-Semitic and no friend of the German Occupation. The desire to maintain the publication of *Annales* at any price, even the removal of Jewish names, was his response to a political objective, as he explained in a letter to Marc Bloch: 'It is because *Annales* is a French periodical . . . and its demise would be a new death for my country'. Letter of 19 April 1941, in March Bloch and Lucien Febvre, *Correspondance*, vol. 34, Paris: Fayard, 2003, 130–31. Febvre hoped to continue 'normal' activity. We simply have to remember that this was all that the Nazi occupiers wanted of Parisian producers of culture and entertainment. On Lucien Febvre as a university politician, see Maurice Halbwachs, 'Ma campagne au Collège de France', *Revue d'histoire des sciences*

end of the war, with the help of subsidies from the Rockefeller Foundation, Febvre managed to establish on a secure basis the sixth section of the École pratique (sciences économiques et sociales), naturally becoming its first director.[32] The establishment would soon be combined with the prestige of the periodical (whose title was changed to *Annales: Économies, sociétés, civilisations*), and go forward to world acclaim.

Robert Mandrou and Fernand Braudel were the closest disciples of Lucien Febvre. Despite both being historians with an impressive body of work, they did not enjoy equal status in the field of academic power relations. Mandrou was to a large extent the continuer of Febvre in terms of theory, while Braudel, influential and brilliant, appeared his natural heir in university politics. Soon after the death of Febvre in 1956, Mandrou, the 'Trotsky' of the *Annales* revolution, was dismissed from the board of the journal and the direction of the École, and Braudel became its all-powerful director. The socioeconomic orientation was confirmed as the hallmark of the journal for the next twenty years, thus continuing to a large degree what had been prevalent before and during the war. Braudel, whose interest lay essentially in what can be called 'medium long time', consecrated slow socioeconomic mutations as the most respectable and venerable historical time.

From now on, the study of structures would definitively supplant that of events: tables, diagrams, curves and maps increasingly invaded articles and the majority of doctoral theses. All students preparing higher degrees turned to 'scientific' and very 'objective' quantitative work; by doing so, they sought to increase their chance of being able to lead a university career and publish their thesis under a prestigious imprint. The unprecedented

---

humaines, 1, 1999, 189–229.

32   This financial generosity clearly had a political purpose: the dangers of Communism for the future of France. Joseph H. Willit, head of the social science department of the Rockefeller Foundation, was explicit on this subject in 1946. See Dosse, *L'histoire en miettes*, 120.

development of higher education in the West in the 1950s and 1960s was accompanied by a growth in the number of lecturers and their battalions of assistants. For the first time in history it became possible to use many 'little helpers' in gathering statistical data about economy, society and demography. Quantitative history was crowned queen of the day, first of all in France, then in Great Britain, the United States, and even Germany.

The historical context of the first two decades after the war seemed to validate these new tastes and subjects. The growth of economic production, the rise of urbanization, the advent of the welfare state in the Western world (and to a lesser extent in the Eastern bloc), did much to help people forget the terrifying nightmare of the 1940s, while politics in France, particularly after the defeat in Indochina, seemed to many people a series of isolated acts, unimportant in the best of cases, and too painful in the worst (Algeria).

A whole generation of French intellectuals, including young historians, rallied for a decade to a kind of national Stalinism: a fashion that is explained, among other things, by the attitude of the bourgeois elites during the war, by the Communists' aura of heroic resistance under the Occupation, and also by the echo of the victory of Stalingrad. Very quickly, however, most of them left politics behind to devote themselves to 'pure' historical research, which in their minds had become no less 'scientific' than Marxism. The *Annales* school seemed to them a home and an ideal refuge.

As against what happened in England, where historians ceased to be Communists but remained faithful to Marx, continuing to infuse their work with a very sophisticated kind of historical materialism, the French scholars grouped around *Annales* were very 'materialist', yet neutralized the dimension of conflict in their representations of the past, which they stripped as far as possible of any political charge. Whereas contemporary Parisian intellectuals were beginning for the first time to seriously confront Marx's thought, and called on their colleagues to seriously engage with the problems of the day (Jean-Paul Sartre, Henri Lefebvre, Louis Althusser, and later Michel Foucault), a significant part of the French historical field, with *Annales* in the leading role, remarkably managed to avoid socio-political conflict, in both past and present. In France, since the start of intensive industrialization, historians at the heart of historiographical production increasingly chose to interest themselves in the peasants of the Middle Ages rather than in modern workers, to study rural life rather than urban develop-ment. This is why we do not find, in the *Annales* school, the French equivalent of a work like *The Making of the English Working Class*, published by E. P. Thompson in 1963 – and this is certainly no accident.[33]

This resembled a general return to the 1930s, but this time with a still greater insistence on the 'scientific' sacralization of the existing. The *Annales* school, in the time of Fernand Braudel, created a positivist historiography in the full sense of the term, despite some gestures in the direction of popular Marxism and the collaboration of the socialist Ernest Labrousse with the jour-nal. The term 'positivism' should not be understood here in the meaning it was given by its founders, in the late 1920s, but rather that conferred by the Frankfurt School, and particularly Herbert Marcuse – in other words, the recording and sacraliza-tion of reality, both past and present, with a neutralization of the critical dimension in its understanding and deciphering (a conception also shared by certain representations of the future that apply existing values, whether consciously or not). This kind of history writing, which rejects any projection towards the future, is generally accompanied by a loss of meaning; which is

---

33   This book was not translated into French until 1988. So as not to wrongly 'blame' French historiography, I should add that historians from the Sorbonne (after the war!) such as Georges Lefebvre, Albert Soboul and Ernest Labrousse displayed in their work, on both a historical and a political level, a far livelier critical sense than the inner circle of *Annales*, even if this was not always exempt from a certain doctrinal rigidity.

why the strong influence of social history began at a certain point to decline.[34]

The irruption in the second half of the twentieth century, at the heart of the Western world, of an intellectual youth that opposed the existing institutions with the utopian demand to bring imagination to power, upset the calm and regular progress of university research. Quantitative, demographic and economic history suddenly appeared less attractive and relevant as against the questions that concerned the young generation. The volume of goods crossing the Mediterranean in the sixteenth century compared to the fifteenth may be important for history, but certainly not for attracting the best energies of youth. The ups and downs of cereal prices in the twelfth century are essential for understanding the lives of the peasants of that time, but would only interest an ever more limited public. What is the use of history if those engaged in it find no responses to the intellectual and political needs of its students, or at least to their elementary curiosity?

As we all know, the student revolt of the late 1960s and early 1970s did not lead to a political revolution. It had scarcely any impact on the social balance of forces, while the global ideologies that it drew on fell pitifully into the margins of history. Yet in a certain way, the student movement did correspond to a kind of cultural mini-revolution: it gave public expression to profound developments, previously hidden in the deep unconscious of Western society.

The early 1970s saw the start of a new and significant socio-economic revolution. Intensive industrialization and the spectrum of activities connected to it began to disappear from the cities. In the last quarter of the twentieth century, automation and the delocalization of productive companies to regions outside

---

34   Huizinga was already aware that 'historical thinking is always teleological'. See his 'Historical conceptualization', in Fritz Stern (ed.), *The Varieties of History: From Voltaire to the Present*, London: Macmillan, 1970, 293.

the Western sphere would alter social stratification and the organization of work in many sectors. The working class lost power and its political representation went into decline. Manual labour in production (as opposed to services) became a minority occupation and gradually gave way to work with signs and symbols. An ever more abstract culture prevailed in production and turned the wheels of the global economy.

In parallel with this, a culture of leisure increasingly developed, both less private and more 'individualist'. On the one hand, it became more accessible, though dependent on state communication and private television channels; audiovisual media burst into every home, with their quota of 'authentic' and 'fictional' stories about the present, past, and even future. On the other hand, the leisure culture also involved care of the self: sensuality and sexuality, family relations (establishing differences of taste between generations), everyday life, illness, diets, ageing and even the end of life.

'Public' debate in the media replaced the collective political forms that had previously characterized national culture, focusing above all on the immediate satisfaction of the spectator. Consumer culture is not a culture with a long time, but rather a short-time culture that hops and zaps from one button to another, changing at breakneck speed.

One after another, historians who had formerly worn heavy socioeconomic garments renewed their wardrobe accordingly. The previous goods had lost their attraction for consumers and had to be changed. The hour of cultural history or history of mentalities had arrived. And if imagination did not take political power, it certainly seized the attention of historiography, as we have seen, to the point of transforming all studies of the past in the Western world.

Only shortly before this time, in 1961, the discreet Robert Mandrou, who had chosen not to follow the furrow traced by Fernand Braudel, set out to continue Marc Bloch and Lucien Febvre's pioneering writings on 'mentalities'. His groundbreaking book *Introduction to Modern France* aroused scarcely any echo – but this did not deter him, in 1968, from returning to the charge with his doctoral thesis, *Magistrats et sorciers en France au XVIIe siècle*.[35] Philippe Ariès was another of these pioneers not to have benefited from public recognition. This determined investigator, outside the academic establishment, who defined himself as a 'Sunday historian', published in 1960 a remarkable work, quite marginal to the historiographical field, *Centuries of Childhood*.[36]

Ariès was a born historian. His rejection of political history, so precocious at a time of structuralism and 'scientific history', was also bound up with the repeated defeats of the nationalist monarchism that he championed. His initial interest was demography, guided by his concern about the declining population of the great 'French nation'. With great intellectual honesty, he reached the conclusion that the causes of this phenomenon were neither of a political order (as his friends on the far right believed), nor economic (as Marxists assured him), but that the explanation was rather to be sought precisely in mental attitudes. The evolution of relations within the family (between men and women and between parents and children), the ways of everyday life, the relation to illness and death, and other factors of this kind had generated this depressing demographic change.

In *Centuries of Childhood*, Ariès put forward the thesis that the conception of childhood prevalent in our modern life is a relatively recent phenomenon in human history. In premodern Europe, a child who had not yet reached the age of reason was seen as an object of entertainment, rather like a small pet animal.

---

35   Robert Mandrou, *Introduction to Modern France, 1500–1640: An Essay in Historical Psychology*, Teaneck, NJ: Holmes & Meier, 1976; and *Magistrats et sorciers en France au XVIIe siècle*, Paris: Plon, 1968.

36   Philippe Ariès, *Centuries of Childhood: A Social History of Family Life*, New York: Vintage, 1965.

Engravings of the time show how children were represented as little adults; the idea of childhood differed completely from that current today. The frequent death of young children (50 per cent before the age of five) prevented the development of strong relations of dependence. Affective relations towards infants and small children certainly underwent some modification, but it was only in the eighteenth century that a basic change in the relationship occurred: the 'creature' who lacked reason began to be perceived as a potential human being. The reduction in infant mortality modified the emotional pattern and the modern nuclear family crystallized, before undergoing its own spiritual and relational changes in the course of time.

Ariès attracted the wrath of critics for not having paid sufficient attention to social classes, for a lack of nuances between different eras, for having focused above all on the nobility, and also for not having included in his analysis aristocracies outside the kingdom of France. Nonetheless, it is incontestable that this was a pioneering work that opened the way to the appearance of new themes in historiography, and a contribution of a particular quality that finally brought its author academic recognition. The book was reissued in 1973 by a major French publisher, and five years later, at the age of sixty-four, Philippe Ariès was appointed director of studies at the École des hautes études en sciences sociales.

We also need to recall certain other events perhaps lost from sight. In 1971, the British historian Keith Thomas published *Religion and the Decline of Magic*; two years later saw Jean-Paul Aron's *The Art of Eating in France*; 1975 was the year of *Montaillou* by Emmanuel Le Roy Ladurie (certainly the best sales ever in France for a history book); and in 1976 Carlo Ginzburg brought out in Italy a new bestseller, *The Cheese and the Worms*.[37] Beyond

---

37   Keith Thomas, *Religion and the Decline of Magic: Studies in Popular Beliefs in Sixteenth and Seventeenth-Century England*, London: Weidenfeld & Nicholson, 1971; Jean-Paul Aron, *The Art of Eating in France: Manners and Menus in the Nineteenth Century*, Chester Springs, PA: Dufour Editions, 1975; Emmanuel Le Roy Ladurie,

their diversity, these books, along with some others, may be viewed as markers of a significant change in research orientations towards the past in the Western world.

Starting in the mid-1970s, while traditional national identity was ebbing, the attention paid to the 'cultural' in all its forms would become an obligatory passage in the writing of the past. This phenomenon was further strengthened and expanded by the interest of the general public in these new objects. In the space of a few years a cluster of stimulating works appeared, of which the following particularly stand out: Jean Delumeau's *Sin and Fear* (1978), Georges Duby's *The Three Orders* (1978), Michel Vovelle's *La mort et l'Occident* (1983), Natalie Zemon Davis's *The Return of Martin Guerre* (1983) and Robert Darnton's *The Great Cat Massacre* (1984).[38] We could add several more titles to this list, at the risk of taking up the remaining space in this chapter.

Did this new historical production have a common denominator, in form or in method, or a single theoretical foundation? The British historian Lawrence Stone, who has tried to characterize it, sees it as the great return of narrative after years spent in the desert.[39] Historians who were confined in quantitative structuralist models had exhausted their pseudo-scientific experience. Figures, tables and curves, certainly important for the reconstruction of the past, became increasingly less accessible to

---

Montaillou: The Promised Land of Error, New York: George Braziller, 2008; Carlo Ginzburg, *The Cheese and the Worms: The Cosmos of a Sixteenth-Century Miller*, Baltimore: Johns Hopkins University Press, 1992.

38   Jean Delumeau, *Sin and Fear: The Emergence of a Western Guilt Culture, thirteenth to eighteenth Centuries*, New York: St Martin's Press, 1991; Georges Duby, *The Three Orders: Feudalism Imagined*, Chicago: The University of Chicago Press, 1982; Michel Vovelle, *La mort et l'Occident*, Paris: Gallimard, 2000; Natalie Zemon Davis, *The Return of Martin Guerre*, Cambridge, MA: Harvard University Press, 1983; Robert Darnton, *The Great Cat Massacre: And Other Episodes in French Cultural History*, New York: Basic Books, 2009.

39   Lawrence Stone, 'The Revival of Narrative: Reflections on a New Old History', *Past and Present*, 85, 1979, 3–24.

intellectual readers without a specialism in the subject, all the
more so as, in terms of knowledge, the great quantitative moun-
tains often gave birth to very small mice. Quantitative analytical
history, whatever might be said of it, most often failed to answer
the question 'why'. In the 1970s historians understood that, if
they did not want to lose their connection with the wide cultivated public, they would have to produce accounts that could
associate the general and the particular, the social, societal and
individual. Thus the new historians, like their forerunners in the
nineteenth century, began to draw from contemporary novelists
more reliable techniques for elaborating historical narrative.

Stone's analysis is quite convincing, though he was himself
aware that the diversity of narrative strategies made it impossible
to locate a uniform common basis. Beyond the narrative, the
dimension of analysis continued to be integrated into this writing in different ways, with the result that it was no longer too
clear what kind of text one was reading. The hypothesis Stone
ended up with was very clear: if it was sociology that had posed
a challenge to historiography up to the 1970s, it was now anthropology and psychology that had taken over this role. Moreover,
if the accounts of traditional narrative historiography had focused
on visible individuals, political or intellectual – kings, leaders,
military chiefs, inventors and major thinkers – in the new anthropological history, whether more analytical or more narrative, the
heroes were almost always anonymous individuals. Groups of
peasants or workers, women or minorities, or at least individuals
representative of these, were the new focus of attention. The
villagers of Montaillou, and Carlo Ginzburg's extraordinary
miller, became heroes of poignant historical dramas, soon
followed by the wife of Martin Guerre.

Stone's article dates from 1979. There can be no doubt that a
decade after the great youth revolt, accompanied in France by a
general strike in the world of labour, a large section of historical
research had acquired a new coloration. The radical state of mind
of the young intelligentsia and the counterculture dissolved very

quickly, but it left behind all the same certain 'scars' that were not immediately forgotten. The political logorrhea uttered in the name of the masses had manifestly failed and gone off the rails; a fringe of historians, however, felt sympathy for the questioning and challenging of existing hierarchies, which they translated into a wave of empathy for the distant past.

One can also formulate a hypothesis in a 'long-time' perspective, and see the promotion of the 'common people' that marked the choice of historical subjects in the 1970s as the culmination of the victorious march of liberal democracy in the West, after a century of maturation. The signs of this democratization were already visible in the 1920s with the debut of the *Annales* school, and later with its many imitators, as well as the breakthrough of Marxist historiography, particularly in Britain. When the sovereign became ever more dependent on the will of the masses, in all national states, a certain empathy towards these was also created in the 'dominated stratum of the dominant class'; in other words, the intellectual field, including historians. 'Pay Caesar what is due to Caesar', the New Testament tells us (Mark 12:17), even if we are not obliged for all that to believe in the divinity of the venerated emperor. The electorate, pseudo-emperor of the twentieth century, was thus enthroned for a time as the main actor in many narratives of the new history.

This assertion needs a small correction. It is actually truer for Britain than for France, where, as we have seen, the best narratives, from Marc Bloch to Emmanuel Le Roy Ladurie, were devoted to the ancestors of the modern masses; in other words, the peasants. It is also interesting to note that the demographic decline of workers on the land gave rise to a correlative expansion in the number of doctoral theses and popular historical accounts devoted to them. The new research, structuralist as well as narrative, was seized with nostalgia for the traditional agricultural past, which leads us to a problematic at the very heart of the new cultural history.

Silent and Forgotten by History

It is well known how, since the birth of 'scientific' history in the early nineteenth century, the political, legal, military and religious elites who act on history more or less consciously have been the object of predilection for teaching and research. The kingdom, the principality, the church and then the nation-state (its institutions, leaders and political parties) have claimed pride of place for the investigation of the past.

The past in question here, moreover, was generally reconstructed on the basis of archives left behind by these same elites, or by the intellectual circles that accompanied them. The distance between written traces, documents and testimonies, and those who produced them was relatively short. In other words, the ruling strata, who 'made' history, were also those who deposited its traces and testimonies.

The changes in historical objects did not greatly modify these sources. Initially, the registers of births, marriages and deaths kept by churches; inventory books of goods; tax receipts; wage contracts; police reports; and so on provided material for quantitative historians, who put the lives of the masses into figures and quantified their behaviour. Almost all traces of the people 'below' came from 'above', in the form of monarchical, feudal and religious institutions or apparatus of power. Only those able to write left evidence behind them, and only a very small number, almost always dependent on the ruling powers, had this capacity. The 'scholars' of the past did not enjoy the relative autonomy that exists in modern liberal democracies. The masses, on the other hand, always remained silent. They wrote nothing, and their presence in history, with the exception of a few moments of rebellion and insurrection, has always been pieced together by the gaze of others, close to power.

When the new history, also known as the narrative history of mentalities, began to blossom, from the start it came up against a set of problems that it was not always conscious of, or, to put it another way, that it preferred to ignore. The three best-known works of this kind provide a good illustration of this: Le Roy Ladurie's *Montaillou*, Carlo Ginzburg's *The Cheese and the Worms*, and Natalie Zemon Davis's *The Return of Martin Guerre*. The protocols of the Inquisition provide the raw material for the first two of these, while the third is based on a report concerning a royal judge in Toulouse in the sixteenth century. In each of these cases, there is no direct testimony from the actors in these judicial dramas. And as always with legal matters, we are dealing with singular cases, outside the ordinary, as distinct from the routine and monotonous way of life of the labouring population, subject to the heavy work of yesterday's world.

The first book tells the story of a village in south-west France in the late thirteenth century, inclined to heresy and won to the Cathar faith. In other words, a rebel village, atypical, which challenged the Catholic papal hegemony. In this book Le Roy Ladurie based himself on the sworn enemies of heresy, in particular the records of the bishop Jacques Fournier, who would later become Pope Benedict XII. The investigations conducted by the inquisitor were both very detailed and very wide-ranging; they collected a mass of information, not only on the beliefs of the accused, but also on their way of life, their work, and their social imaginary. Le Roy Ladurie drew on this source to piece together, quite brilliantly, whole swathes of the life of this village community. However, this attractive reading leads us to forget that the Inquisition did not possess recording machines, and that we are not hearing or receiving the voices of Cathar villagers. These expressed themselves in Occitan dialect, while the transcripts were written in Latin. The villagers responded to questions put to them under very harsh conditions, certainly not on a psychoanalyst's couch. We can never know what the interrogator, cultivated and cunning, adjusted, added, or passed over in silence. Indirect testimonies collected under torture have never constituted proof of 'truth' about the past. Aristotle excellently said,

'For no less under compulsion do men tell lies rather than the truth.'[40]

What interested Le Roy Ladurie, however, was the everyday life of the peasants, and his book is a brilliant example of the new anthropologically oriented historical writing. The author searched in the sources for characteristic elements of the life of the peasantry in the late thirteenth and early fourteenth centuries, and he explored this subject, down to the extraction of lice as an act of love, to the best of his ethnological imagination. He was not particularly interested in heresy, or in the particular character of the Cathar rebellion. He was little concerned with ideological and political conflict, seen as insufficiently representative of the era being studied. The problem, though, is precisely that heresy lay at the root of this trial, and without it we would not have 'historical sources'. Jacques Rancière, in a criticism of the book, rightly pointed out that Le Roy Ladurie had had to 'bury the heretics condemned to death to bring the peasants of Montaillou to life . . . It would be wrong to say that the historian does not want to know the Inquisition. What he does not want to know is heresy.'[41] In this way, we indirectly join in the historical action of the church, which aimed to destroy heresy in order to unite the whole of the faithful in a pacified and subjected rural 'normality'.

If, by dint of their heresy, the inhabitants of Montaillou were precisely not 'representative' peasants, they had to become so in order for a history to be written that was not reducible to a particular and singular narrative. This is the same method that Carlo Ginzburg employed in his brilliant essay on Menocchio, a simple miller who lived in the sixteenth century in the north-east of Italy, who was also condemned to death by the Inquisition. Once again, we find ourselves faced with a micro-history

---

40   Aristotle, *The Art of Rhetoric*, London: Penguin, 1992, Book I (1377a), 70.

41   Jacques Rancière, *Les noms de l'histoire: Essai de poétique du savoir*, Paris: Seuil, 1992, 151.

supposed to instruct us about macro-history via a very indirect route. As in Montaillou, we have an attempt to lead from the particular to the general, the individual to the social. And here again, the greater part of the sources come from the protocols of a trial in which the protagonist faced the grave accusation of heresy.

Menocchio, the village miller, was not an educated man from good society; yet despite his modest origin, and by way of varied reading, he reached heretical conclusions about the Holy Trinity. In an eclectic fashion he developed a naive pantheism, according to which, starting from a great block similar to a ripe cheese, angels were created like worms, and God among them. It goes without saying that the church did not at all appreciate this exegesis, and still less the questioning of its monopoly on the truth; once again, after a certain hesitation, it condemned the candid rebel to death.

While the majority of sources that mention him were hostile to the autodidact miller, Ginzburg, coming from the 1960s left, showed evident sympathy. Menocchio served him as a lever to expand the place of oral popular culture, at the expense of the dominant culture of the upper classes. The miller Menocchio could read and perhaps write; with his inveterate curiosity, he is the constant dream of every enlightened socialist. Notwithstanding the political desire of the Italian historian, Menocchio did not resemble any of his peasant colleagues, uneducated and rather passive, as Ginzburg himself agrees at the start of his book. The miller, however, was not selected at random from the anonymity of the silent and subjected lower orders, to be judged and executed. Unfortunately, he wrote nothing and, like the heretical peasants of Montaillou, all that we know of him comes from other people's mouths. What the miller apparently thought and imagined, we draw from the accounts of brutal investigators who extorted declarations from the victim and his terrified neighbours, and indeed in a language different from that of the written source. Micro-history, in other words, pieces together its enthusiastic narratives on the basis of indirect testimonies.

It was indeed founded for this very purpose. This historical narration is certainly legitimate and arouses curiosity. Let us compare it, however, with Giordano Bruno. The astronomer and philosopher perished at the stake in 1600, the same year that Menocchio was executed; but we have first-hand knowledge of him, not simply gathered by distant and hostile intermediaries. Bruno left a great deal of writing, which began to be published only three years after his death. Consequently, and though it is not easy to reach agreement, the deciphering of the intellectual's mental world seems far more reliable and well-founded than are the indirect testimonies gleaned from the records of the Inquisition. At the same time, the knowledge of the world left us by Bruno enlightens us better on his contemporaries of the same social class, both his supporters and his opponents, which is absolutely not the case with a marginal figure such as Menocchio. Thus, by following the traces of Giordano Bruno we come back to the old narrative history of elites; in other words, we situate ourselves once again in history seen 'from above': less democratic, less popular, and, it must be confessed, far less original.

Natalie Zemon Davis's essay comes up against the same basic difficulties. As against the two accounts just discussed, the history of the usurper who presented himself as Martin Guerre was already familiar: Alexandre Dumas had used it in a novel. In the early 1980s, it attracted this American historian because it reflected her conception of the world and matched particularly well the spirit of the time. Like Ginzburg, Davis came from the intellectual left that in the 1960s had focused on the history of class conflicts. From the early 1970s, she turned increasingly towards cultural history, crossed with a productive and stimulating feminism. Davis was not the only historian whose prism for observing the past had changed, in parallel with the decline of the proletariat and the rise of women's struggles for equal rights. Feminist historiography experienced a quickening along with the advent of cultural history, to which indeed it made a very marked contribution.

Was Bertrande de Rols, the rich and cunning peasant, a kind of sixteenth-century feminist, living in a small quiet village at the foot of the Pyrenees? Davis was very likely correct in deeming it impossible that a woman, even when her husband and the father of her child had been absent for eight years, could be mistaken and certify in good faith that the usurper was indeed her legal companion (at the time of their marriage, her husband had been fourteen, and she was still younger than him). Bertrande was still young; she needed a husband and accepted the risk of being accused of deception and adultery in order to satisfy her material, emotional and sexual needs. But how many peasants, simple people, would have shown in those days such a determined will, such fierce independence and audacity in the face of danger as the abandoned wife of Martin Guerre? And above all, can we connect this extraordinary tale with any other similar event lived by a woman in the same period, who overcame her fears and a long oppression to take her destiny in hand, even by a ruse?

Just like the audacious autodidact Menocchio, Bertrande de Rols was in all probability a courageous individual worthy of imitation, but despite everything, she represents a rare strand in the human panorama of the premodern peasantry. In this story, the historian seems to have projected her own sensibility, her imagination and her own aspirations, on the basis of the writings of one of the magistrates brought in to judge her crime, and who condemned the impostor to death. Bertrande de Rols did not leave behind the least written testimony; so in this case, too, the historiographical interpretation had to be based on distorted sources that already constitute a male interpretation of the era. To interpret interpretations is certainly a legitimate part of the historian's work, but, contrary to what Davis believes, this extraordinary and dramatic tale does not necessarily contribute to deepening our understanding of the sexual or emotional imaginary of representative women of the oppressed class in the sixteenth century. Knowledge of this imaginary is likely to be always sadly lacking in the history of humanity: working women were still more silent than the majority of working men.

It seems that at a certain point in time, 'cultural' historians perceived that their writing of a history 'from below' was not sufficiently based on reliable firsthand sources. As the years of the counterculture slid into the past, they felt more ready to return to the history of cultural elites, for which documentation has always been far more direct and plentiful. In this way, the silent slowly began to disappear again from the historiographical field, without anyone being particularly upset by this.

The publication of *A History of Private Life*, the imposing collective work edited by Philippe Ariès and Georges Duby and continued by other *Annales* figures in the conservative decade of the 1990s, may be seen as the culmination of this change of orientation.[42] This clearly focused on individual and family aspects of the long 'Western culture' that supposedly continued without interruption from the Roman Empire to our own day.[43] It is logical that only the rich and powerful had a private life, something that the book's illustrations amply confirm. They had ceremonies, taste and style, and they sent their children to study in schools – children whom, in contrast to peasants, they soon began to love. At the end of the day, it emerges from this work that, ever since the Roman Empire, the rich were the precursors of the individual and comfortable modernity in which 'we ourselves', readers of books, live, which is a pleasant sensation. To read the various articles in this collection from the *Annales* school, we are almost nostalgic for characters like the Montaillou peasants or Menocchio – these superhuman heroes of the 1970s.

---

42   Philippe Ariès and Georges Duby (series eds), *A History of Private Life* (5 vols.), Cambridge, MA: Bellknap Press, 1987.

43   Paul Veyne tried with difficulty, in a very odd way, to justify the choice of periodization: Paul Veyne (ed.), *A History of Private Life*, vol. 1, *From Pagan Rome to Byzantium*, 2.

The world is essentially given to us by way of stories, which we grow up and reach maturity with. It is natural, then, that seeing historiography return to the writing of dramatic tales has had a refreshing and enthusing effect, after socioeconomic history's long period of apathy. Cultural production, however, also takes other channels: novelists, journalists and film-makers generally reconstruct stories better than even the most talented historians. It is in no way surprising, therefore, that the initial enthusiasm bound up with the return of narrative should have fallen off after a decade or so, although several other historians sought without great success to integrate stories from folklore into what was considered, wrongly, in my view, the 'truth' of the common people of the past.

In 1974, Jacques Le Goff and Pierre Nora published their three volumes on the new history, with the ambition of including in this tremendous undertaking the 'new problems, new approaches and new objects' (the respective subtitles of the three volumes of *Faire de l'histoire*) that contemporary historians were concerned with. These problems and objects clearly did not include the stories of Vichy, Stalinism, colonialism or decolonization, still less so the war in Algeria – not even the imprint of nationalism in the formation of modern history. But there was, of course, a religious history of former times, likewise a history of science, a quantitative demographic history, and histories of art and literature. The history of economic crises, of archaeology, of the book, of myths, of the generation gap, as we already saw, occupied a respectable place in this very varied panorama of Parisian historical research.

Let us return for a moment to some striking events of the intellectual context in which the writing of the 'apolitical' cultural history of the 1970s took place. In 1969, the Franco-American film-maker Marcel Ophüls directed *Le chagrin et la pitié*, a historical documentary on the behaviour of ordinary French people under the Occupation, which aroused tremendous anger and was banned from being broadcast on public television

(ORTF). Programmed in a small cinema in the Latin Quarter, it became a cult film of the student youth, but it was not until 1981 that it was shown on television. Then, in 1972, the first publication to deal seriously with France under the German Occupation, and the persecution of Jews in that period, was the work of an American historian, Robert Paxton. The book was translated into French a year before the publication of *Faire de l'histoire*, but a whole decade would pass before it made any impression on indigenous French research.

If the elite of French historians found 'event' subjects distasteful, these did inspire mainstream cinema, independent of state or institutional finance (university salaries or research grants). In 1976, the American Joseph Losey made *Monsieur Klein*, precisely in Paris. This remarkable and revealing masterpiece was one of the first to dare to present the historical and moral context of the round-up and deportation of French people and foreigners of Jewish origin in Paris in 1942, the so-called 'Vél d'Hiv raid'.[44]

Moreover, in 1966 the Italian film-maker Gillo Pontecorvo had released his much-praised film *The Battle of Algiers*, which was banned in France until 1971 (and until 2004 on French television channels). In 1972, there was the low-budget film *Avoir vingt ans dans les Aurès*, by the leftist René Vautier, the commercial distribution of which was cleverly disrupted. And in 1973, after many efforts, Yves Boisset managed to complete the filming of *RAS*, which courageously deals with the bloody 'events' of the 1950s in Algeria. Finally, in 1977, the British author Alistair Horne published his impassioned book *A Savage War of Peace*, translated into French three years later.[45]

---

44   A low-budget film by Michel Mitrani dealing with the roundup of Jews in Paris, *Les Guichets du Louvre*, was released in 1974. On French cinema's handling of the Occupation period, see my book *Le XXe siècle à l'écran*, Paris: Seuil, 2004, 311–17.

45   Alistair Horne, *A Savage War of Peace: Algeria 1954–1962*, New York: NYRB Classics, 2006.

The war in Algeria ended in 1962, but for the *fine fleur* of French historians in the 1970s, the era of decolonization was still too close for them to concern themselves with it. Besides, this was still a time when event history had not again begun to seem pertinent. It was only from the 1990s, after the elites who had collaborated with the German Occupation, along with the champions of *Algérie française* (sometimes the same people), had finally left the stage of history, or even the world of the living, that French historians found it in them to begin cautiously to tell their stories – or, more often, those of their families, friends and acquaintances. The generational problematic is a major factor for understanding the turns taken by historiography, and the evolution of its centres of interest. As far as I am aware, this subject has not yet attracted the attention it deserves.[46]

There was also in the 1970s a 'non-event' history that did not find a place in the production cycles of the new French historiography. In 1976, Eugen Weber's *Peasants into Frenchmen* appeared in the United States before being published in French in 1983 under a less bold title.[47] It was scarcely surprising that this book met with a lukewarm and sometimes highly critical reception. Weber developed the thesis that in the second half of the nineteenth century French society was still far from forming a consolidated nation. Until compulsory education was instituted and military service generalized, and until a new administrative apparatus was established that deeply penetrated the agricultural world, a large proportion of peasants still did not know

---

46   See Karl Mannheim, 'The Problem of Generations', in *Essays on the Sociology of Knowledge by Karl Mannheim* (ed. P. Kecskemati), New York: Oxford University Press, 1952, 276–320. This pioneering article from 1923 encouraged a long series of works, but historians have generally abstained from turning the generational problematic on to themselves. An exception is William Palmer, *Engagements with the Past: The Lives and Works of the World War II Generation of Historians*, Lexington: University Press of Kentucky, 2001.

47   Eugen Weber, *Peasants into Frenchmen: The Modernization of Rural France, 1870–1914*, Stanford: Stanford University Press, 1976. Published in French as *La fin des terroirs*, Paris: Fayard, 2011.

that they were French; their identity and their political consciousness scarcely went beyond the limits of the province in which
they lived and worked. Hypotheses of this kind were still totally
unacceptable to French historiography, whether traditional or
new, being so opposed to the republican logic that saw the French
Revolution as the apogee of the formation of the *grande nation*.
Weber's book appeared before the pioneering works of Ernest
Gellner and Benedict Anderson, and the realization that nations
are a phenomenon of 'short time', a time far more constricted
than historians had previously imagined, had not yet reached
Paris.

This sketch, if somewhat impressionistic, does indicate a
'lacuna' in the research and teaching of history until the 1980s,
leading us once again to formulate a basic question: what does
history respond to and what is its purpose? If professional history,
having regard to its scientific character and its great political
caution, imposes on itself such a break between past and present,
and if the cinema, fiction, and even philosophy and political
sociology make a better and bolder job of comparing the distant
past with the problems of today, what part remains for historians? Should they accept being increasingly drawn towards an
apolitical esoteric folklore, in other words to fragments of
marginal cultural history? The impasse and the growing scepticism that the historical profession experienced in the late twentieth century have challenged the self-confidence of more than
one accredited specialist in the past.[48]

A minority, coming from the group of historians who had
contributed to the *Faire de l'histoire* collection, distanced themselves from this and returned to contemporary political history,
focusing their interest especially on political culture and its intellectual aspects rather than on concrete political action. This may
have some connection with the fact that these were historians

---

48   Apropos awareness of the crisis that shook *Annales*, see the editorial article
'Histoire et sciences sociales: Un tournant critique?', *Annales*, 43, 1988, 291–3.

closely linked with the world of the media, such as Jacques Julliard, Marc Ferro and François Furet.[49] For others, the ultimate elegance before the twentieth century came to a close was to mobilize for a new field of research: nostalgic history, better known under its byword '*Les lieux de mémoire*'.

The Invention of a Nostalgic Memory

Just ten years after *Faire de l'histoire*, Pierre Nora began publication of a series of volumes, *Realms of Memory*.[50] This was not only the end of a decade, but also marked the end of a kind of hegemony in the French research field. The new cultural history had not yet completed its triumphant progress, the provincial fringes of Western universities being still unconquered, yet the first cracks had already appeared at its nerve centres, affecting the discipline's vigour. If Pierre Nora had not previously written any particularly striking historical work, he certainly knew how to seize opportunities, thanks to a brilliant ability to capture and decipher shifts in public sensibility.[51]

In 1985, a year after the publication of the first volume of *Realms of Memory*, Claude Lanzmann's marathon documentary *Shoah* was released, made up of a great tissue of remembrances. These two successful projects are very different, but they also present certain common features. One is exclusively interested in

---

49   In 1984, Furet founded, under the aegis of the EHESS, the Institut Raymond Aron, with a proclaimed liberal orientation and the object of refocusing on intellectual political history. With this aim in mind, and in the wake of Lucien Febvre, Furet turned to American foundations to finance the project. See, on this subject, Christophe Prochasson, *François Furet: Les chemins de la mélancolie*, Paris: Stock, 2013, 298.

50   Pierre Nora, *Realms of Memory* (abridged in 4 vols.), New York: Columbia University Press, 1992. *Les lieux de mémoire*, t. 1, *La république*, Paris: Gallimard, 1984; t. 2, *La nation* (3 vols.), Paris: Gallimard, 1986; t. 3, *Les France* (3 vols.), Paris: Gallimard, 1992.

51   We should note here that two years previously Yossef Hayim Yerushalmi had published *Zakhor: Jewish History and Jewish Memory*, Seattle: University of Washington Press, 1982.

French memory, while the other uniquely honours Jewish memory. In the first, places of different types play the leading role, while in the second, it is various groups of witnesses. They each reject any direct historical debate, despite the implicit hypothesis that confrontation with remembrance leads to a greater knowledge of historical truth. Both present themselves as processes of critical investigation of places and witnesses, while fitting into a sophisticated positivist approach that neutralizes any possibility of developing a serious critical position towards the two 'national narratives'.[52] These two great productions give the impression of a kind of historical simulacrum, to use a notion brilliantly analysed by Jean Baudrillard in the field of instant culture.[53] Both works are presented, in fact, as a memory of memory, staking a claim to 'truth' that has no need of other proof than the place of remembrance or the witness who remembers. Both take responsibility for a very particular memory, which we can describe as neither conflictual nor disturbing, hence the enthusiastic consensus of their reception.

Memory, as we know, is very selective. Remembering and forgetting are a two-faced Janus, both turned to the past and inviting a convergence with the present, or even expunging under the effect of shame. Mnemosyne in Greek mythology, with her great creative intelligence, is the goddess of memory (Clio, the muse of history, is one of her seven daughters), and this is also the name of the spring of memory that flows alongside Lethe, the river of oblivion. The dead souls that reach here must drink of her water to forget the past. And yet, forgetting is an immanent part, conscious or unconscious, of the process of

---

52   The references to the *longue durée* of the French nation, made in several articles in the volumes edited by Pierre Nora, are full of surprising anachronisms. It sometimes seems that the French people and their national identity have existed for a thousand years. See the critical article by Steven Englund, 'De l'usage de la Nation par les historiens et réciproquement', *Politix*, 7/26, 1994, 151–8.

53   Jean Baudrillard, *Simulacra and Simulation*, Ann Arbor: University of Michigan Press, 1995.

memorization; and so anything that is not fixed forever in the cultural schemas of remembering did not really exist in the past, as we know nothing, or very little, about it. This is why, as a matter of simple logic, there is no mention of forgetting in *Realms of Memory*.

The seven volumes of the series contain many places: monuments commemorating victories, heroism and sacrifice, the tricolour flag, the national anthem, the Louvre, the Panthéon, festivals, national funerals, national historians and so on. On the other hand, Napoleon's great defeats seem never to have existed, not being engraved in the national memory. The Vichy regime, having left no *lieu de mémoire* behind it, seems not to have needed any serious reference and is thus left aside. Moreover, while Pierre Nora had as a younger man written on the Algerian war, this historiographical enterprise on the *longue durée* 'forgets' the acts of repression and pillage perpetrated by French colonialism since the nineteenth century. From Dien Bien Phu to the Battle of Algiers, the bloody liberation struggles with their 'processions of suffering' have been removed from history. Forgetting of this kind follows completely from Pierre Nora's editorial logic: in the absence of an official place of commemoration for these 'marginal' crimes, why integrate them into this reorganized collective memory?[54]

Surprising as it may appear, Claude Lanzmann also 'forgets' Vichy. While his film is French, even very French, it does not 'remember' the Drancy camp; no French trains are seen in the film, only German and Polish ones. In the same vein, there are neither French murderers nor French victims, and consequently no French Jewish memory apart from the 'supreme memory' organized by Lanzmann. It is thus only logical that, helped by this forgetting of the terrible role played by the Vichy regime, the

---

54   Having met with criticism on this point, Pierre Nora was reluctantly compelled to add in the final volumes published in 1992 some references to the 'dark' pages in France's glorious history.

modest contribution to collaboration of French-Jewish organizations, particularly in relation to the round-up of 'Jewish' foreigners without French nationality, should have also disappeared
from Lanzmann's *Shoah*. The film was thus able to benefit from
generous subsidies on the part of both French and Israeli govern-
ments. Lanzmann's work was praised to the skies by the entire
French cultural establishment (the Israeli one as well), in contrast
to the cold reception given to Hannah Arendt's merciless and
incisive book on the Eichmann trial, let alone the painful essay
that the journalist Maurice Rajsfus, who as a child escaped the
raid of summer 1942, had written on the collaboration of certain
Jews with the persecutors.[55]

Nora's volumes experienced just as enthusiastic a reception as
Lanzmann's consensual film. The fact of focusing essentially on
sites that the national state and its various arms had configured
and maintained for decades, or on consensual places of culture,
ran no risk of coming up against a wounding and tormented
memory. And if pain filtered in despite everything, this was
generally experienced, and not inflicted.[56] With a purified and
painless imaginary past (non-controversial except perhaps for
the Vendée and the Paris Commune, whose wounds have had
time to heal), it is possible to go on living calmly and even cultivate a controlled nostalgia. Knowing that there is scarcely any
place of national memory dedicated to the evils inflicted on
others, the high cultural bodies did not spare their praise, and
the gates of the Académie française were opened to the author.[57]

---

55   Hannah Arendt, *Eichmann in Jerusalem*, Harmondsworth: Penguin, 1963.
Maurice Rajsfus, *Des juifs dans la collaboration. L'UGIF 1941–1944*, Paris: EDI,
1980. If Arendt's essay had to wait thirty-seven years before being translated into
Hebrew, Maurice Rajsfus's rare testimony aroused no interest at all in Israel.

56   This did not preclude *Realms of Memory* from containing some stimulating
critical articles on the nature of government commemorations. But by being few and
far between, these actually provide an alibi for a 'cultural' and apolitical overflow in
conformity with the best *Annales* tradition.

57   The Académie had previously 'immortalized' several 'responsible' historians;
Pierre Nora took over the chair of Michel Droit, a former journalist on *Le Figaro*,

Both Nora's *Realms of Memory* and Lanzmann's *Shoah* thus themselves gained the status of adulated and sacralized *lieux de mémoire*.

In 1984, the same year that Pierre Nora published the first volume of his project on memory, which would be completed in 1993, a young writer named Didier Daeninckx published a modest police novel titled *Murder in Memoriam*.[58] The fictional plot was inspired by a strong sense of history, referring, by way of the story of two individual murders, to the mass murders committed with the involvement of the French governmental authorities: the imprisonment in the Drancy camp of East European and French Jews awaiting deportation to Auschwitz, and the killing of Algerian demonstrators in the heart of Paris on 17 October 1961 (the exact number of victims, between one and two hundred, is unknown). Daeninckx's book appeared rather too soon: in 1984, these two events, marked by fear and shame, were still banished to the margins of national places of memory in France, despite being part of the remembrance of French Jews and Algerians respectively.

Over the three decades that have passed since the mid-1980s, 'memory' has flooded the shelves of bookshops and historical documentary films. It is not, of course, just Nora or Lanzmann who awakened memory and drew it out of its refuge. If it has become the central axis of our reference to the past, the explanation must be sought in signs of the time: something began to stir in the intellectual climate of the late twentieth century, apparently summing up the era better than the critical writing of its history. Works of historical research largely ceased to assuage the public's thirst for veridical narratives of the past.

---

who had railed against Serge Gainsbourg for having composed a reggae version of the *Marseillaise*, thus desecrating one of France's most sacred places of memory. And by being Jewish, Gainsbourg had supposedly contributed indirectly to the rise of anti-Semitism.

58   Didier Daeninckx, *Murder in Memoriam*, Brooklyn: Melville International Crime, 2012.

This phenomenon also indirectly revealed a fissuring of modern collective identities, the national, democratic, social and socialist consciousness that had each carried with them a fundamentally optimistic relationship with time. Among the factors that made a notable contribution to the upsurge and success of the memory industry, we should count the feeling that, with economic and cultural globalization, the certainties of the marvellous national 'two hundred years of solitude' had unravelled. Pierre Nora understood this better than the other historians he involved in his enterprise: the spectre of the nation's death agony, which hovers over Western Europe, is also the infectious spirit of the triumph of memory.

The formula that 'when there is less future, there is more past' is not exact and needs refining: 'when there is less future, remembrance of yesterday replaces the imagining of tomorrow.' The expansion of this phenomenon cannot simply be attributed to the collapse of visions of the future and their power of mobilization – whether it is a question of utopias, the belief in progress, or even political programmes. The growing force of individualism, concerned to draw from the present the maximum immediate satisfaction, has also contributed to the loss of credibility of a 'scientific historical' past, in the face of witnesses who distil the authentic account of their personal memory. Representations of the past in the form of cinematic fiction, almost always embodied by particular individuals, have certainly accustomed consumers to privilege the apprehension of collective memory by way of personal stories.

In this debate on 'memory' we should begin with an analysis of the concept. There clearly is an individual memory, the nature of which thinkers in the Mediterranean culture already pondered. Aristotle deals with it in detail as an integral part of human knowledge.[59] Cicero refers to it as a major element of rhetorical ability; Saint Augustine, in his *Confessions*, sees it as a

---

59   Aristotle, *On Memory and Reminiscence*, at classics.mit.edu.

determining factor in the consolidation of human reason. Later on, Giordano Bruno, and others after him, investigated how to develop and retain remembrances. And yet memory never really again received the attention it deserved until the late nineteenth and early twentieth centuries.[60] In 1895, Sigmund Freud, together with Joseph Breuer, made the act of personal reminiscence, by way of the free association of ideas, a main axis of psychotherapy.[61] A large part of Freud's future work would consist in developing certain fundamental positions formulated in this essay. *Matter and Memory*,[62] the pioneering and intricate work by Henri Bergson, published in 1896, constituted a new opening on the relationship between sensation and reminiscence, in particular between the automatic memory that pertains to habit and the more reflexive memory of the past that Bergson sees as the genuine image of authentic memory. It is not surprising that Marcel Proust, a student at the Sorbonne in the 1890s, should have attended Bergson's lectures: *À la recherche du temps perdu* is one of the most important masterpieces ever written about the act of reminiscence in mechanisms of awareness and action. Proust only began to write his novels in 1907, but he followed Bergson's teaching in the very years that the philosopher was researching the problematic of memory.

Bergson had another disciple, initially at the Lycée Henri IV, where he had begun his teaching career, then at the École normale supérieure. This was Maurice Halbwachs, remembered as the first sociologist to have widely explored the significance of collective memory. His book *On Collective Memory*, published in 1925, contains several references to his former teacher.[63] And it

---

60 For a good insight into the place of memory in Western culture, see Frances Yates, *The Art of Memory*, Chicago: The University of Chicago Press, 1966.

61 Joseph Breuer and Sigmund Freud, *Studies on Hysteria*, vol. 2 of Sigmund Freud, *The Standard Edition*, London: Hogarth Press, 1971.

62 Henri Bergson, *Matter and Memory*, New York: Digireads, 2010.

63 Maurice Halbwachs, *On Collective Memory*, Chicago: The University of Chicago Press, 1992.

was by way of this confrontation with Bergson that Halbwachs came to develop a new field of original research, which sadly did not have immediate successors either in sociology or in historiography.

'Memory-images', a key concept of Bergson's, formed the starting point for Halbwachs. And yet, as a sociologist in the Durkheim school and in the broad sense a functionalist, he criticized the individual view of his teacher, transposing remembered images to the level of social utility. Memory based on the accumulation of personal experience is neither hermetic nor pure; it is entirely pervaded by components arising from the environment in which the individual acts and the needs that this generates. The environment of memory is constituted chiefly by the family, social class, and wider social circles; and Halbwachs meticulously analyses the formation of memory within the various collectives and contexts in which these act.

However, if it is religion and religious communities that hold pride of place in Halbwachs's analysis, this also displays certain lacunas. In 1925, but also in Halbwachs's later uncompleted writings, we find no serious reference to the nation-state, which officiates as high priest and fashions the transformation of sectorial memories – those of churches, communities, political movements – into a unified grand memory. Similarly, when he discusses differences between collective memory and history, Halbwachs avoids entering a debate about the ideological frameworks in which this 'history-memory' is elaborated, to become a major integral part of modern collective identity.[64] Halbwachs was too much of a republican to be able to look at his national republic from outside. It is curious how this highly observant scholar, one of the very few in 1920s France to refer directly to both Sigmund Freud and Max Weber, did not integrate into his

---

64   See the chapter 'Mémoire collective et mémoire historique', in Maurice Halbwachs's last uncompleted essay, *La mémoire collective*, Paris: PUF, 1968, 35–79.

book the innovative contributions of Ernest Renan to the problematic of national memory.[65]

At the end of the twentieth century, it was clear that without the modern state, with its educational system, schools and textbooks, it would be impossible to speak of a collective memory. The historical imaginary of populations, in the course of the same century, was strongly marked by systems of national education, backed up by such non-state bodies as political parties, municipalities, regional administrations, community representatives and so on. Cinema, television and newspapers clearly also played an active and decisive role in the construction of various memories. With the rise of the Internet, a plethora of specialized sites won an ever-growing space on the market for the diffusion of specific knowledge, often heavy with nostalgia for the past. And yet, at least until the early twenty-first century, we can maintain that the nation-state, whether liberal or authoritarian, kept its grip on 'historical memory', in parallel with its mission of elaborating a common language and public culture.

In his introduction to *Realms of Memory*, Pierre Nora, concerned to refine the distinction between history and memory, had recourse to the following theoretical formulation:

> History, because it is an intellectual and secular production, calls for analysis and criticism. Memory installs remembrance within the sacred: history, always prosaic, releases it again . . . memory is by nature multiple and yet specific; collective, plural, and yet individual. History, on the other hand, belongs to everyone and to no one, whence its claim to universal

---

65   Halbwachs referred to Freud's *The Interpretation of Dreams*, which had not yet been translated into French. See Halbwachs, *On Collective Memory*, for example 167. Similarly, Max Weber's *The Protestant Ethic and the Spirit of Capitalism* was then only accessible in German (Halbwachs, *On Collective Memory*, 85). On Maurice Halbwachs, see also Gérard Namer, *Mémoire et société*, Paris: Méridiens-Klincksieck, 1987, 11–158; and Paul Ricoeur, *La mémoire de l'oubli*, Paris: Seuil, 2000, 146–51.

authority . . . At the heart of history is a critical discourse that
is antithetical to spontaneous memory.[66]

Happy the believer! Institutional historians, who live from their
craft, very often tend to emphasize what separates history from
memory, the 'objective' from the 'subjective'. They like to make
a distinction that confirms them in their perception of the scientific dimension of historical research, as distinct from the memorial culture of the public, which is not 'objective'. Their insistence in marking this strong contrast between the two 'categories'
that deal with the past and seek to recycle it proceeds from the
assumption that history seeks the truth, while memory is indifferent to this 'scientific' quest. This point of view contains a share
of illusion that is far from negligible, clothed in the form of
debatable self-celebration. As I see it, it is important to point out
that the historical discipline, in both research and teaching, has
been and remains a central vector in the process of construction
of national memory. Without the teaching of history, the modern
world would have scarcely anything in the way of common
remembrances, and if it did, these would be different from those
we are familiar with today. I do not think it possible to conceive
a collective memory that is really spontaneous; at least, no such
creature has been seen up till now.

It is true that some waves of personal memory do flow in and
out of our consciousness in a relatively spontaneous way; in other

---

66   Pierre Nora, 'Between Memory and History', in Pierre Nora (ed.), *Realms of Memory: The Construction of the French Past*, vol. 1, *Conflicts and Divisions*, New York: Columbia University Press, 1996, 8–9. In 1978, in a brief initial article on collective memory, Nora had already made a distinction between emotional and symbolic memory on the one hand, and unifying and scientific memory on the other. See here *La nouvelle histoire*, 398–9. Much later, Nora applied this distinction in his autobiography, according to which his interest in memory constituted 'the embodiment of a Jewish identity; and in the historical dimension, a way of appropriating for myself French identity . . . Memory refers to the Jewish side, and history to France' (Pierre Nora, *Esquisse d'ego-histoire*, Paris: Desclée de Brouwer, 2013, 47).

words, without being controlled or steered. We have our intimate and unprogrammed 'places of memory': a landscape of our childhood, a portrait, a phrase, an expression, a word or a pun, a meeting with a figure from the past – all signs that bring back to us things and moments that have been experienced, forgotten, denied or rememorized. The hegemonic collective memory differs substantially from these personal cognitive processes, which is why it is highly questionable to supply the storehouse of public remembrance by transposition or conceptual borrowing from the domain of individual psychology (repression, negation and so on). Collective memory has a far more instrumental character, more steered and directed than personal remembrance; it may remarkably agree with the needs and political imagination of those who created it, and those who re-create it. Places of memory, far from corresponding with the fragments of spontaneous and fluid remembrance that time has frozen, are in fact almost always defined in advance.

Ancient tribal memory was an oral transmission that left hardly any traces behind it. There may be, in our day, a certain perception of this in the form of anthropological studies of closed groups that have remained almost remote from the outside world. This type of memory, however, the main instrument for the transmission of traditions, was maintained and accumulated from generation to generation by the sorcerers, elders and priests of the tribe, those who always 'know' more than others.

In premodern agricultural societies, collective memory was essentially religious, often mixed in with communal remembrances that revolved around sacred characters, festivals, legends and local ceremonies. In the age of paganism, with its rich mythology, then with the monotheism of the Old and New Testaments, the evocation of the past and the construction of cultural places of memory were designed to confirm the divine power, as well as, of course, the presence of its earthly representatives. As a consequence, it was theology, for a long time the dominant discipline in European universities, that among its other intellectual functions completed the crystallization of the long memory of the church.

At the same time, within the nobility and power apparatus of all kingdoms, a monarchical memory was written and preserved, in order to assure and transmit the legacy of the central power. Court functionaries, the scribes and literati of the religious institution, took on the imposing task of writing dynastic chronicles, sometimes going back hundreds of years. The public for whom these remembrances were designed was not yet made up of the illiterate 'masses', but only those who at different levels exercised power in the kingdom: from the prince to the humblest knight, each had to know the noble origin of the primus inter pares. The first official memory, therefore, was always what we can define as a power-memory.

In the modern world, the nation granted itself the lion's share of collective memory, founded, financed and maintained by intellectual and political elites, the masters of speech and image. They sometimes supplemented it with local popular traditions, and drew amply from both religious and monarchical memory, while conferring on these fragments of remembrance a new quality and characteristic. In the national movements that preceded the constitution of the nation-state, avant-garde elites invented the founding myths and sacred symbols. At the same time as the foundation of the state, the same elites established monuments to the dead, public statues, museums, hymns, street names, postage stamps, teaching curricula, history textbooks, and subsequently audiovisual immortalization, increasingly diffused via electronic communication.

These elites included politicians, writers, playwrights, journalists, and later screenwriters and film directors. We also find painters, sculptors, photographers, architects, archaeologists and geographers. And yet, since the late nineteenth century, the priests of the official cult, charged with selecting and fashioning the places of memory and public immortalization, have been professional historians. All the intellectuals, politicians and other representatives of the public in the nation-state learned in their youth from official history books. They had perhaps heard talk in their family of Julius Caesar, Vercingetorix, Arminius, Boadicea, Joan of Arc or Bar Kokhba, but it was school that stamped the seal of official truth on the heroic tales of the past.[67] Those who gave names to railway stations (Austerlitz, Waterloo) or public squares (Trafalgar, Leipzig) knew these battles not because an ancestor of theirs had taken part in them, but rather because they were products of the official systems of pedagogic indoctrination.

This holds also for the majority of writers, and later for the creators of both fictional films and documentaries dealing with historical subjects for the cinema or television. Aside from a few exceptions, some of which we have already mentioned, the majority of creators of the 'artistic' historical imaginary began by using history books as a model, even if taking a great liberty with them; and by doing so they played a growing part in the formalization of key elements of public memory. The modern 'historiophoty', to use the term that Hayden White coined to denote historical films, could not have existed without the written history that served it as a springboard.[68] Historians and scholars are to national memory what poppy growers and dealers are to drug users; they supply the greater part of the commodity.[69]

Since the nineteenth century, liberal democracies have no longer needed to maintain an official censorship in order to

---

67   See on this subject Marc Ferro, *The Use of Abuse of History: Or How the Past Is Taught to Children*, London: Routledge, 1984.

68   Hayden White, 'Historiography and Historiophoty', *American Historical Review*, 93/5, 1988, 1193–99.

69   An image that I take from Eric Hobsbawm (see above, p. xxv). I should point out here that very close to the time that Pierre Nora brought out *Realms of Memory*, this British historian published, together with Terence Ranger, a captivating book on *The Invention of Tradition* (Cambridge: Cambridge University Press, 1983), a diametric historiographical antithesis to Nora's enterprise.

control heterodox or heretical stories. The accredited investigators of the past, and the sworn professors of history, have in general been official personages and responsible citizens who were not going to disappoint the political institutions. Throughout the twentieth century, they were well capable of deeply inspiring national values, and showed proof of the caution required in bringing to light scars of memory that were still highly sensitive. It is true that the relative autonomy of intellectual strata in the context of liberal democracy generates from time to time particular circumstances when criticism can be expressed towards the higher institutions that finance the production of memory. In the main, however, the guild of historians has displayed not only a great sense of discipline towards the rules of its profession, but also, almost always, a great respect for the fundamental conventions imposed by the national state.

The silent strata of society have always participated in the process of creation of memory only in a marginal way; they have generally been passive consumers of the 'memory industry'. From time to time, in periods of crisis or radical change, their irruption into the public arena and their indirect pressure on the apparatus of power has managed, with the help of critical intellectuals, to generate an atmosphere propitious to the creation of new or different collective remembrances. The appearance of counter-remembrances, on the margin of the cultural battlefield, has prepared the ground for the emergence of an unforeseen dissident memory. If, in the past, socialist movements tried to maintain a distinct memory apropos workers' struggles and organizations, so decolonization, the rise of feminism, and in the United States the struggles of African-Americans for civil rights have pressed on the walls of the traditional dominant memory, if without breaking them down.

If an additional remembrance added in this way includes a conflictual and self-critical tone, it almost always appears at the moment when the subjects concerned by the earlier memorial image have fulfilled their role. Hegel's expression about the 'owl of Minerva', the goddess of wisdom, that does not take flight until the end of the day, applies very well to this discordant and critical aspect of collective remembrance; it appears at twilight, when the facts in question are finished, and above all when their main protagonists have disappeared.

At the end of the twentieth century, the owl of the new memory, less monolithic and a bit less national, is enthusiastically aloft in the media, coming to challenge the ideological apparatus of power. The state, for a hundred years, saw historians as sworn priests of official memory. A certain margin of creativity was left to them, as a sign of tolerance but liberality, but at the same time the state always reserved the last word for itself whenever it was a question of fashioning memory for the public. We have also seen, at the end of the century, a series of additional new days of commemoration, designed to meet the demands of new memories. This is certainly a mark of cultural globalization, and, in particular, of a media proliferation that is almost uncontrollable, while traditional national emphases are undergoing a certain softening under the pressure of the new particular identities (community, religion or ethnicity) that have begun to corrode the unity of the hegemonic official memory. What is most surprising is that, alongside these days of remembrance, we have had for the first time new laws, backed up by sanctions, that lay down not only what must be commemorated, but also what is true and what is false in the narration of the past.

It is hardly surprising that professional historians should suddenly have felt rather ashamed, even mortified, when it turned out that their autonomy had always been more relative and limited than they had imagined. Some of them even rebelled and organized themselves in order to defend their monopoly of the representation of the past, which seemed at the beginning of the new century to be in the process of being dismantled. In France, for example, Pierre Nora, the high priest of academic memory, was elected president of the association Liberté pour l'histoire.[70]

N.B.

In 1986, a law was passed in Israel that prohibited denying or minimizing the Shoah. The same principle was imported into France, in 1990, in the form of the *loi Gayssot*, followed by similar legislation throughout almost all of Europe in the following years. I viewed the spread of this legislation with a certain sense of disappointment and concern. The deep disgust that I feel towards those who deny or trivialize the mass extermination perpetrated by the Nazis did not prevent me from seeing such laws as a violent ideological act, designed to impose by law and the force behind it what one is authorized to remember, and consequently what one is allowed to forget. I believed, and continue to believe, that the battle against those who are customarily called 'revisionists' or 'negationists', however marginal they may be, and not including any professional historians, must be waged freely and in broad daylight in the public sphere; in other words, in a cultural and pedagogic context. If historians should not have a monopoly on truth, then still less should this fall to the state.

The date of the founding of the state of Israel also marks, as we know, that of the flight and mass expulsion of the Palestinian population in 1948. From the 1970s, Israeli Arabs started to publicly express on that day their mourning and grief. In 2011, however, a law was brought in, with the support of the government, stipulating that any public institution (for example, Arab municipalities) that referred to this date as a day of mourning would be penalized and refused any subsidies. In the Israeli media, these measures are known as the 'Nakba Law'.

No doubt some people will object that the injustice created by the Zionist project can in no way be placed on the same footing

---

70   See lph-assoc.fr.

as the crimes of the Nazis, and that any attempt to make a parallel between them is stupid – an objection that is quite right and proper. And yet the fact that any government whatsoever should use law, with all the force this implies, to wipe out the painful places of memory of cultural minorities living under its authority is no less intolerable, even in a state that views itself as a permanent victim of the course of history.

We may also deplore that the official and institutional descendants of the 'people of remembrance' across the world, so sensitive to their own past, and who boast of a sublime Jewish morality, have expressed no protest against the Nakba Law, which is a law against memory. Certain things, it seems, are fated from the start to be thrown into the dustbin of history; and these are always components of the painful memory of other people.[71]

---

71   On the politics of remembrance and forgetting in Israel, and on places of memory more generally, please see the Afterword to my book *The Invention of the Land of Israel: From Holy Land to Homeland*, London: Verso, 2012, 259–82.

CHAPTER 3

Probing the Truth of the Past

*The renewal of France's history, which I pointed out was very
much needed, presented itself to me under two aspects: one scientific and the other political . . . In short, I asked that with the aid
of science combined with patriotism, our old chronicles might give
rise to stories capable of stirring the fibre of the people*
            Augustin Thierry, Dix ans d'études historiques, 1834

*The practical significance of historical studies lies in the fact that
they, and they alone, brandish before the state, the people or the
army, its own image. More particularly, historical study is the
foundation of political progress and culture. The statesman is the
historian in practice, capable of seeing realities and doing the
things that have to be done*
            Johann Gustav Droysen, Grundriss der Historik, 1867

In 1985, ten years after leaving it as a student, I returned to the
University of Tel Aviv to teach history there. The lectures I gave
were on nineteenth- and twentieth-century Europe, which
required me to plunge back into the study of a vast field, far
beyond the narrow specialization to which my doctoral thesis
had confined me. I immersed myself with delight in the

boundless ocean of knowledge known as history, and thanked the profession that had granted me this privilege. I understood very soon that, if the writing of research work encourages a general tendency to empiricism, teaching completes this process, impelling the historian willy-nilly towards a historiographical positivism that is ever more palpable.

The efforts involved, on the one hand, in the construction of an 'entire' past on the basis of various fragments, the laborious accumulation of a knowledge capital on the basis of crumbs, and, on the other hand, in the determination to transmit this to others, necessarily induce the deep conviction, conscious or otherwise, of the solid veracity of the said knowledge. When historians write texts, or enter the classroom to teach, they are supposed to be perfectly familiar with the account they are going to deliver, on top of which they must convince their listeners and readers of the validity and reliability of their explanations. Even if their rhetoric is tinged with the modality of doubt ('perhaps', 'probably', 'it seems'), it is not wrong to maintain that 'practical realism' or 'relative objectivity' are intrinsic to the historian's craft.

The legitimacy of teaching history and living comfortably from it, as I have been able to do for a large part of my life, rests on a well-anchored assumption: that it is possible for us to approach the truth of the past and perhaps even attain this. Given the right methodology, a critical attitude towards sources, correct deciphering, and the ability to avoid prejudices of a political and ideological nature, it will be possible to present a reliable and solid history. While I was writing my thesis, however, I already came up against the acute scepticism of Georges Sorel regarding the scientific character of all social research, both present and past. I knew very well that it is impossible for us to reach 'what actually happened in the past', but I felt a moral and professional obligation to mobilize all my intellectual strength to approach this and cling to it. It was relatively comfortable, I admit, to teach the metanarratives of the contemporary West, particularly the history of France, without questioning too much either the theoretical problematic on which historical representations are based, or their effect in terms of pedagogy.

Few 'pure' historians have taken the trouble to formulate theories on the historiographical discipline itself, and the majority of those who have risked this were concerned above all with methodology rather than epistemology. This should hardly be surprising: very few great writers have been at the same time good literary critics. In both cases, in literature as well as in history, the writing of accounts devoted to persons, events, and even processes seems to require far more in the way of creative imagination, rhetorical talent and ability to memorize, than it does in the way of systemic reflection. It is no accident that many thinkers and philosophers, from Hegel via Karl Marx to Nietzsche, or from Jean-Jacques Rousseau via Auguste Comte to Jean-Paul Sartre, not only made a free use of 'history' and extracted from it with remarkable selective capacity the materials that they needed, and that they also did not hesitate to define it, characterize it and problematize it without waiting for a go-ahead from historians.

The writing of history, in my view, can be divided into two main periods. Until the early nineteenth century, in many different cultures, history was not a discipline but rather a literary genre that essayists used to relate past events. François Furet formulated this very strikingly: 'If history did not exist in the teaching of the classical age, and thus as a scholarly discipline, this is because it did not exist as a discipline at all.'[1] Even in Athens, blessed city of learning, there were seminars in philosophy and medicine, but not in history. Starting in the sixteenth century, a few isolated and marginal chairs were established in some European universities, but it was not until the start of the nineteenth century, and hesitatingly even then, that the first

---

1   François Furet, 'La naissance de l'histoire' [1979], in *L'atelier de l'histoire*, Paris: Flammarion, 1982, 101.

professional communities of historians appeared, and history began to be regularly taught.

Over the next two centuries, on the other hand, an academic and pedagogic discipline steadily established itself, spreading to universities and teaching establishments throughout the world. From a prestige product, reserved for centuries to a thin stratum of learned elites, it was transformed into an article of mass consumption, offered to all students in the schools of the modern state not just as a right but as an obligation. Along with reading and writing, knowledge of the historical past was dispensed to citizens as a central axis of teaching. A proper understanding of this mutation is an important preliminary to any serious debate on the question of what historiography is, and what roles it plays in history.

History as Political Literary Genre

From the time of the hydraulic civilizations through to the Age of Enlightenment in Europe, a countless number of stories have survived to give evidence of their time or that of previous eras, in a wide diversity of narrative forms. The primitive myths of which we have fragments, and the chronicles of the kingdoms of Mesopotamia, Egypt and China, are presented as truthful accounts of the past, even if the main characters in them are not always human beings, and the events described are intermingled with pure miracles.

The majority of chronicles of the great Asiatic kingdoms of antiquity are lost, with the exception of those written rather later in China. We know for certain, however, that these existed, and that they even included autobiographies. Authentic manuscripts have been found at archaeological sites in both Mesopotamia and Egypt, as well as evidence from their Greek and Jewish 'margins'. Herodotus himself spelled this out, referring essentially to the Egyptian priests: 'The Egyptians . . . by their practice of keeping records of the past, have made themselves much the most learned of any nation of which I have had experience.'² In the Bible we read, about the kingdom of Persia, 'That night sleep eluded the king, so he ordered the chronicle of daily events to be brought; and it was read to him' (Esther 6:1). And in the first century BCE, Diodorus of Sicily referred, in his *Historical Library*, to 'the royal records, in which the Persians in accordance with a certain law of theirs kept an account of their ancient affairs'.³

As I explained in the first chapter, the Greek myths drew very largely on the literary imagination of Babylonian, Egyptian and Persian scholars, though they infused these with new poetry and zest. Homer's epics, which date from the eighth century BCE and relate mythic stories of the past based largely on oral traditions, pervaded the memory of the educated elites of the Hellenic cities. The biblical Jahehwist accounts that are the cradle of Mediterranean monotheism also took over much from the epic poems of nearby Asia and Africa, giving these a renewed vigour. The principal actor was still a supreme force who steered and directed, but alongside this there now appeared a number of human figures, sometimes even 'realistic', whose desires were grafted on to the imaginary tales.

In the fifth century BCE, when anonymous Hebrew authors imbued with a burning faith were wrestling with their mythic-historical stories, the Greek cultural space saw the appearance of texts of a new kind. There had previously been other accounts, but Herodotus's 'investigation', known under its Greek name

2 Herodotus, *The Histories*, London: Penguin, 2003, Book 2 (77), 125. See also Book 2 (100), 133, where Herodotus describes the priests' use of their annals. The Egyptian historian Manetho of Sebennytos, in the third century BCE, drew on ancient Pharaonic evidence in writing *Aegyptiaca*, his great essay on Egyptian history. See on this subject Arnaldo Momigliano, 'Persian Historiography, Greek Historiography and Jewish Historiography', *The Classical Foundations of Modern Historiography*, Berkeley: University of California Press, 1990, 5–32.
3 Diodorus Siculus I, *The Historical Library*, Sophron, 2014, Book II (32), 94. The kings of Judaea also had their historians, one of these, Shaphan the scribe, being mentioned several times in the Bible.

Ἱστορίαι, is the earliest preserved in its entirety. Divinities and miracles have not yet disappeared, but they remain on the margin in a separate domain, while the human eye now verifies, filters and assumes responsibility for these accounts. Another parallel development was no less important: the new historians had names; they were citizens and not just subjects (a fact that is perhaps more than accidental); and, above all, they judged what was truthful or probable, and what did not meet this criterion and was to be rejected. From now on, the past was no longer used simply as direct support for the power of the sovereign or divinity, but became to a large degree an object of research and questioning.

Herodotus, if he is often described as the first historian of all time, has also been seen as a pioneer of historical fiction. Thucydides, the 'second' known historian, already accused his predecessor of relating untruths, and many subsequent scholars echoed this judgement. It is true that Herodotus was not like the majority of researchers of the past who succeeded him. He exhibited a disturbing scepticism, and readily admitted being not always certain that the things he described actually corresponded to the truth. He liked to offer diverging parallel accounts without making a definite choice between them, declaring, for example, 'as for myself, I keep to the general plan of this book, which is to record the traditions of the various nations just as I heard them related to me'.[4] The 'first historian' believed that history relied above all on competing accounts, and this lack of 'scientificity' he displayed has been hard to pardon.

Thucydides, on the other hand, saw himself as a bearer of truth, writing basically as he did about his own time, and about facts of which he is said to have had firsthand knowledge. This is actually inexact: his book contains a number of rhetorical inventions, but ever since this first 'positivist' historian, the

---

4   Herodotus, *The Histories*, Book 2 (123), 145, likewise Book 7 (152), 468.

majority of his successors have continued to believe that they relate the strict truth, and to accuse their fellow historians, especially those of the generation preceding their own, of distorting the past and inventing fallacious myths. The new generation may well be well-founded in its criticism, yet they do not expect to be themselves contradicted just as quickly by their own successors.

There are many respects in which Thucydides may be seen as the 'genuine' father of the historical genre, on top of his claim to give a truthful account. If we find in Herodotus a comparative cultural history, almost anthropological, inserted in the midst of political facts, Thucydides, on the contrary, bequeathed to the majority of his successors the view that history fundamentally consists in a series of political, diplomatic and military events (in fact, the first two works of this genre that have survived are both devoted to the description and explanation of wars). Xenophon continued in the line of Thucydides, followed by a plethora of other chroniclers. This is probably why Aristotle, who much preferred epic poetry, recognized at least that 'the political speaker will find the researches of historians useful'.[5]

This important remark by the Athenian philosopher opens up a series of questions about the political function of the historian in premodern civilizations and, leading on from this, about his social status. Who were historians writing for, and why were they writing, before the creation of the modern teaching establishments that bring history to the masses? What did they live on, and who paid them? We know, for example, that in all agrarian civilizations the number of people able to read was extremely limited: generally between 5 and 7 per cent, perhaps rising to 10 per cent in exceptional cases (though there is no certainty about these figures). We may equally suppose that many of the literate population had little or no interest in history, so that the readership for historians was basically made up of young people from

---

5   Aristotle, *Rhetoric*, at bocc.ubi.pt, Book I (4).

the nobility and high officials of the state, in other words very slender and extremely elitist. As a consequence, history was written by the erudite, for the sociocultural strata to which they belonged, and generally with the authorization of the rulers whom they served.

The socio-professional status of historians, and their relationship with the established power, casts an essential light for understanding both the context in which they wrote and the content of their writings. The well-known dictum that historians are the children of their time does not say that they are also the children of their social class and its culture (a fact that historians themselves have scarcely sought to emphasize). What people write is infused by the geographical, cultural and temporal space in which they are writing, as well as by the sociopolitical place from which they express themselves.

This is why it is important to examine biographical data for the historians of the long premodern past, even if information is often scanty at best. We know several hundred authors of historical narration, who often practised this among other creative genres, and it is only possible here to refer to the most famous among them, in particular those whose historical reasoning has acquired such fame that it is perceived as self-evident. The list still remains quite long and detailed, and I appeal to the reader's patience.[6] The impatient, or those interested only in 'major' and prestigious historians, are welcome to skip the following section – even though the devil always lies in the details.

We know very little on the life of Herodotus, the 'father of history' (482–425 BCE), except that he was born into a well-to-do family from Halicarnassus, in Asia Minor, and that he possessed several slaves. Thucydides (460–395 BCE) was an Athenian noble and the owner of a much larger number of

---

6   Kelly Boyd (ed.), *Encyclopedia of Historians and Historical Writers*, London: Fitzroy Dearborn, 1999.

slaves, some of whom worked in his family's mines in Thrace; in contrast to Herodotus, he led an army and was also involved in high politics. Xenophon (428–354 BCE) also belonged to the Athenian nobility and was likewise a military commander; he entered the service of the king of Sparta, who gave him a large property.

Polybius (203–120 BCE), the 'father' of Roman – or even of 'universal' – historiography, was a Greek noble and politician, originally from Arcadia; he became adviser to Scipio Africanus, whom he faithfully served for a long period. Titus Livius (59–17 BCE) was close to the Emperor Augustus, and tutor to the future Emperor Claudius. Tacitus (56–117 CE) was born into a rich equestrian family; he held various political functions, and was particularly a Roman senator.[7] Plutarch (47–127), the descendant of a king of Thessaly, began his career as a priest at Delphi and ended it as a Roman governor and a friend of the Emperor Trajan. His colleague Suetonius (69–122), born apparently in North Africa, was also a friend of Trajan, and served as loyal secretary to Emperor Hadrian. Dio Cassius (155–235), son of a Roman senator, was born in Asia Minor and himself became a senator, having served as governor and consul.

Sima Qian (140–86 BCE), the father of Chinese historiography, was appointed astrologer and adviser to the emperor, a position that his father had held before him; Ban Gu (32–92 CE) came from a particularly rich noble family, directly connected to the Eastern Han dynasty. Sima Guang (1019–86) occupied a high position in the imperial administration; his works were authorized and published by the emperor immediately after they were written.

Eusebius of Caesarea (256–339), the father of clerical history, was archbishop and protégé of Emperor Constantine I; Procopius

---

7   Flavius Josephus (37–100), the great Jewish historian, from an influential priestly family in Jerusalem, was also a military leader. He never wrote on Roman history, but he was active in Rome, where he composed a good part of his work under the aegis of emperors Vespasian and Titus.

of Caesarea (500–65) was close to Belisarius, the Byzantine army leader whom he accompanied on several campaigns; Anna Komnene (1083–1153), very likely the first known woman historian, was a Byzantine princess, the daughter of Emperor Alexis I.

Al-Mas'udi (896–956), the father of Arab historiography, came from an influential Baghdad family that descended from one of the companions of Muhammad; Ahmad Al-Maqrizi (1364–1442) was active principally in Egypt; born into a particularly opulent family, he became a high official of the regime. Ibn Khaldun (1332–1406), also from a family of Islamic aristocracy, was adviser to several rulers, including Muhammad Al-Ghani, sultan of the emirates of Granada.

Gregory of Tours (539–94), father of European historiography, was the son of a noble and senator; he was appointed archbishop, as had been two of his uncles before him. The Venerable Bede (672–735), father of English historiography, belonged to a rich family; he became a monk and was made 'doctor of the church' by the Pope. Jean de Joinville (1224–1317), likewise born into the high nobility, grew up at the court of the comte de Champagne and became councillor to the king of France.

Jean Froissart (1337–1405), from more modest origins, became chronicler at the court of the queen of England, and ended his days as a man of the church, under the protection of various nobles. Niccolò Machiavelli (1449–1527), born to a noble family in Florence, held high office in both politics and diplomacy, and entered the service of various patrons. Francesco Guicciardini (1483–1540) was also from a rich Florentine family. He served the Vatican as an ambassador, while being at the same time vice-governor of Reggio d'Emilia, Modena, Parma and Bologna.

In the Age of Enlightenment, as we know, Europe boasted several philosophers, some of whom also wrote famous works of history. They included Giambattista Vico (1668–1774), who, despite not coming from a particularly well-off background, finally obtained a university chair in rhetoric and ended his career as historian at the court of the Kingdom of Naples. Voltaire (François-Marie Arouet, 1694–1778) was the son of a notary. He managed to build up a personal capital, but for reasons of status and prestige needed to add a title of nobility to his original name. He spent part of his life under the protection of a famous marquis, and later went to live in the palace of the king of Prussia. Edward Gibbon (1737–94) was born into a richer family, and came into a legacy that enabled him to live in opulence for the rest of his life. He was for a while a member of Parliament.

From Herodotus through Ibn Khaldun and Gibbon, the authors of chronicles, and those mainly responsible for the historical representation of the figures of their time, all belonged to the upper classes, and almost all wrote in the protective shadow of the ruling authorities. In this respect they were no different from the majority of men of letters: philosophers, artists or poets who circled around the centres of political power from which they drew their subsistence. If we leave aside the advantages they may have gained personally, their works basically served as explicit political models for the education, consciousness and identity of the elites of their time.

True, there were sometimes (rarely) disputes between certain individual historians and their protectors, and the former did not always assume the role of direct spokesmen of state authority that seems to have been the case with chroniclers in the hydraulic monarchies. There was no equivalent there of a Socrates, a Giordano Bruno or a Spinoza – not a single one. The historical knowledge produced and diffused at that time had a very restricted margin of autonomy, if any at all.

History has always been written from above and, no less important for the subject, it has been essentially based on documentation likewise elaborated within the dominant strata, religious or secular, who were themselves most often part of a monarchical administration. In all premodern societies, written matter bore the seal of those possessing political, religious or economic power, who were also the masters of all that was written. It is clear that without this production, full of unparalleled information on bygone times, we would be almost completely ignorant of the past; however, all debate on the status of historiography must begin with the basic clarification that all those who live, depend and write on the side of power are themselves part of power, and, above all, that they write about power.

This holds, as we have just seen, from the chroniclers of the Asiatic kingdoms through to Gibbon. History, without being a discipline, was always a kind of storehouse of accounts of the past, most often political. The acts described in time were, in general, events outside people's everyday experience. Whether monuments to the glory of oriental despots, Greek epics, Roman histories, ecclesiastical chronicles or stories of modern times, preference has always been given to war, conquest, victories and peace treaties. Power struggles, descriptions of the functioning of royal administrations, portraits of monarchs and warriors, and biographies of great martyrs also came within the purview of customarily accepted chronicles.

On the margin of this narrative torrent we sometimes find a small stream of information on human activities outside 'high' politics, whose revelation casts a precious light on wider social strata. But we should right away raise a point that I shall return to at the end of this chapter. Historians have sometimes tended to resort to deceptive globalizing concepts, which weigh heavily on the construction of the past. Premodern historians, just like the majority of their modern successors, have described peoples and nations that did not actually exist. The collective identities of elites, as expressed in historiography, in no way resembled those of groups who had only limited and episodic communication with one another. In each valley, and behind each range of hills, labouring men and women spoke different dialects, and only ceremonials in honour of the gods, or later the worship of one god, created wider cultural networks than those of the tribe, the village, or neighbouring localities. The great majority of these working people played almost no part in historical events, unless they were enrolled in them by force, or compelled to hand over their children to bands of mercenaries.

In fact, interaction between force and event formed the core of historical narrative, from its origins to the stabilization of democracy in the twentieth century. Force gave rise to events, while events explained, directly or indirectly, the origin of this force (earthly or transcendental). Politics is at the end of the day a human activity seeking to organize social relations, and so dramatic political events were milestones on the roads of history writing.

History as Professional Discipline

Starting in the early nineteenth century, a slow and gradual process saw the writing of history divide along two main pathways. The broader path was one on which 'independent' essayists continued the tradition of writing history as it had prevailed until the late eighteenth century. Alongside this, however, a new path appeared, still narrow, on which those investigators of the past who were organized in universities and other research institutions advanced with a hesitant step. In Europe, famous historians such as Thomas Carlyle (1795–1881), Thomas Macaulay (1800–1859) and Henry Thomas Buckle (1821–1862) in England, and Augustin Thierry (1795–1856), Alexis de Tocqueville (1805–1859) and Hippolyte Taine (1828–1893) in France, did not join the university departments that were being established; in terms of their sociopolitical status (along with the majority of less celebrated historians of their time) they were far closer to Gibbon and Voltaire than to the professional historians of today.[8]

---

8   Carlyle unsuccessfully sought an appointment at the University of St Andrews.

The majority of their number were free from any material worries, by virtue of their close integration into social, political and cultural elites. They often successfully followed a political career of their own, while still devoting a substantial part of their time to writing. In this way, they published essays that are still seen today as precious summits in the development of historical narration. Make no mistake, the value of these works does not just lie in their literary quality. It is impossible not to be impressed by the way in which the most talented of their number used original sources and evidence, sometimes quite systematically, as well as by their understanding of history, despite their lack of the organizational supports possessed by the profession today.

Alongside this traditional form of history writing, a specific academic discipline labelled 'history' now began to emerge step by step. The first historians recruited to the universities were themselves autodidacts; their doctoral theses were very short essays, and publications were not the main criterion for obtaining a position. William Stubbs (1825–1901) was appointed to an Oxford professorship in 1866, and John Dalberg-Acton (1834–1902) only gained this position at Cambridge in 1895, though their French colleague François Guizot (1787–1874) became a Sorbonne professor as early as 1812, rather by chance. Stubbs, however, was at the same time Archbishop of Oxford, while the two others were deeply involved in politics: Acton as a Member of Parliament, Guizot as minister and then prime minister. Their historical work was no less significant, and they are recognized today at least as much for this as for their intense political activity.

Jules Michelet (1798–1874), on the other hand, was more of a pure historian, and perhaps the most productive of his time. His interest in politics was no less than that of his colleagues, but he abandoned a career in public life to become a lecturer in history and philosophy at the École normale supérieure in 1827, then an assistant professor at the Sorbonne in 1830, before obtaining a chair at the Collège de France. Numa Denis Fustel de Coulanges (1830–89) was a wide-ranging historian who devoted himself completely to academic life; appointed to the University of Strasbourg in 1860, he obtained a lectureship in Paris ten years later, at the École normale supérieure, and after eight more years was appointed to the prestigious chair of history at the Sorbonne.

Ernest Renan, who became the best-known historian of Christianity and Judaism in France, obtained a coveted position at the Collège de France in 1862, not in history but in Hebrew (some university positions at this time still combined two subjects). A famous scholar who intervened in many fields, he was inspired by the Prussian victory over France in 1871 to write *The Intellectual and Moral Reform of France*, in which he held up German science and education as the supreme model for building a powerful and victorious nation.[9] Renan's political conclusions, tinged with monarchism and aristocratic conservatism, are clearly such as to arouse scepticism; yet the fact of drawing attention to the German educational system was quite unprecedented at that time. Renan held that in terms of scholarship Germany had reached far higher results than France, and invited his country to take this as a model for imitation. As far as changes in the writing of history during the nineteenth century are concerned, Renan was certainly correct, and he drew the corresponding lesson in terms of pedagogy.

It would not be wrong to maintain, in fact, that monarchical and conservative Prussia was the birthplace of history as a professional discipline, almost half a century before Great Britain, France or the United States. The working methods accepted today throughout the world have their origin in early nineteenth-century Prussia, and their paternity can be ascribed to Leopold von Ranke (1795–1887), who became professor of

---

9   Ernest Renan, *La réforme intellectuelle et morale de la France*, Paris: Perrin, 2011.

history at the University of Berlin in 1825. Other particularly prolific scholars would continue and indeed expand on his achievements. Johann Gustav Droysen (1808–1884) was appointed professor at the University of Kiel in 1840, later at Jena, before ending his career at the prestigious University of Berlin. Heinrich von Sybel (1817–1895) was professor first in Munich, then Bonn. Theodor Mommsen (1817–1903) began his career at the University of Leipzig and continued it in Zurich, before obtaining the Berlin history chair in 1861. Heinrich von Treitschke (1834–1896), a colleague and popular competitor of Mommsen's, also acquired a professorship at the same university in 1874.

This series of eminent scholars, to which we could add others, made a great contribution to the professionalization of modern history and its transformation into a specific discipline, arousing in its time the envy of their counterparts across Europe.[10] By the mid-nineteenth century there were already twenty-eight history professors in nineteen German-language universities; sixty years later, just before the First World War, the number had risen to 185.[11] Germany's famous 'historicism' was maintained by a far larger number of accredited agents than that of any other national culture.

This striking professionalization, which apart from prestige was accompanied by a certain social mobility, in no way meant that academic historians, any more than their 'dilettante' colleagues, had renounced public careers. All of them, without exception, wrote political, diplomatic and military history, and at the same time almost all openly cherished political ambitions. These two sectors of activity went hand in hand, each supporting

---

10   We should add that the professionalizing of history happened in close parallel with that of political activity.

11   On this subject, see R. Harrison, A. Jones and P. Lambert, 'The Institutionalization and Organization of History', in Peter Lambert and Phillip Schofield (eds), *Making History: An Introduction to the History and Practices of a Discipline*, London: Routledge, 2004, 10.

the other. And if the notion of 'pure objectivity' was advanced in history writing, no one put forward the idea that it was incumbent on the historian to preserve 'pure neutrality' in the public sphere. They sat in parliaments, were ministers or government advisers, edited major newspapers, or were involved one way or another in matters of state and diplomacy. In other words, almost all were 'committed' intellectuals, with clear ideological positions. We can distinguish among them convinced monarchists, consistent conservatives and moderate liberals, but there was no socialist professor to be found, no woman, and throughout Europe no professor of Jewish origin.[12]

Was it a matter of chance that the need for an accelerated nationalization of the masses found expression precisely in a cultural and linguistic space not yet unified into a single political framework by a long-standing monarchical tradition (as opposed to England and France)? And was it jealousy of the already established West, after the upheavals caused by the Napoleonic conquests, that required a more assured and stable professionalization of history in Prussia? The aim of this professionalization was above all to create a consistent historical past. The trade of historian, qua university specialist, seems to have been born precisely when and where the greatest need for history made itself felt: the need for a unifying collective imaginary, going back in time right to 'ancient' Rome, the 'Middle Ages' and the first

---

12   Wilhelm Zimmermann (1807–1878) was one of the rare historians to openly express sympathy with the left, but despite completing a doctoral thesis he did not obtain a university position, and had to be content with teaching for a short while in a *gymnasium* and a polytechnic. Leopold von Ranke had several students of Jewish origin, the most brilliant of whom, Philipp Jaffé (1819–1870), became a famous medieval historian; Jaffé reached professorial level at the University of Berlin, and converted to Christianity to be more suitable for an official appointment. But his candidacy was rejected, and this seems to have been the reason for his suicide. Hedwig Guggenheimer-Hintze was the first woman to be awarded a doctorate in history at the University of Berlin, and obtained a lectureship there in 1928. Of Jewish origin, she fled to Holland with the rise of Nazism, and also committed suicide, in 1942, when faced with deportation.

German Reich, not to mention the need for a modern history of the rising power of Prussia.

It is hard to be certain about these broad questions. Other factors certainly contributed to the fact that the first professional guilds dedicated to history appeared in one of the most conservative environments in Europe. We should not lose sight of the fact that this same environment was also one of the most advanced in terms of the pace and level of material production. The advance of industrialization, coupled with the Napoleonic conquests, broke the old social structure of estates. Did these processes have an effect, even indirectly, on the emergence in the universities of new bodies of ideological production? This question, too, cannot be definitely answered. We may, however, advance the hypothesis that the guilds of narrators of history, under the surveillance of the state and with financing from it, were destined among other things to work at joining the now dislocated identities of yesterday with the newly emerging identities of the present.

It is interesting to note that the hierarchical organization of the discipline and its growing specialization, along with the absence of solidarity, the prevailing egoism and the modes of dependence in these academic guilds that have persisted to our own day, evoke the unpleasant memory of the premodern guilds of artisan–artists that precisely left the historical stage at that time. Is it accidental that the flame of knowledge should have been transmitted in such a context? The question remains open to all kinds of interpretation.[13]

We should perhaps designate as the pioneer of the new historiography Barthold Niebuhr, official historian of the German Empire, who was appointed to his Berlin professorship when the university was founded in 1810, not to mention the great

---

13   On the hierarchical structure of the academic mandarinate, see the interesting book by Jean Chesneaux, *Du passé faisons table rase?*, Paris: Maspero, 1976, 73–83.

linguist Wilhelm von Humboldt, himself a founding father of the university, whose intellectual inspiration fostered the birth of the new discipline.[14] And yet, from both a literary point of view and a narrowly technical one, the roll of honour among these pioneers is rightly headed by Leopold von Ranke: historians throughout the continent, whatever their cultural background and political tendency, have almost all agreed on this.[15] Lord Acton, for example, in summing up his relation to history writing at the turn of the century, referred to the Prussian historian as 'my own master', and added, 'by his influence on able men, and by the amount of knowledge which mankind receives and employs with the stamp of his mind upon it, he stands without a rival'.[16]

The historian's craft as we know it today does indeed owe much to Ranke. It was the Prussian historian, following the rudimentary model that existed already at the University of Göttingen, who established the framework of the research seminar that is still the norm in universities today. His critical philological approach, methodically applied to each document and piece of evidence, seems in broad terms a distant descendant of Spinoza's *Tractatus Theologico-Politicus* of 1670, as well as a kind of modern continuation of Mabillon's *De re diplomatica* of 1681. And it is of no lesser importance that we owe to Ranke and no other the systematic addition of the footnote, that cornerstone of 'historical truth'. Earlier theological exegeses certainly contained footnotes, but these now assumed a quite different status.[17] Ranke,

---

14 Humboldt's speech on the historian's mission, in 1821, was a powerful stimulant on the emergence of the new historiography. See 'On the Historian's Task', *History and Theory*, 6/1, 1967, 57–71.

15 On Ranke's place as seen by later historians, one may consult the article by Georg G. Iggers, 'The Image of Ranke in American and German Historical Thought', *History and Theory*, 2/1, 1962, 17–40.

16 Lord Acton, *Lectures on Modern History*, CreateSpace, 2015, 8 and 10.

17 See on this point the stimulating work of Anthony Grafton, *The Footnote: A Curious Story*, Cambridge, MA: Harvard University Press, 1997. The author makes copious reference to Ranke (34–93).

whose doctoral thesis was devoted to Thucydides, believed like his subject that only a history based on firsthand sources was seriously worth transcription. Until Gibbon, the custom of historians had been to turn to a variety of archives and testimonies, then on the basis of this material to summarize the unfolding of events and integrate these summaries in their accounts; from now on, a document as object of research had to be quoted word for word, with this decisive proof appearing as an appendix to the historian's own text.

At this stage, history had to be political history if it was to be recognized as an 'objective' discipline. Footnotes could not for the moment guide readers towards social, economic or cultural situations, nor did they seek to do so. Neither the fate of workers on the land (and still less that of peasant women), nor the work of artisans, nor the way in which soldiers died were of interest to the professional historian. Footnotes had to refer to governmental archives, to the diaries of great men of state, to diplomatic correspondence and treaties – material that it was easy to access. And all the more so, in that the local powers that subsidized the new historians spurred them to use official sources; that is, documents preciously sorted and preserved by the existing elites. Universities, under the aegis of empires or principalities, looked favourably on the construction of a new memory among the emerging bourgeois elites, perhaps to obtain some legitimacy after the destabilization of the old order with the Napoleonic Wars. Nothing could be more political and more ingenious than to transform heavy romantic nostalgia into 'science', or to see the enchanting and deceptive fictions of Walter Scott as 'authentic' accounts. Romanticism, as we know, was very good at feeding a spirit of return to the past, without itself being the agent of this.

This helps us understand not only why Ranke was seen as the pioneer of history professors, but also why he was appointed in 1832 as editor of a new journal, enjoying wide circulation and generous government support, with the significant title of

Historische-politische Zeitschrift. In 1859, Ranke's disciple and follower von Sybel founded a more strictly professional journal with the simpler title *Historische Zeitschrift*; the 'political' label was removed in order to give research a more objective appearance. This publication, which still exists today, served as a model for all historical journals. In parallel with seminars and academic chairs, such journals were thus an important element in tracing the professional frontiers of the new guild.

Ranke's first book, on which dozens of articles have been written, was titled *History of the Latin and Teutonic Peoples.*[18] Though an explicit national label is still absent, the conservative Ranke initially researched what united 'civilized' Europeans (excluding Slavs and Hungarians), and indirectly laid down the markers for subsequent historical narration.

With this book, we see the birth of modern history as a new political theology, preparing to dethrone the old metaphysical theology that had marked European culture for many centuries.[19] For this Prussian Protestant, who had himself been destined for theology before turning historian, and who wrote a good deal and sympathetically on religion, 'states are the thoughts of God'. It is clear enough today that states do not arise from the meditations of a divine power, but are the instruments of completely earthly forces. However, what Ranke expressed, in a brilliant narrative, was the sense that the kingdoms still ruled by conservative elites were at a decisive turning point for their future, after the upheavals of the French Revolution and their defeats by Napoleon: politics would now have to pay more consideration to the nations in process of formation, whether

---

18   Leopold von Ranke, *Geschichte der romanischen und germanischen Völker von 1494 bis 1514,* first published in 1824. This book is full of footnotes. The English translation, *History of the Latin and Teutonic Peoples from 1494 to 1514* (London: Bell, 1909), does not contain the original preface.

19   It is perhaps not accidental that the four most prominent German historians of the nineteenth century were all sons of Lutheran pastors: Ranke, Droysen, Sybel and Mommsen.

this was welcome or not. With the emergence of new crowds, historical truth had to be unambiguous.

Many historians over the years have pondered the meaning of Ranke's declaration at the start of his book: 'To history has been assigned the office of judging the past, of instructing the present for the benefit of future ages. To such high offices this work does not aspire: It wants only to show what actually happened (*wie es eigentlich gewesen*).'[20] The debate revolves principally around the ambiguities of the German word *eigentlich*. Did the author mean 'really', 'essentially', 'effectively' or 'truthfully'? Was Ranke the father of historiographical positivism, who believed that his narration 'reflected' the past? Was he a naive historian, like many researchers who followed in his footsteps, starting from the principle that written history actually (*eigentlich*) is the history that happened?

It is not merely by chance that modern historians, following in this respect their predecessors, have never deemed it necessary to mark a terminological difference between Herodotus's Greek term Ιστορίαι, meaning 'investigation' (history as writing about the past) and the object of this writing, the past 'itself'. No one has taken the trouble, up to now, to invent a professional term to deal with the past, as is the case in all other domains: 'geography', 'archaeology' and 'sociology', followed by 'anthropology' and 'psychology'. For history, at least in etymological terms, there is apparently no difference between what has been written about the procession of facts and the facts themselves.

Yet we should not deceive ourselves. Despite his very realist style of writing, Ranke was neither a complete positivist nor an essayist lacking a personal consciousness. In the end, it is not that important to know precisely what he was thinking when he

---

20   Leopold von Ranke, 'Preface to *Histories of the Latin and Germanic Nations from 1494 to 1514*', in Fritz Stern (ed.), *Varieties of History*, New York: Vintage, 1973, 57. See also Felix Gilbert, *History: Politics or Culture? Reflections on Ranke and Burckhardt*, Princeton: Princeton University Press, 1990, 19.

wrote *eigentlich*.[21] It may be that he meant 'essentially', and if the preface to his book is read in this way, his assertion was then clearly intended to confer certainty on his research, as well as to distance himself from speculative philosophy, in particular that of Hegel. Moreover, Ranke always considered the writing of history an artistic act, even a kind of literature: he was aware of the portion of subjectivity that any historian carries with him.

The cardinal problem of Ranke's declaration, as of the 'scientific' writing of history in general, is the meaning given to the question 'what happened?' Beyond its preface, Ranke's book offers in response to this question a series of political events, from wars to diplomatic agreements, on which he collected a wealth of evidence taken from government archives. It would be logical to conclude from this that, from the point of view of historians and their readers, what does not figure in the archives is not really part of the past. This basic principle for reconstructing the past would guide historiographical research for years to come; Ranke's students and those of other professors would adopt it in full and transmit it to their own students, in both universities and secondary schools. And it is clear that this phenomenon, far from being specific to Prussia and Germany, soon became in all modern countries a guiding principle of historical research, and a fortiori of its teaching.

I shall leave aside for the moment the problem of the relation between testimony or written documentation and the events to which these relate, as well as the relationship between the conceptual tools we create and what we call 'processes' and 'events'. Everyone is well aware of the impossibility of representing the past in its totality, particularly given its limitless character. If the past that interests us is the ensemble of human activities that took place, it evidently remains beyond the grasp of a human

---

21   See on this subject the remarks of Peter Novick, *That Noble Dream: The 'Objectivity Question' and the American Historical Profession*, Cambridge: Cambridge University Press, 1988, 21–31.

being – even a being who claims descent from a god. A large part of 'what happened' has disappeared forever, without leaving the least trace that would enable us to locate and identify it. As for what remains of the past, as this steadily builds up it forms a mountain of diverse data that it is impossible to master without proceeding to a selection, as a function of values and preferences that are often arbitrary. This is why Ranke's proclaimed objective of showing 'what happened' bears a heavy imprint of naivety, at least if not removed from the context of his text, or alternatively an imprint of bad faith. Ranke should have written that he wanted to show 'what happened' according to the archives that he had access to and those that he chose to search.

Behind the question formulated by Ranke lie two main postulates: the first is the guarantee given the reader that the historian's objective is to reach 'an identification between reflection and the facts', with the objective that 'what happened and the science (of what happened) . . . entirely coincide'.[22] In other words, to tend towards objective truth, with all the difficulties this involves. It means that what the historian writes cannot simply be an interpretation of documents sufficient in themselves; this type of interpretation, concerning situations experienced in the past, is often erroneous. The historian's work must lie rather in piecing together a jigsaw puzzle on the basis of actual fragments of the past, arranging them correctly in order to obtain an adequate image of what was once a reality. Despite the application of a critical method, the danger is that documents themselves become a historical fact.[23]

The second postulate is that the craft of the new historian, as distinct from traditional history or philosophical ethics, is not intended to educate, instruct or guide people in their lives, but simply to familiarize them with the past. It follows from this

22   See Catherine Devulder, 'Histoire allemande et totalité: Léopold von Ranke, Johann Gustav Droysen, Karl Lamprecht', *Revue de synthèse*, 2, 1987, 178.

23   For a different verdict on Ranke, see Gérard Noiriel, *Sur la 'crise' de l'histoire*, Paris: Belin, 1996, 49–55.

that, for the writer, history is not a political or an instrumental discipline, but a 'pure science'. Just as physics studies the phenomena of movement, and biology examines living organisms, so the only mission of history is to teach what happened in the past. In other words, the study and teaching of history exist in a disinterested fashion, and not for the Prussian emperor or the king of Bavaria (among other major financiers of the professionalization of history). This is where 'scientific' history received its initial formulation and set out on its long trajectory. From now on, the professional historian would be increasingly financed by the modern state, while independent historical writers and dilettantes were driven from the stage.

The instrumentalization of the natural sciences is clearly a matter for debate. We can express doubts as to the relationship between the experimental sciences and their more abstract counterparts on the threshold of the modern age. Sceptics may also have reservations about the idea that the work of humanity on nature, the needs created by this interaction and the experience accumulated, provided the necessary springboard for technological advances and scientific revolutions. And yet there were several reasons behind the definition of history as a science, after the model of physics and chemistry, biology and zoology. In the last analysis, a science is not just a collection of concrete or abstract knowledge of the world, even if many historians still believe this today.

'Science' and the Magic Power of Facts

Descartes, in the seventeenth century, refused to consider the writing of history as scientific research. Vico, however, in the early eighteenth century, chose to title his work on the philosophy of history *The New Science*. He believed, contrary to Descartes, that it is easier for us to understand human history than to know external nature or our own mind, given that history is what we have done (the principle of *verum factum*). This conception is based on the postulate that the men and women who acted before us are an integral part of our consciousness; there is thus an identity between them and us that makes it possible to give a scientific explanation of the past. The Neapolitan philosopher and historian was sufficiently cautious not to equate the dynamic that drives historical life with the laws of nature, which pertain to God. (Ranke, on the other hand, was persuaded that if the historian paid proper attention to the facts, divine providence would lay down the laws of history.)

From Vico until the early nineteenth century, when the comte de Saint-Simon sought to make science the new religion of the industrial age, many thinkers in the field of the study of humanity and society began to envy the aura of experimental science with its rapid ascension. The philosophers of the Age of Enlightenment, seduced by scientific rationalism, already aspired to introduce this into the observation of human social development. Advances in life sciences such as biology and zoology, moreover, aroused an increasing desire to transpose the concept of science from the world of life into that of the study of man that was part of life. *Wissenschaftlichkeit* or 'scientificity' became a kind of password, a guarantor of truth, in many channels of European culture, at least until the second half of the nineteenth century.[24] This 'scientific' fashion also infected several novelists of the time, for example in the form of a realist and impersonal style of writing. With Honoré de Balzac, Gustave Flaubert, Charles Dickens, Leo Tolstoy and Émile Zola, to take only such major figures, the passion for social and psychological realism expressed a demand to know all life precisely and systematically.

In Ranke's time already, the idea that past and present human society could be dissected with the aid of scientific tools had already come to prevail among intellectual elites, both in Europe

---

24   On the intellectual climate of the era, see Heiko Feldner, 'The New Scientificity in Historical Writing around 1800', in S. Berfer, H. Feldner and K. Passmore (eds), *Writing History: Theory and Practice*, London: Bloomsbury Academic, 2003, 3–22.

and in the New World. In this way, a foundation was gradually created for what today are reverentially called 'social sciences' or 'human sciences'. Many elite thinkers of the 'scientific' century undertook to study both the laws that governed social relations and those that ruled over human time. We can briefly present three famous examples here, in order to illustrate the contours of the ideological climate that came to prevail in many erudite milieus.

Auguste Comte (1798–1857), the father of social science; Karl Marx (1818–83), father of scientific socialism; and Herbert Spencer (1820–1903), father of social Darwinism, were none of them historians, and yet history played a key role in the formation of their doctrines. Though each of these three thinkers beat a distinctive new path, they all believed in the primacy of society over the individual, the possibility of formalizing human relations and of identifying constant determinants in these. (All three also had in common the fact of not having obtained academic employment and of having to live either from their writings or from the support of their friends.) Their contributions to assimilating historical development to natural science had a long-term effect, directly or indirectly influencing the writing of history through the twentieth century. Comte and Spencer were more famous in their own time, though Marx's thought has had a far more lasting effect on modern culture. Despite their differences, these three thinkers also showed many points of convergence, intellectually, morally and politically.

Auguste Comte did not fall into philosophical essentialism, but he liked to think that historical phenomena exhibited a constant set of laws, and saw himself in this respect as the direct heir of Descartes and Leibniz. This led him to develop what he called 'social positivism', and conceive a schema of humanity's progression in three decisive stages: the theological or fictive stage, the metaphysical or abstract stage, and the positive or scientific stage. In this last stage, that of Comte's own time, the sciences had reached a summit of perfection, in which the science of sociology (a term Comte himself coined) would organize and regulate all the others. The object of this science was the forms of organization of human society and its modes of development. Only knowledge of the laws according to which social relations evolved would make it possible to rationally guide and act on the latter.[25]

Karl Marx likewise believed in a conception of the development of human society through successive phases, according to laws of history. In his view, the engine of progress and change was twofold: there was first of all the contradiction arising between the developing means of production and the relations of production (in other words, between the dynamic force of technology and the forms of property and domination in which this was harnessed); then, as a result of this contradiction, the constant struggle between social classes. A final confrontation, in the wake of industrialization and the accumulation and concentration of capital, would lead to the rising power of the proletariat, whose victory would make possible the advent of a classless society and mark the end of history. Engels, in 'Socialism: Utopian and Scientific' (extracted from his book *Anti-Dühring*), synthesized Marx's more complex and nuanced viewpoint, with a certain schematism but effectively.[26]

Herbert Spencer shared with Marx the view of history as a succession of permanent struggles. Or rather, his view was not one of confrontations between classes but rather of competition between individuals for survival, followed by conflicts of social groups to obtain more. Spencer was to a certain degree already an evolutionist and 'Darwinist' before reading the masterwork of the famous zoologist. It is true that after he read *The Origin of Species* he used the expression 'survival of the fittest', and there are also references in his work to a competition between races,

25   Comte's own summary of his views can be found in Auguste Comte, *A General View of Positivism*, London: Trübner, 1848, available at archive.org.

26   Frederick Engels, 'Socialism: Utopian and Scientific', *Marx–Engels Collected Works*, vol. 24, London: Lawrence & Wishart, 1989.

but in the last analysis he was an English-type liberal, also explor-
ing the notion of human progress though on a different path
from those of Comte or Marx. Like them, he sought to exhibit
historical laws that society had to conform to in order to advance
and improve itself. He dreamed of achieving a unifying synthesis
of all the sciences, in order to approach the truth about nature
and history. He believed that the laws of nature were equally
applicable to society, and that it was enough to be able to discover
these in order to maximize competition and thus promote and
generalize wealth.[27]

These three thinkers already proclaimed the victory of the
'rationalist' bourgeoisie over the traditionalist forces that had
sought to obstruct its progress by recourse to old beliefs. All three
translated in their own way the values of the new world, and the
widespread sense that history, having reached the industrial age,
had attained a culminating point of maturity, even though it still
had to take an additional great leap forward. Each of them
conceived this leap in a different form, while basing it on a 'scientific logic' rather than on human voluntarism. What is fascinating about them all is their ability to decipher the codes of their
environment better than their contemporaries. Unfortunately,
however, they did not stick to this, but went on to erect the
dynamics of conflict characteristic of their era into general and
timeless historical laws.

The prodigious scientific achievements that revolutionized
production expressed a growing domination over nature and
helped to fuel a utopian vision of the future. Science and its laws
were closely imbricated with progress. Historians of this time
participated in this attractive ideological process, transposing it
into a study of the past with the explicit aspiration of guiding the
present and building the future. The facts that they set out to
reveal with systematic rigour were arranged in 'scientific' fashion

---

27   Herbert Spencer, *Principles of Biology* [1864] (2 vols.), Amazon Digital
Services, 2014.

according to eras, centuries, kingdoms, nations, cultures, revolutions and decisive wars. Objective truth about the worlds of yesterday seemed within grasp.

Two famous historians, the Englishman Henry Thomas Buckle and the Frenchman Hippolyte Taine, clearly sought to identify history with the new natural sciences.[28] Buckle's famous *History of Civilization in England* served as a standard work of reference for many scholars in the second half of the nineteenth century.[29] Buckle, who was incidentally a great chess player, sought to arrange the past in a succession of regular processes that could be grasped not only with the tools of logic, but also with those of 'science'. He maintained right at the start of his major work,

> I entertain little doubt that before another century has elapsed, the chain of evidence will be complete, and it will be as rare to find an historian who denies the undeviating regularity of the moral world, as it now is to find a philosopher who denies the regularity of the material world.[30]

According to Buckle, there exists despite certain differences a coherent continuity between nature and history; accordingly, with the effort of intelligence, the laws that are common to them can be brought to light. Initially it was the geographical and climatic environment that conditioned the first steps of human

---

28   Other less prominent historians also sought to establish a science of human time. See, for example, the early essay by the 'Saint-Simonian' historian Philippe Buchez, *Introduction à la science de l'histoire ou science du développement de l'humanité*, Paris: Paulin, 1833; the book by the Italian Nicola Marselli, *La Scienza della storia*, Turin: Loescher, 1873; and the later work by Paul Lacombe, *De l'histoire considérée comme science*, Paris: Hachette, 1894. We may also recall the peremptory assertion of Fustel de Coulanges, 'History is a science; it does not imagine, it simply sees' (*Histoire des institutions politiques de l'ancienne France, la monarchie franque*, Paris: Hachette, 1888, 1).

29   Henry Thomas Buckle, *History of Civilization in England* [1857], Cambridge: Cambridge University Press 2011.

30   Ibid., 31.

societies. The physical world shaped the beginnings of humanity and set the direction and ways of being of civilization. To make this comprehensible, social relations should be analysed starting from the following fundamental components: soil, climate, food, and the other accidents of nature. And whereas European civilization managed to overcome the constraints of its physical environment, other civilizations continued to be subject to these. As a result, and as distinct from the rest of the world, deciphering the history of advanced Europeans had to focus chiefly on the laws of the intellectual and mental domain, and less on the natural environment. Historical advances now depended on cultural developments, and these claimed priority for historians' attention. Nonetheless, these must make sure to base their writing on the inductive principle, as was the rule in the exact sciences.

Hippolyte Taine was neither less popular nor less 'scientific' than Buckle; he also believed that identical laws governed both nature and history. Taine's view was that with the help of the experimental method it was possible to characterize the determinant factors of human development, which were race, milieu and moment. However, given the impossibility of re-creating these data in a laboratory, it was important to promote the system of historical investigation, based on a precise analysis of the facts, their rigorous classification, and a proper formalization of the relations between them. Using such methodological tools, it would become possible to transcribe historical processes in the same way as biological life. Armed with these theoretical premises, Taine undertook between 1875 and 1885 the publication of his monumental work: *Les origines de la France contemporaine.*[31]

Taine's work found great resonance within the community of French historians, and despite meeting certain criticisms, its reputation rose again after the death of its author. Gabriel

31   Hippolyte Taine, *The Origins of Contemporary France*, Lenox, MA: HardPress Publishing, 2013.

Monod, for example, the founder and editor of the *Revue histo-rique* in 1876, and a leading member of the new professional historiography of the late nineteenth century, published in his journal a glowing obituary in praise of the 'scientific' historian who so distinguished himself as against the mode of writing of his Romantic colleagues.[32]

Buckle, in contrast to Taine, encountered fierce criticism despite the great popularity of his books. Professional histori-ans did not appreciate his self-assuredness and hasty generaliza-tions; besides, his cutting anti-religious materialism was repug-nant to those who refused to abandon God. Lord Acton, for example, who upheld free will in history, wrote about Buckle in 1858,

> The whole system of positive philosophy is the work of under-educated men, adepts in physical science, but ignorant of the principles of any other, who insist that science must have the same method as theirs and that the metaphysical realities must be measured and explained by physical laws. We state this to show that Mr Buckle's absurdities and dishonesties are not his own but those of his school.[33]

In expressing this distrust of positivist philosophy, Acton's particular target was Buckle's champion, John Stuart Mill. Acton, a Catholic historian who would become a pillar of British

---

32   Monod ('Hippolyte Taine', *Revue historique*, 52/1, 1893, 113) summed up Taine's project in the following words: 'Whereas the positivist is content with analysing facts, establishing their correspondence or succession without claiming to grasp any certain relationship of causality, Taine, in the name of his absolute determinism, sees each fact as a necessary element in a group of facts of the same nature that determines it and is its cause. Each group of facts is conditioned in turn by a more general group which is also its cause, and it is theoretically possible to go back, group by group, to a single cause that would be the condition of everything that exists.'

33   Quoted by G. A. Wells, 'The Critics of Buckle', *Past and Present*, 9, 1956, 76.

historiography, did not reject historical 'scientificity', but as against Buckle and Mill he preferred Arthur de Gobineau and his racist *Essay on the Inequality of Human Races* (1853–55). Acton found Gobineau's work more convincing, as it explained the hereditary tendencies that each race manifested in its relation to religion and God. Acton's disdainful criticism was in fact hardly serious, and it was rather from Germany that a far more interesting new reaction appeared at this time.

Johann Gustav Droysen, the great historian of Hellenism (a term that he himself coined) was, to my understanding, the first modern historian to pen a specific essay designed to explain and justify the foundations of his craft. In 1858, using material from his public lectures, he published the work generally referred to as his *Historik*, a stimulating essay that appeared in successive reworked and enriched versions between 1862 and 1882.[34] Droysen's book was one of a number of important attempts in the nineteenth century to characterize in a basic and systematic fashion, albeit somewhat opaquely, the codes of historical narration. Its importance, recognized by its translation into French in 1887 and English in 1893, requires us to dwell on it at some length here.

While a large part of the book turns out to be an indirect and very cautious critique of the legacy of Ranke, Droysen devotes an appendix to Buckle and his conception of history, with the express purpose of refuting this. The fact that Buckle made no appeal to human will in his configuration of historical time (no more than he did to divine providence) offended the liberal world view of the German *Bilderbürgertum* that was the ideological wellspring of this penetrating historian of Hellenism.[35] Similarly, the risk of political passivity inherent to the writings of many historians led Droysen to seek an alternative to absolute

---

34 J. G. Droysen, *Outline of the Principles of History*, New York: Howard Fertig, 1967.

35 See also on this subject Hayden White's critical article '*Historik* by Johann Gustav Droysen', *History and Theory*, 19/1, 1980, 76–7.

objectivism, whether in Ranke's realist version or Buckle's determinist one.

Droysen did completely accept the conception of progress
common to all historians of this generation. However, in a
similar spirit to Acton, the liberal Catholic, he always sought
the imprint of human will, believing that this played a decisive
part in the structuring of historical time. For him, each man
was a social subject, constructing around him a set of values,
in which could be detected, among other things, the aspiration to liberty that was the principal stimulant of progress. The
deceptive alternative between materialism and idealism should
be rejected: 'Historical things have their truth in the moral
forces, as natural things have theirs in the natural "laws",
mechanical, physical, chemical, etc.'[36] Communities such as
family, society, people and state were bearers of specific sets of
norms and played an important part in the formation of the
inter-human fabric; and it was necessary therefore to have
recourse to a specific methodology, distinct from that of the
hard sciences, in order to understand the logic and scope of
their choices in any given phase. Ranke's profound erudition
and the enthusiasm of Buckle were both indispensable to
producing historical knowledge, but it was important not to
rest on the 'scientific' laurels that these brought. On the
contrary, professional tools of a new type had to be forged. The
historical hermeneutics practised on documents should integrate a conceptual apparatus different from that of the natural
sciences, without, for all that, drifting into speculative
metaphysics.

According to Droysen, 'The science of history is the result
of empirical perception, experience and investigation.'[37]
These are based on identification with human experience and
personal comprehension, which form a whole. The process of

---

36   Droysen, *Outline of the Principles of History* (15), 16.
37   Ibid., (8), 12.

understanding is both synthetic and analytic, inductive and deductive. This does not mean that everything that happened in the past has equal value in the eyes of the historian, whose job it is to arbitrate and emphasize the simple acts from which history emerges (*wie aus Geschäften Geschichte wird*).[38] And Droysen adds that, if political acts are decisive and form the core of history, research should not dwell solely on these acts: the moral expressions, intellectual actions and social situations that make up civilization are also a source for the historian.

Buckle's attempt to make history a science actually proved dangerous, and risked compromising the discipline. Exhaustive knowledge of human actions was an illusion, and if the past continues to pervade our existence and our actions, by definition it no longer exists, and its totality will always escape us. In a theoretical development exceptional for his time, drawing on Kant and especially on Hegel, Droysen asked his colleagues, 'Has the "guild of historians" actually not yet made the observation that objective facts are a different thing from the manner in which we know them?'[39]

The historian must be aware of both his capacities and his limitations. Contrary to what Buckle and the positivists thought, history was a domain where the quest is not for laws but only for a meaning. The prudent historian should constantly bear in mind this essential point:

We have already remarked that if there is to be a science of History, this must have its own method of discovery and relate to its own department of knowledge . . . Fortunately there are between heaven and earth things related as irrationally to

---

38   Ibid. (45), 72.

39   Ibid., 70. See also Thomas Burger, 'Droysen's Defense of Historiography: A Note', *Theory and History*, 16/2, 1977, 168–73. On the presence of Hegel in Droysen's approach, see M. J. Maclean, 'Johann Gustav Droysen and the Development of Historical Hermeneutics', *History and Theory*, 21/3, 1982, 347–65.

deduction as to induction . . . things which demand not to be 'developed' or 'explained' but understood.[40]

Droysen suggests a basic separation between the 'mind sciences' (*Geisteswissenschaften*, or, as we would now say, 'social sciences') and the 'natural sciences' (*Naturwissenschaften*).[41] Whereas the researcher in natural science seeks to explain (*erklären*) physical, chemical or biological phenomena, the mission of the researcher in social sciences is to understand (*verstehen*) human phenomena.

Wilhelm Dilthey, in broad terms a disciple of Droysen and subsequently acclaimed as one of the most important philosophers of history, took over from his teacher the distinction between 'explanation' and 'understanding', on which he built a systemic hermeneutics with wide ramifications. He had already supported Droysen in rejecting Buckle's theory of science, and in a brief but important article on the British historian's book, published in 1862, he complemented Droysen by formulating a position that aimed to preserve empiricism while rejecting the objectivism that he saw as characteristic of the history writing of his time.[42]

The methodological difference between 'understanding' and 'explaining' was increasingly recognized in many fields. German historians, philosophers and sociologists would in future brandish this habitual distinction in order to crown their analyses with the aura of a true science. From Max Weber to Hans-Georg Gadamer, the human and social sciences would be recognized as independent disciplines, certainly different from the exact sciences, but likewise called to join these under the prestigious

---

40   Droysen, *Outline*, 76.

41   The German term *Wissenschaft* is somewhat broader and more flexible than the word 'science' in other languages.

42   Wilhelm Dilthey, 'History and Science: On H. T. Buckle's History of Civilization in England', in *Hermeneutics and the Study of History*, Princeton: Princeton University Press, 1996, 261–70.

label of 'science' that united all academic researchers: physicists, chemists, historians and sociologists formed an imposing scholarly bloc.

To sum up, Buckle can be credited with an intellectual honesty that was wanting in a majority of his colleagues. He had well understood what a science was, and set out to make history scientific, naively but with success. One question remains without a fully satisfactory response. Why was it precisely in the nineteenth century, at a time when historical narration was far closer to literature than it is today, that historians made such an effort to be defined as scientists? It is clearly impossible to identity a single explanatory factor; as always in history, any phenomenon has a multitude of causes. We have to accustom ourselves to the fact that, even in the best of cases, only some of these will be revealed.

Marc Bloch, the Last Great Positivist?

From Johann Gustav Droysen's *Historik* to Marc Bloch's *The Historian's Craft* written in 1943, a number of historians sought to debate the problematic of historical writing, but the results were rather scarce and mediocre. Only scholars of the past who were also brilliant philosophers (R. G. Collingwood or Benedetto Croce, for example), left works that are still readable today. The *Introduction to the Study of History* by Charles-Victor Langlois and Charles Seignobos, published in 1898, was in some respects an exception;[43] like Droysen's book, this was also based on a series of lectures designed for history students. The authors, both 'craftsmen' par excellence, with high academic qualifications, made a plea for the 'scientific method in history'. They knew Droysen's book, which had been translated into French, and

---

43   Charles-Victor Langlois and Charles Seignobos, *Introduction to the Study of History* [1898], CreateSpace, 2009.

judged it 'heavy, pedantic, and confused beyond all imagination',[44] even contributing to stifling in the cradle any potential interest for it in France. They did not appreciate at all the idealist hermeneutics of the German historian, sometimes excessively abstract, even if (ironically) they reached conclusions that were close to Droysen's though expressed carelessly and in a totally different terminology.

Langlois and Seignobos also maintained at the start of their book that the method of historical science had to be radically different from that of the sciences based on direct observation. The fact that history investigated specific situations made it hard to define as a science, since science always deals in abstract fashion with generalizations, and with the fixed and permanent relations that these contain. History could not proceed in this way, as it was a science of a different kind, dealing with realities that were constantly changing, and for that reason it had to content itself with description rather than the search for exhaustive formulas.

The book is full of hypotheses of all kinds, and contains unresolved contradictions. According to the two authors, for example, history is a science when it bases itself faithfully on archives. The collection of sources is the laboratory of the researcher into the past, and the cosmos from which his undertaking is launched. However, alongside peremptory assertions of this kind, we find in the book serious positions that few historians would dare formulate explicitly even today: 'History is only the utilization of documents. But it is a matter of chance whether documents are preserved or lost. Hence the predominant part played by chance in the formation of history.'[45]

It is not said, after such an assertion, how history can still be defined as a science; and the authors, like many other historians, appear unaware of the problem. Yet they have no hesitation in maintaining with much aplomb,

---

44   Ibid., 6.
45   Ibid., 316.

The historical sciences have now reached a stage in their evolution at which the main lines have been traced, the great discoveries made, and nothing remains but a more precise treatment of details. We feel instinctively that any further advance must be by dint of investigations of such extent, and analyses of such depth, as none but specialists are capable of.[46]

This prostration before sources as all-powerful divinities of historical writing led Langlois and Seignobos to be seen as 'positivists', a term that had now lost its early lustre. Thus the founders of *Annales* and their heirs looked back suspiciously at these predecessors, whom they saw as conservative historians, always ferreting in political archives in quest of truth. However, if we closely consider the state of mind of the majority of historians, French or otherwise, until the late 1970s, we can note that the profession's epistemological approach had not evolved much since Langlois and Seignobos: sources were still taken as proof, and they alone guided historical reconstruction. The issues of *Annales* in the 1930s and 1940s, apart from a mere few remarks, contain no basic debate on historical writing and its perspectives. The editors and contributors to the journal were certainly not worshippers of theory: philosophy of history was repugnant to them and they preferred empirical work, the historian's true kingdom. That is why *The Historian's Craft*, which Marc Bloch wrote under the German Occupation, only a short while before being shot, can be viewed as an exceptional manifesto of the *Annales* school.

In discussing this book I feel the need to recall a personal memory; when I read it for the first time, my command of French was still rudimentary. I read it therefore in English, in its initial and still incomplete version, and only later, in the 1980s, did I come to know the important additions that had been made to it. In my mind, Bloch embodies an epigram of Nietzsche's:

---

46   Ibid., 77.

'The fine historian must have the power of coining the known into a thing never heard before and proclaiming the universal so simply and profoundly that the simple is lost in the profound, and the profound in the simple.'[47] Bloch's writing struck me as a model of clarity to be imitated, strong both in his diagnosis and in his presentation of the proper technique for historical writing. *The Historian's Craft* figures as the last great example of the sophisticated positivism that dominated historical reconstruction for more than a century: the resonance of the work was felt for some three decades after it was written, and left unfinished by the death of its author.

There is every reason to think that Marc Bloch would have been exasperated to read these last lines. He saw himself, in fact, as a definitely anti-positivist researcher, radically rejecting simplistic empiricism and the conception that sees the historian as explorer of the past after the model of a traveller setting out to discover exotic lands. And yet, if we rigorously follow his argument in favour of history as 'a science in movement', 'a science in its infancy' or 'a science of men in time', we have to conclude that he remained a tireless defender of the idea that with the progress of this 'young science' it would be possible to arrive at the objective truth of past worlds. According to Bloch, if for many years history rather resembled literature, it was now on the royal road to becoming a science, despite being, as Fustel de Coulanges had put it, 'the most difficult of sciences'.[48]

But what kind of science was it? Just like Droysen, Bloch appeared to reject the positivist tradition that Buckle and Taine had sought to translate into historical language, and that claimed to exhibit constant laws in the human sciences. According to him, this theoretical process had an echo in the sociological tradition, but there was no place for it in an approach to history

---

47   Friedrich Nietzsche, 'Second Untimely Meditation: On the Use and Abuse of History for Life' (trans. Adrian Collins), at wikisource.org.

48   Quoted in Bloch, *The Historian's Craft*, 13–14.

that was conscious of itself and its limitations. Yet to abandon science and see history only as an aesthetic work would be profoundly unsatisfactory.

What we find here is the effect of the 'science syndrome' already present with Droysen and almost all other historians: history for them was, in the last analysis, a science of a different kind, one based on a professional approach to the materials that it dealt with, and on a critical reading of documents and evidence as the basis for constructing a historical narrative. Marc Bloch presents to his readers a series of brilliant formulas, along with subtle warnings that sharpen the understanding of techniques of historical narration. Historians must start by having full awareness of the direction in which they wish to advance, and the problematic they seek to decipher. They are supposed to be attentive to the dialectical connection between past and present, and also to the fact that historical research, far from being autarchic, has constantly to be supplied with data and evaluations from other domains. The abundance of advice that this book contains is certainly manna for the novice historian, and over the years I have regularly recommended students to read it.

However, Bloch was no more inclined than his predecessors to be satisfied with a view of history reduced to a critical and systematic elaboration of debris collected in the past, from which possible accounts of the world of yesterday might be composed. He was resolved to see history as an authentic science, with a Cartesian logic and solid causal explanations. One novelty introduced by Bloch lies in his comparison of history with the major new turning point in physics. This comparison is a central pillar of his assumptions, and those of historians who came after him, which is why it seems necessary to me to quote it in full, all the more so as I have long held to it myself:

The kinetic theory of gases, Einstein's mechanics, and the quantum theory have profoundly altered that concept of science which, only yesterday, was unanimously accepted.

They have not weakened it; they have only made it more flexible. For certainty, they have often substituted the infinitely probable; for the strictly measurable, the notion of the eternal relativity of measurement . . . Hence, we are much better prepared to admit that a scholarly discipline may pretend to the dignity of a science without insisting upon Euclidian demonstrations or immutable laws of repetition. We find it easier to regard certainty and universality as questions of degree. We no longer feel obliged to impose upon every subject of knowledge a uniform intellectual pattern, borrowed from natural science.[49]

According to Bloch, therefore, the questioning of positivist certainties in certain domains of the natural sciences makes the science of history in a certain sense their younger sibling, with a fine future ahead. Yet the comparison between quantum theory and the new history with its potential for advance leaves itself open to objection and critique. In reality, the share of uncertainty in certain fields of exploration of nature does not imply the disappearance of laws in most other domains, nor of the experimental capacity to discover new ones. The fact that Copernicus's heliocentric system supplanted Aristotle's geocentric one does not mean that there is a relationship of the same type between Einstein's theory of relativity and the laws of Newton. It is true that the view of time as a solid and immobile entity has been challenged, but Einstein did not displace Newtonian physics, rather he reduced its validity and proposed a law that applies to speeds close to that of light.

Can the different interpretations of the French Revolution, between a conservative historian such as Hippolyte Taine and a radical historian such as Albert Mathiez, whose writings Marc Bloch was very familiar with (or between Albert Soboul and François Furet, whom Bloch could not have known), be explained

---

49   Ibid., 17.

by a revision in the paradigms of the historian's craft in the light of accumulated knowledge? In 1939, on the eve of the deadly maelstrom that the world would collapse into, two major works on the medieval era were published: the first part of Marc Bloch's *Feudal Society*, and *Land and Lordship* by the Austrian historian Otto Brunner, who the same year successfully applied for membership of the Nazi Party.[50] The distance between the historical approaches represented by these two works, and the conclusions drawn about the period in question, are in no way comparable with a theoretical controversy in physics. Moreover, the fact of being based on the same documentary sources does not prevent historians from reaching different and even opposing conclusions.

Bloch knew very well that it is impossible to authenticate a result of historical argument by way of experiment, given the singular character of the interaction of human phenomena. As we have seen, it is not in our power to permanently observe the consequences of social processes, and to rectify or amend our assessments in this light. Historians never operate in a laboratory, and do not view the past from a contemporary observatory; accordingly, their analyses of cause and effect will never be identical, or even similar, to those of the sciences of nature and life. Yet for all that, historians have clearly not ceased proposing possible causal relations in order to understand history; otherwise their work would have no sense. However, they have no means of certifying the scientific validity of the explanations they offer; all their analyses pertain to the domain of logical hypothesis – and logic is not always best distributed among historians.

The discovery of the theory of relativity does not prevent our ability to construct and fly a plane on the basis of a mechanics based on the laws of Newtonian physics. Marc

---

50   Otto Brunner, *Land and Lordship: Structure of Governance in Medieval Austria*, Philadelphia: University of Philadelphia Press, 1992. The book's original title in 1939 after the Auschluss was *Land und Herrschaft: Grundfragen der territorialen Verfassungsgeschichte Südostdeutschlands im mittelalter.*

Bloch, however, certainly never imagined that an aeroplane could be built using the relative 'scientificity' of previous historians, or even that of his most intelligent contemporaries. He also knew in all probability the decisive difference between the scientific work of a physicist who happens to be a liberal in politics, and the 'scientific' research of a liberal historian; between a conservative and nationalist chemist and a historian of the same stripe: there is no such thing as a liberal physics, any more than a conservative chemistry. Historiography, on the other hand, can indeed be liberal or conservative. What is most surprising, however, in *The Historian's Craft*, is the author's total lack of interest in the political character of sources and their connection with social class, or in the growing instrumentalization of historical work.

In the previous chapter I criticized the historians of mentalities of the third *Annales* generation for focusing on the culture of 'common people' without taking into account that these have always been silent in history, and that everything we know of them comes 'from above'. The starting point of this blindness is already to be seen in the writings of Bloch, who demonstrated a great critical sense apropos the subjective character of testimonies, suspecting their invented or romanticized dimension, but did not hesitate at the same time to maintain, 'We shall never penetrate the mentality of the men of eleventh-century Europe, for example, as we can that of the contemporaries of Pascal or Voltaire; since we have from them neither private letters nor confessions.'[51]

We know, however, that the overwhelming majority of contemporaries of Pascal or Voltaire wrote neither letters nor confessions, for the good reasons that they could neither read nor write. We may even assume that the mental distance between the two philosophers and the mass of peasants of their time was

---

51   Marc Bloch, *Apologie pour l'histoire*, Paris: Armand Colin, 1997, 74. [This passage does not appear in the English edition of *The Historian's Craft*. – Tr.]

in certain respects greater than the mental and intellectual gap between the two of them and Bloch himself. There is also every reason to think that during the First World War the young historian Marc Bloch saw at close quarters soldiers writing letters to their families. This would be one of the rare moments in history when 'common people' had not only learned to write but also wrote about themselves, on account of their enforced distance from home. The moment would soon disappear with the invention of the telephone and other more recent means of communication, whose traces disappear immediately after use. We have, therefore, to recognize that the great mass of the human population did not leave behind them any written traces, and very few traces at all.[52]

As a social historian, Bloch clearly knew that testimonies of the past and their transmission are the product of apparatus and institutions designed for the strata of high society, and not for village communities, artisan guilds, or the modern working-class world. The founder of *Annales*, who sought to look at the world 'below', had constantly to depend on concepts and images coming from the world 'above'; he had, therefore, to explore and use accounts of data, inventories and institutional evidence to elaborate a view of mass behaviours. However, Bloch did not attempt a systematic deciphering of the political and class language that all these sources express. A critical dimension of this kind does not figure in the reflections of this historian, who until his tragic end saw the Third Republic as the pure expression of the nation's general interest; and from this point of view, his work is an aspect of a certain republican consensus that stood above class.

At the end of his book, Bloch lambasts those who expect the historian to be a judge. Just like Ranke 120 years earlier, he

---

52   We can assume that the intelligence services today record millions of phone conversations, but it is likely that they select for preservation only a few of these, and that what interests them will not necessarily interest the future historian.

maintains that the 'science' of history aspires to neutrality in terms of values, with the exception of the initial motivation that inspires it: to be of service to human society, always trying to develop intelligence and knowledge. Every effort of scientific research is thus ultimately based on a moral foundation. Bloch saw in science, by the rationalism and critical spirit inherent to its system, a concentrate of historical progress.

One question remains, to which I have so far hesitated to give a definitive answer: why should we reject the current use of the term 'science', to which Bloch and his colleagues were so stubbornly attached? We always need names to refer to phenomena, but these also answer to the names of wider families. Cats and dogs are different species, but both belong to the category of mammals. Should the same logic not lead us to divide the 'family of sciences' into such secondary concepts as 'natural sciences' and 'social sciences'? In other words, if dogs only bark and cats only meow, does this mean they are not both animals? And likewise, in the case that concerns us here, are we not just dealing with different 'sciences'? Marc Bloch, like many historians, sociologists and economists before him, liked to think so. All of these sincerely believed that their discipline was a science in the course of development, with the sole objective of being of service to humanity. The moral progress of human society necessarily stimulated study not only of the world external to it, but also of its own components and internal wellsprings.

The exact sciences and the life sciences appeared and developed in parallel with humanity's taking possession of nature, and with the objective of aiding this project. Understanding and explanation of the external world did not proceed from a disinterested study or from simple curiosity, even if the latter always played an indispensable role. It was the modern state that was its principal driving force. In fact, the rivalry between neighbouring political entities, and the need to respond to the fundamental needs of production and competition on the capitalist market, led it to take responsibility for and include in its institutions the organizing and perfecting of the hard sciences. Did the 'human and social sciences' grow up and prosper in the same context and for the same reasons, in other words the desire to strengthen the state's domination? The answer would probably be positive, and yet the question that then arises is, domination over what?

The 'Scientific' Imaginary and the Invention of Peoples

We can well doubt whether the bodies of researchers into humanity and society were at any time scientific; but we should be aware, all the same, that the state needed certain basic knowledge in order to function and ensure the modern organization of society. Contrary to what Marc Bloch and his forerunners believed, however, a specialization is not yet a science, even if it is based on a growing knowledge and develops specific methods of work. In almost all professional, artistic, and even literary fields there is a specialization, but in the majority of cases this has never claimed to be a science. We have specialist tailors, specialist architects, ultra-competent computer hackers – in other words individuals who have built up systematic knowledge but still do not claim to be scientists.

To develop elementary education, however, without which the industrial economy and the developed division of labour could not have existed, the modern state needed schools and, at a later stage, compulsory education for all. The pedagogic system needed teachers, and trainers of teachers. Educational establishments grew ever more complex, leading to the growth of universities that were gradually transformed from institutions reserved for ecclesiastical elites into centres dedicated to government elites. For many years, these were frequented only by the sons of the upper socioeconomic strata; the children of the rising bourgeoisie would now be more educated.

Whereas the teaching in premodern universities was basically law, medicine and theology, philosophy being a branch of the latter, the new human 'sciences' or 'humanities' saw the addition of philology, history, geography, archaeology and literature. In due course these were joined by their younger sisters, still more heavily decked out in 'scientific' terminology, with the names economics, sociology, political science, psychology, anthropology and so on. Of course, not all these subjects were required for basic education, and they were not taught in the context of the general instruction of the masses. Pupils learned to read and write, and acquired a basic familiarity with scientific subjects: mathematics first of all, followed by physics, chemistry and other natural sciences. At the same time, they studied four salient areas of the 'humanities' or 'human sciences': language, literature, history and geography. In all modern states, these formed an organic part of the formation of culture, consciousness and collective identity for all students. From now on, alongside a national language and a unifying literary and cultural imaginary, students would also possess a common collective past and a distinct national territory.

It was quite logical that the pedagogical culture that was being formed did not aim to teach the rudiments of law, economics or philosophy to the new heirs, who by this time came from every stratum of society. Although school played a major part in the formation of citizens, it did not need to inculcate in the mass of students a conception of fundamental rights or a basic knowledge of the law. Similarly deemed superfluous was the teaching of economics, which would have endowed students with a critical perspective on the nature of their expenditure and needs, and perhaps made them aware of their social situation. While philosophy had the mission, at least in principle, of teaching *how* to think, history consisted above all in teaching students *what* to think – a key distinction that contributed more than a little, in primary and secondary schools the world over, to history being taught as a compulsory subject, whereas its younger philosophical sister only enjoyed in the best of cases the status of an optional one, at the end of secondary education.

The key question for understanding the discipline of history and its position, both in academic institutions and in the cartography of general culture, is, 'What is thought in history?' A quotation from Michel de Certeau offers a good point of entry: 'Each "discipline" maintains its ambivalence of being at once the law of a group and the law of a field of scientific research. The institution does more than give a doctrine a social position. It makes it possible and surreptitiously determines it.'[53]

The institutional position of the modern historian has been largely conditioned by the fact that he figures among the visible midwives of the nation. Professional historians have sought to reconstruct the past, distant or near, in the shadow of a political identity in the course of construction. For more than a hundred years – broadly in the period from 1825 to 1950 – many accredited scholars wrote essays whose conceptual apparatus inspired the national romance. Almost all throbbed with a patriotic ardour that fuelled their aspiration to create and cherish their own nation-state.[54]

For example, if the unification of Germany was finally achieved by the Prussian monarchy, rather than by a democratic popular force, growing strata of intellectuals, and hundreds of new students in particular, had already become German thanks to their eminent history professors. And if Joseph de Maistre had seen the executioner as the pillar of traditional monarchy, to which Ernest Gellner would more recently add that in the modern state this function had been honourably transferred to the professor, there is every reason to believe that, in the growing community of teachers, historians had pride of place. Along with

---

53   Michel de Certeau, *The Writing of History*, New York: Columbia University Press, 1992, 61.

54   See on this subject the excellent article by Daniel Woolf, 'Of Nations, Nationalism, and National Identity: Reflections on the Historiographical Organization of the Past', in Q. E. Wang and F. L. Fillafer (eds), *The Many Faces of Clio: Cross-cultural Approaches to Historiography. Essays in Honour of Georg G. Iggers*, New York: Berghahn, 2007, 71–103.

their philologist and geographer colleagues in the establishments of higher education, historians contributed to the construction of national identity and attachment to the fatherland, instructing new state officials, judges, journalists and publicists on this path, and preparing the hearts of military volunteers and the thousands of conscripts of compulsory national service, itself now under expansion.

In a stimulating article on the new professional historians and their relation to the nation, Thomas N. Baker defined them as 'post-Enlightenment thinkers'.[55] Whereas Voltaire and Gibbon had no hesitation in exhibiting, in the events of the past, an endless chain of human stupidities caused by religious belief, ignorance and a general lack of culture, the 'popular' past was now idealized and glorified by the men of 'science'. And if the majority of Enlightenment thinkers had evoked the unity of the human race, nineteenth-century figures, building on the original considerations of Johann Gottfried von Herder, began to emphasize ever more the 'ethnic' specificity of different human groups. The foundations of the new national particularism that appeared in the course of the modernization process were referred back to a distant ancient time.

In 2002, the year that Baker's article appeared, the American medieval historian Patrick Geary published his pioneering book *The Myth of Nations*,[56] in which he demonstrated the construction process of a fictional ethnicity in nineteenth-century historiography. According to Geary, such ethnic groups as 'Celtic', 'Gothic', 'Gaelic', 'Lombard', 'Teuton' and so on, far from lying at the ancient origin of national creation, should rather be perceived as distinctive imaginary identities, resulting directly from the ideological production of modern historians. Early

---

55   Thomas N. Baker, 'National History in the Age of Michelet, Macaulay, and Bancroft', in L. Kramer and S. Maza (eds), *The Blackwell Companion to Western Historial Thought*, Malden, MA: Blackwell Publishers, 2002, 186–89.

56   Patrick Geary, *The Myth of Nations: The Medieval Origins of Europe*, Princeton: Princeton University Press, 2002.

Europe experienced waves of migration, a dizzying mixture of various tribes with a multiplicity of dialects and customs, but there were no identifiable 'ethnic' divisions of either peoples or nations. These were invented, as the work of an exuberant and very 'scientific' imagination, by modern engineers, specialists in the past, who claimed a right of priority for their new homelands.

At the same time, historians focusing on 'ancient' and imaginary national roots displayed scant respect for or interest in concrete and living local traditions when these went against the construction of the national metanarrative, which had to be one-dimensional. They deliberately expunged various 'savage' cultures, regional or provincial, to give pre-eminence as far as possible to the hegemonic superculture; likewise, dialects had to disappear in the face of the official language issuing from the central state.

In 1819 the *Monumenta Germaniae Historica* was founded in Prussia, an impressive collection of sources and documents that gathered every piece of knowledge about the past of all 'Germans' from the fall of the Roman Empire. The first volume in this collection, which is still continued today, was published in 1826. This 'scientific' initiative was very soon emulated in every European state.[57] The work bears the Latin epigraph *Sanctus amor patriae dat animum*, or, in free translation, 'Sacred love of the homeland gives courage'. The primary object of the enterprise was in fact to explore the primitive sources of the eternal German nation.

In 1840, a year before being chosen as official court historian of the kingdom of Prussia, Ranke had published the five volumes of his *German History in the Age of the Reformation*, followed immediately by his *Nine Books of Prussian History*.[58] In these

---

57 In 1833, François Guizot launched the Collection des documents inédits sur l'histoire de France, and in 1860 the Rolls Series began to appear in England.

58 Leopold von Ranke, *Deutsche Geschichte im Zeitalter der Reformation*, Berlin, 1840–1847; *Neun Bücher preussischer Geschichte*, Berlin, 1847–1848. At around the

two wide-ranging series, soon imitated by other historians, Ranke depicted the course of Germany's religious and national formation from the time of Martin Luther, comparing the Protestant revolt against the papacy to the rising of the German tribes against the Roman Empire. Ranke indeed wrote more than this: other historical works on the papacy, on England, on France, even on world history, but his political writings on the kingdom of Prussia were the pinnacle of his historiographical work.

After resigning in 1849 from his mandate to the Frankfurt Parliament, Droysen embarked on his first historical and patriotic work: *The Duchies of Schleswig-Holstein and the Kingdom of Denmark from the Year 1800*, which enjoyed a tremendous success.[59] Despite his specialization as a historian of Hellenism, and his many publications in this field, the popularity of Droysen's anti-Danish essay spurred him to write an enormous new work, in fourteen volumes, titled *History of Prussian Politics*.[60] A brilliant researcher, Droysen saw Prussia as the political power (a modern Macedonia) that had unified the Germans (the modern Hellenes), and sought accordingly to magnify the past of the Prussian kingdom. From now on, and in a different direction from that taken by Ranke, this past became far less religious and increasingly political and secular. The publication of the first volumes led to Droysen being invited to take up a professorship at the University of Berlin, where he began to teach alongside his older colleague.

In 1875, chancellor Otto von Bismarck appointed Heinrich von Sybel, Ranke's closest disciple, as head of the Prussian royal

---

same time, George Gottfried Gervinus published *Geschichte der deutschen Dichtung* (1835–42). This work, a history of poetry, made a more decisive contribution to German national consciousness than did Ranke's later works.

    59   Johann Gustav Droysen, *Die Herzogthümer Schleswig-Holstein und das Königreich Dänemark seit dem Jahre 1800*, Hamburg, 1850.

    60   Johann Gustav Droysen, *Geschichte der preussischen Politik*, Leipzig, 1855–1856.

archives. The eminent historian thus gained access to official documents that no researcher before him had been able to consult. A former liberal, and the author of a patriotic essay (*The German Nation and the Empire*),[61] he now embarked enthusiastically on the writing of a seven-volume work on *The Foundation of the German Empire by Wilhelm I*,[62] a further hymn to the national unifying power of the Prussian kingdom, which had accomplished its modernization and whose historical destiny it was to build a great and powerful nation state.

At the risk of repeating myself, I must emphasize that the history of 'Germany' was not the original field of specialization of these three leading historians. In each case, their publications included many works on the history of other past kingdoms, as well as on contemporary European states. However, if the echo of current politics is always heard in any work devoted to the distant past, each of these felt the need to emerge from his 'professional' field of study and directly make his contribution to the establishment of German unity that was so greatly desired. This is why their works stimulated history textbooks, dozens of more popular writings and thousands of newspaper articles, which formed the ideological cauldron for the construction of the Second Empire.

Heinrich von Treitschke, on the other hand, was a 'pure' historian. His own multi-volume work on *German History in the Nineteenth Century*, which began to appear in 1879, met with great success and won him admirers among teachers, journalists, politicians and government officials.[63] Treitschke was at the same time an active Reichstag deputy, and a talented essayist

---

61   Heinrich von Sybel, *Die deutsche Nation und das Kaiserreich: Eine historisch-politische Abhandlung*, Düsseldorf, 1862.

62   Heinrich von Sybel, *Die Begründung des deutschen Reiches durch Wilhelm I*, Munich, 1889–94.

63   Heinrich von Treitschke, *Deutsche Geschichte im neunzehnten Jahrhundert*, Leipzig, 1879–94; *Treitschke's History of Germany in the Nineteenth Century*, London: McBride, 1915–19, available at archive.org.

who wrote several historico-political articles. The 'direct descendants of the Teutons' found in this historian a highly gifted storyteller, who explained, with complete 'scientific' certainty, that Germany was the most sublime of nations, and that its particular long history could serve as a moral and political model to other nations. Treitschke's striking narration was interrupted by his death, but the scent of Germany's triumph in the war of 1870 against France rises from every line of his writing.

The 'Myth-story' of National Territories

The military confrontation of 1870 between the kingdom of Prussia and the French Empire remains an important event for the understanding of modern historiography. It was also a golden opportunity for subsequent historians of the conflict who were not particularly conservative to publicly express their national pride, and reveal at the same time the share of emotion and sentimentality that deeply pervades those of their works with a more 'universal' character. The annexation of Alsace-Lorraine to the newly established German Empire had the effect of unanimously and selflessly mobilizing, in defence of their homeland's 'ancient' soil, the leading historians of both nations.

Institutional German intellectuals viewed Alsace and part of France's Moselle department as an integral part of Germany, on account of their populations speaking a German dialect. Their French counterparts, in chorus, saw things in a diametrically opposite sense. This was in a way a dress rehearsal for what would be the future positions of their spiritual heirs, on both sides, in the First World War (and perhaps even of most intellectuals in all the twentieth century's territorial conflicts). On the German side, historians stressed a national argument based on historical rights: the cities of Metz and Verdun had been annexed by the French monarchy in 1543, Alsace in 1639 and Strasbourg in 1683, yet despite this the great majority of their inhabitants were still marked by a local culture closer to their neighbouring communities to the east than to those to their west.

It is hardly surprising, then, that Treitschke should have immediately seized the flag and published his stirring essay *What Do We Demand from France?* even before hostilities ended.[64] July 1870 saw the start of a public epistolatory exchange between David Friedrich Strauss and Ernest Renan, both authors of standard works on the life of Jesus that had brought them worldwide acclaim. According to Strauss, a moderate and cautious scholar, France had violated the peace, and had consequently to pay the price in territorial terms; he went on to maintain, as an eminent historian, that the former line of separation was not a natural frontier between distinct cultural and linguistic communities, hence the obligation to redefine it. Renan rejected from the start national demands based on ethno-culturalism, upholding the more moral, and more modern, political principle of the self-determination of the inhabitants.[65]

In August of the same year, Theodor Mommsen, also a prestigious historian and a specialist in Roman history, as well as a consistent liberal, wrote three open letters that were published initially in Italy.[66] He called on his Italian readers to support Prussia's territorial demand, and expressed the point of view that too many German-speaking people lived in regions dominated by foreign powers (the Austrian and Russian empires, Switzerland), although the new Germany, out of moderation and maturity, did not demand their annexation. As far as Alsace-Lorraine was concerned, however, the war had created a particular situation that fully justified territorial annexation and the rectification of an injustice. Modern history taught that it was proper for the framework of political sovereignty to correspond

---

64   Heinrich von Treitschke, *Was fordern wir von Frankreich?*, Berlin: G. Reimer, 1870.
65   This exchange is reprinted in L. Rétat (ed.), *Renan: Histoire et parole*, Paris: Robert Laffont, 1984, 639–55.
66   Teodoro Mommsen, *Agli italiani*, Florence: Tabilimento Civelli, 1870.

with culture and language. We should remember that Mommsen felt repugnance for Treitschke's ethnocentric and anti-Semitic nationalism, and that in all his historical work on the Roman Republic and Empire he supported open and inclusive collective identities. Though pragmatically supporting Bismarck (the modern 'Caesar'), he dreamed of a great Germany, republican and unified, based on the rights of man and the citizen. Yet despite all this, egoistic national primacy proved decisive even for the sole historian ever to receive a Nobel prize. For Mommsen, too, when the guns roared the soil of the homeland became sacred, and it remained so even after they fell silent.

On the French side, the first to react to Mommsen's essay was the historian Auguste Geffroy, professor at the École normale supérieure,[67] soon joined by his colleague Fustel de Coulanges. Both of these opposed the German historian, whom they admired, with patriotic themes based, as we saw with Renan, not on history and culture but precisely on politics: the future and identity of the inhabitants of the occupied regions should be decided by their own free choice. French historians – who in the past had shown little sign of enthusiasm for democracy, prefer- ring rather to express ethnocentric and nationalist conceptions – suddenly maintained, spurred by national and territorial inter- est, convictions of republican patriotism that were far more democratic: Alsatians and Lorrainers were French, because they wanted to be part of the French nation. It was not the long course of history that should provide the criterion for membership of a nation, but solely the right to self-determination of the popula- tion. Fustel de Coulanges hastened to formulate this principle, addressing himself directly and publicly to Mommsen:

You, monsieur, are an eminent historian. But, when we speak of the present, we should not fix our eyes too much on history.

---

67   Auguste Geffroy, 'Manifeste prussien de M. Th. Mommsen à l'Italie', *Revue des deux mondes*, November 1870, 122–37.

Race is a matter of history and the past. Language is again history, the residue and sign of a distant past. What are current and living are desires, ideas, affections. History perhaps tells you that Alsace is a German land; but the present proves to you that it is French. It would be childish to maintain that it has to return to Germany because it was part of Germany a few centuries ago.[68]

It is true that Germany did not offer its new inhabitants of 1870 a referendum; democracy was not among the new empire's founding principles. And yet, contrary to the violent accusations made against him, it would be hard to tax Mommsen with racism: he sought to base his conception of the fatherland on culture, language and history. To complete and balance the picture, we should remember that after the (re)conquest of Alsace and Lorraine, at the end of the First World War, French historians also did not ask their government to organize a referendum, and accepted the French annexation of these territories as a matter of course. The victors generally do not bother too much with 'irrelevant' details when it is a question of the sacred territory of the fatherland, and French historians are no exception. We may also note that they were later on among the last intellectuals to support the right of self-determination for the insurgent populations of the colonies.

The confrontation between Treitschke, Strauss and Mommsen on the one hand, and Renan, Geffroy and Fustel de Coulanges on the other, is a perfect illustration of the ways in which nationalism was present in late nineteenth-century historical discourse, even if scholarly and 'scientific' rhetoric has sometimes made it difficult for later historians, nationalist themselves, to distinguish its foundations. Besides, not all texts focus explicitly on the

---

68   Fustel de Coulanges, 'L'Alsace est-elle allemande ou française: réponse à M. Mommsen', *Revue des deux mondes*, October 1870, available at bmlisieux.com. Despite this declaration, Fustel de Coulanges insisted in his subsequent writings that France owed very little to the Germanic legacy with which it seemed to be pervaded.

subject of the nation, and we should emphasize that readers were offered a wide spectrum of different types of nationalism: from pseudo-tribal ethnicism to democratic republicanism. From this point on, at all events, nationalism became completely hegemonic in the main currents of professional history writing. The war of 1870 decisively nationalized accounts of the past, and displayed still more clearly the mechanisms of its production. The imperialist race, in the late nineteenth and early twentieth centuries, completed the process and conferred on historical writing the forms that would be dominant for the next fifty years. Droysen, Sybel and Treitschke had prepared the ground to make national identity more visible, by cultivating an imaginary and homogeneous collective past, while excellent French historians did the same in a different language.

From Augustin Thierry via Jules Michelet and Fustel de Coulanges through to Ernest Lavisse and a bevy of less eminent historians, the long trajectory of the past acquired a stronger French stamp in the course of the nineteenth century. The Romantic Thierry, if his scholarship was probably inferior to that of Ranke, was far more aware than his Prussian colleague of the objectives of the new professional historian. He openly proclaimed the double motivation that underpinned his writings: science and patriotism were welded together in the reconstruction of the past, and formed the very essence of historical narration. In 1820, when still beginning his work, he had already detected the secret of political modernity: 'In difficult circumstances, a nation is always led to cast its eyes back.'[69] That is why the world needed historians of a new type, able to create national narratives, for example in researching the Celtic roots of the French ethnic community. Thierry did not stint himself on the study of 'ancient' France, undertaking research on the Germanic conquests that remained incomplete. His less gifted brother,

---

69   Augustin Thierry, 'Lettres sur l'histoire de France' [1820], in Marcel Gauchet (ed.), *Philosophie des sciences historiques*, Paris: Seuil, 2002, 69.

Amédée Thierry, went on to publish three volumes of a *History of the Gauls* that remained a standard work until the mid-twentieth century.[70]

Jules Michelet, a historian omnipresent in nineteenth-century France, referred rather less to race, but was no less nationalist and Romantic than the Thierry brothers in his quest for the 'long continuity' of sentiments of his chosen group. He also set out at an early age to fashion French identity, which he always saw as particular and incomparable with other collective identities. From his *Summary of the History of France until the Revolution*, published in 1833, to his monumental multi-volume *History of France* (1833–1844); from his booklet *The People* (1846) to his *History of the French Revolution* (1847–1853), Michelet constantly shaped and sculpted, with rare talent, the forms of the great nation – from its emergence in the time of the Celts, via the Carolingian age and Joan of Arc, to end with the great popular Revolution in the late eighteenth century. He spent a great deal of energy establishing the required homogeneity in space and time, and succeeded better than any other essayist, so much so that his construction has scarcely been 'demolished' in subsequent years. With only a little exaggeration, we could say that in late nineteenth-century France, the national consciousness would have been very different without its most talented 'bard'.

Michelet's romantic love of the 'national soul' is expressed in the words of thrilling emotion he pronounced at the end of his life, in his final preface to the *History of France*:

I ask for nothing. What would I ask of you, dear France, whom I have lived my life with and leave with such great regret? I have spent forty years with you (ten centuries) in such community. We have been together in so many passionate,

---

70   Amédée Thierry, *Histoire des Gaulois depuis les temps les plus reculés* (3 vols.), Paris: Sautelet, 1828–45. The 'syndrome' of Gauls vis-à-vis Franks had already surfaced somewhat earlier. See, for example, Abbé Sieyès, *What Is the Third Estate?*, in *Political Writings*, Hackett: 2003, 99.

noble, austere hours . . . I worked for you, I went, came, sought, wrote. Each day I gave all of myself, perhaps even more.[71]

The nation was a person, a body, and the romance with it was not only strong, painful and sweet; it also lasted a long time. Michelet's work devoted to the 'French people' covers a plethora of pages, similarly in this respect to the writings of Droysen, Sybel and Treitschke, written in more or less the same years. Like them, Michelet set out to encompass the total history of all the 'French', and in an almost identical historiographical procedure, he sought to study its organic unity, at the cost of leaving in shadow the cleavages of class and the different cultures of irredentist provinces, the better to reach the national totality.

The great pedagogue Ernest Lavisse took up where Michelet left off, systematically organizing the popularization of the same patriotic stories and devoting still more volumes to immortalizing the nation and the *patrie*.[72] With Lavisse, a professor at the Sorbonne, director of the École normale supérieure and adviser to the Ministry of Education, the teaching of France's national history entered a new stage of development in the means of ideological production, progressing from small-scale manufacture to large-scale industry. Abridged editions of his books were sold by the million, for the millions of students educated by these accounts who would go off to fight the former students of Sybel and Treitschke, or more precisely their students' students, in the First World War.

---

71   Jules Michelet, 'Préface de *L'histoire de France*' [1869], in *Philosophie des sciences historiques*, 358.

72   Twenty-seven volumes in total. Lavisse clearly stated his objective as follows: 'The teaching of history has the duty of making the *patrie* loved and understood . . . Our ancestors are our own past selves, our descendants are our future selves.' Ernest Lavisse, *Histoire de France: De la Gaule à nos jours* [1940], Paris: Armand Colin, 2013, ix. It is worth a mention that Lavisse studied in Germany, and that his first five books, before he became France's 'national schoolteacher', all deal with German history.

This short extract from Lavisse's textbook, published and distributed in 1912, gives a glimpse of the type of patriotic-historical education dispensed on the eve of the catastrophe:

War is not probable but it is possible. This is why France must remain armed and ever ready to defend itself . . . By defending France, we defend the land where we were born, the finest and most generous land in the world . . . France is the most just, the most free, the most humane of countries.[73]

Many of his readers were already infused with the spirit of the 'petit Lavisse' of 1884 when they went off singing to the new colonies that would make France a great empire despite the amputation of Alsace-Lorraine.

The description of the Gordian knot between the nation and the 'science' of history would not be complete if we failed to mention, albeit briefly, the English-speaking world. It is certainly hard to find a British or American equivalent of the German and French historians. However, Thomas Macaulay's *History of England*, written between 1849 and 1859, and George Bancroft's *United States of America*, published between 1834 and 1878, mark the beginning of promising national narratives, which, by their length and their obsession in relating their respective national sagas, readily stand comparison with their German and French counterparts.[74]

Macaulay was a prolific 'Whig' historian. After service in the colonial administration in India, he was for a time minister of war. In his view, the world had always been divided between civilized and barbarian nations; and naturally England was

---

73   Quoted by Pierre Nora, 'Ernest Lavisse: Son role dans la formation du sentiment national', *Revue historique*, 228/1, 1962, 104.

74   Thomas Macaulay, *The History of England from the Accession of James the Second* (6 vols.), London, 1849–59; George Bancroft, *United States of America, from the Discovery of the American Continent* (8 vols.), Boston, 1834–78. Bancroft, like Lavisse, studied at German universities before becoming a historian.

situated at the summit of the pyramid of civilization, which conferred on it a natural right to govern the backward peoples. He was equally persuaded that Hinduism and Islam were retrograde religions that would disappear in the face of the rising power of Western Christianity. In Macaulay's book, the British appear not so much as 'descendants of a pure race' (like the imaginary Germans of Prussian historiography) as 'empire builders' by vocation.[75]

Bancroft also served in government (he was secretary of state for the Navy), but he set out to demonstrate, in a luminous style, that the United States was the most patriotic and democratic nation ever (neither the fate of the Indians under US colonization and territorial construction, nor the African slave trade, are mentioned in his account).

These messages would soon be extended and amplified by other historians over the next hundred years. The project managers of the metanarrative, in the English-speaking world, were no less enthusiastic than their colleagues on the European continent, even if the invention of a long historical time proved problematic for the Americans.[76]

Just as theology could at no point in its hegemony dispense with reference to God, so the history of modern times had to replace this with 'science' in order to ensure its existence as a discipline. There was in fact no other choice after the breakthrough of scepticism and the secular spirit in the Age of Enlightenment. Science took the place of faith in many fields of knowledge, and appeared to everyone as the ultimate recourse after the death of God. The vocation of victorious natural science was to master the physical

---

75   See Catherine Hall, 'Macaulay's Nation', *Victorian Studies*, 51/3, 2009, 505–52.

76   See on this subject the chapter 'History Makes a Nation' in J. Appleby, L. Hunt and M. Jacob, *Telling the Truth about History*, New York: Norton, 1994, 91–225. However, my lack of familiarity with national historiographies outside the European prevents me from discussing this.

world, and the mission of the human sciences was a double one, perhaps after the image of all national politics in the era of democracy: first of all, to work for an organized and regular balance of forces between social classes, and second, to guarantee humanity a reassuring and promising future (after the painful loss of Paradise). This latter function also obliged the human sciences to revisit the origins of humanity in order to explain the present situation.

Almost all the humanities, in the university context, decked themselves with the title of 'science', but where history was concerned this conferred a very particular aspect and status, by the increased certainty given to the facts selected, or to those of which some trace subsisted, and these in return became so many weighty proofs of the truth of narratives devoted to the past.

The modern state that began to provide a pedagogic context for the various sciences had very clear reasons for granting certain privileges to the discipline of history. As we have seen, history was spurred to diffuse its discoveries and points of view at all levels of official education, not just in the university. The state also showed understanding for attempts at writing a universal or comparative history, and accordingly granted researchers a growing margin of autonomy. In exchange, it explicitly required from those historians that they placed at the centre of their intellectual activity the celebration of the collective past, still being formed under the aegis of the nation-state. The strength, status and development of the historical discipline in the academy would depend, if not exclusively then at least in large part, on this decisive ideological contribution.

The teaching of a specific ego-history was a characteristic aspect of each unifying national culture. Historians were not aware that they were less the result of their 'national' past than its actual creators, via their literary and mythological imagination. In their expert hands, multiple and plural identities were endowed with a single essence and combined into a single central narrative. Nomadic tribes were transformed into peoples and national religious communities. The chosen words of scholars living under the protection of monarch or church were interpreted as so many expressions of a sublime patriotic consciousness. Wars between kings and feudal potentates were depicted as confrontations between peoples. The language used by the administrative elites of the cities, the centres of power, was perceived as the national language. The 'truth' was clearly hard to demonstrate in these totalizing narratives, hence in particular their length and the insistence on presenting them as the results of science. On the other hand, it was not easy to refute or contradict such a profusion of works, and there were very few candidates with the desire, or in a position, to do so.[77] This is what made for the strength of these narratives, justifying their description as modern mythologies.

Contrary to what Friedrich Nietzsche believed, the professional historians of the nineteenth century and the first half of the twentieth were not myth-breakers; in fact, they created a 'mythistory' par excellence. This clearly does not negate the fact that many of their number were excellent specialists, rigorous researchers, and in the last analysis quite convincing writers. Their persuasive force, apart from literary quality, was fuelled by their own convictions, the creators of 'hot' myths being, in general, the first worshippers of these.

As distinct from premodern myths, national mythologies did not directly serve to support the power of a despotic sovereign, whether metaphysical or terrestrial. Neither were they literary works designed, as in the past, to maintain the aura of ruling elites. Their main function, beside the proclaimed desire to sincerely explain past events, was to create a new collective identity in the era of rising democracy. This must also be placed in a context in which the sovereign was more dependent on the

---

77   I suspect, for example, without being able to prove this, that one of the reasons for the relative neglect of Tocqueville in the second half of the nineteenth century, apart from his unusual liberalism, was the fact that he was seen by republicans as an insufficiently national historian.

masses once these recognized themselves in their nation-state. As we saw above, it is generally impossible, with rare exceptions, to create a stable and permanent body of citizens devoted to the state and respectful of its laws without a common language and, no less important, without a unifying imaginary past (perhaps also without a war . . .).

Finally, apart from 'erudition', there is a significant difference between ancient myths and the national narratives of the past: the former did not reject other myths, accepting for better or worse an ideological coexistence with all the rest. National historical narratives, however, have generally challenged or even squarely denied the myths of neighbouring peoples and nations. They have proclaimed themselves permanent possessors of a sole authentic truth, which explains among other things the stubbornness of their inventors in defining them as science.

N.B.

When I began this book I omitted to point out that, in my University of Tel Aviv (and the same holds for other Israeli universities) there is no department of history. In Israel, in fact, there have always been three completely distinct departments: general history, the history of the people of Israel, and the history of the Middle East. No similar 'scientific' division is found anywhere else in the Western world. It is, however, an important foundation for the anchoring of the country's historical consciousness and particular destiny, and for the sense of ownership of the country imparted to all those across the world who were born of a Jewish mother or converted to Judaism according to the rules of rabbinical orthodoxy.

I was not initially aware of the convenience of this arrangement, not only for the direct producers of a national consciousness of the past, in other words those historians who deal with the history of the Jews, Zionism and Israel, but also for the rest of us, teachers and researchers in the department of 'general history'. Like my other 'scientific' colleagues in this department, I appreciated my independence from the conceptual apparatus of the nation with its heavily mobilizing vocation. We were thus able to gather in our research spaces and continue to occupy ourselves with our sensitive subjects in all 'objectivity'.

When I decided, after a great deal of hesitation, to undertake a critical study of Zionist historiography, I did not imagine how vehement would be the negative reactions that this aroused. Some of my colleagues, specialists like me in 'general history', had written on Jewish and Israeli history before I did, without provoking the least discontent. They had not been accused of invading a field of research that did not pertain to their own competence. The explanation is that they had piously borrowed the habitual concepts and schemas of their national historians, whereas I had introduced myself, without authorization, into the territory where the Jewish past is elaborated, and proceeded to a critical assessment and systematic deconstruction of its fundamental categories.

A number of Israeli archaeologists, for example, had already challenged the account of the exodus from Egypt. It was only from my own work, however, that I discovered how, contrary to the historical myth in which I had grown up, and which is engraved in the declaration of independence of the state of Israel, the Judaeans were neither exiled by the Romans nor torn from the land that they cultivated. What, then, had become of them? And how did believers in the Jewish faith appear in such large numbers around the Mediterranean littoral in the first century BCE, and still more so a century later? I was amazed to discover that no academic work had been published on the 'act of exile', on the imaginary abandonment of the land of Judaea/Palestine, or again on the massive conversions to Judaism,[78] even though

---

78   With the exception of the important work by Abraham Polak, founder of the department of Middle East history at the University of Tel Aviv: *Khazarie: Histoire d'un royaume juif en Europe* (in Hebrew), Tel Aviv: Bialik, 1951. This book has been expunged from the national memory and been completely forgotten.

in university genetics departments the hunt for a 'Jewish DNA'
has been pursued with all 'scientific' zeal.

As Ernest Renan already said, the building of a nation does
not just need remembrance, it also needs forgetting. Yet he did
not envisage that the share of forgetting can sometimes be greater
than that of remembrance.

CHAPTER 4

Retreating from National Time

My young son asks me: Must I learn history?
What is the use, I feel like saying. Learn to stick
Your head in the earth, and maybe you'll survive.
Yes, I tell him . . . learn your History!
                    Bertolt Brecht, 'My Young Son Asks Me', 1940

'Tell me, Daddy. What is the use of history?' Thus, a few years ago,
a young lad in whom I had a very special interest questioned his
historian father . . . the problem which it poses, with the embar-
rassing forthrightness of that implacable age, is no less than that of
the legitimacy of history.
                    Marc Bloch, *The Historian's Craft*, 1943

Ever since I began to confront the modes of presence of nationalism in historical time, in the steps of Benedict Anderson, Ernest
Gellner and Eric Hobsbawm, historiography and the way its
knowledge was distributed struck me as a far more capricious
domain than I could previously have imagined. Max Planck
wrote, 'A new scientific truth does not triumph by convincing its
opponents and making them see the light, but rather because its
opponents eventually die, and a new generation grows up that is

familiar with it',[1] and I understood that this somewhat excessive assertion is in all likelihood still more applicable to new historiographical paradigms and the controversies to which these give rise.

I continued to teach as if nothing had changed, but I was constantly beset by doubts and hesitations. The weight of arbitrary and ideological words was an increasing burden. For a while, I escaped from routine professional phraseology and occupied myself with moving images, writing a book on the relationship between cinema and history. I believed for a while, in the wake of my friends Marc Ferro and Robert Rosenstone, that the cinema narratives consumed on a mass scale would help me better perceive both the relationship between visual representation and words, and the influence of historical films on the consciousness that populations formed of the past throughout the twentieth century.[2] I understood later that the conceptual torments I had personally experienced were part of a wider semantic and theoretical change that had occurred over three decades in wide sectors and also affected the mass media. The two world wars were a lasting shock to human civilization. If the First World War exacerbated national crystallization in Europe, the Second World War accentuated this phenomenon, even while contributing to the expression of a certain weariness with nationalism. Although the Cold War continued to blow the patriotic embers for a while, the decolonization that took place in the same period, and more particularly the successive defeats of the metropolitan powers in Algeria and Vietnam, were a blow to the pride of the dominant national collectives, as well as to the narratives on which these had been constructed.

---

1   Max Planck, *Scientific Autobiography and Other Papers*, New York: Philosophical Library, 1968, 33–4.

2   My 'visual turn' was spurred by two collections of articles, Marc Ferro, *Cinema and History*, Detroit: Wayne State University Press, 1988; and Robert A. Rosenstone, *Visions of the Past: The Challenge of Film to Our Idea of History*, Cambridge, MA: Harvard University Press, 1995.

In Europe from the 1820s to the late 1930s, national historiography perfectly accomplished its mission. By creating various 'historical pasts', it enabled each individual French, Italian, German and English person to know with certainty that the ancestors of their ancestors had always been French, German, Italian and English, and that their own nation-state was indeed the supreme and definitive culmination of these 'ancient' identities. True, there is no nation whose construction is finally achieved: human recalcitrance works against any total and definitive engineering. Since the second half of the twentieth century, however, the demand that professional historians should pursue the great mythological undertaking has rather weakened. The effort to construct national time with the aid of a grand narrative has slackened, and demolishing winds have arisen and begun to blow in the corridors of the discipline.

The *Annales* group's retreat from political history in the 1930s was perhaps the first indication of this reduced tension. The turn away from politics also corresponded to an unconscious retreat from the national, though this did not mean that the founders of *Annales* were not still in thrall to the paradigm of a long patriotic time. Marc Bloch, for example, could still write on the eve of the Second World War that 'so far as France and Germany were concerned this [national] consciousness was already highly developed about the year 1100'.[3] After the war, the majority of historians in Western Europe preferred to ignore or circumvent this tricky subject, rather than tackling it head-on. For the same reason, they also turned away from traditional textbooks, which

---

3   Marc Bloch, *Feudal Society*, London: Routledge, 2014, 468. Lucien Febvre was a bit more far-sighted in this respect; see, for example, his article 'La nationalité et la langue en France au XVIIIe siècle' [1926], in *Combats pour l'histoire*, Paris: Armand Colin, 1992, 182–200. Braudel, despite having notably contributed to reducing the hegemony of ego-national history in his work on the Mediterranean, resuscitated nostalgia for this in his ultimate book: Fernand Braudel, *The Identity of France* (3 vols.), New York: HarperCollins, 1990–92. See also the pertinent comments of Marcel Detienne on this work in *Comment être autochtone: Du pur Athénien au Français raciné*, Paris: Seuil, 2003, 138–49.

would still serve for many years as the foundation for the formation of consciousness of the national past in schools and colleges.

In parallel with the consolidation of the welfare state, social
and economic historiography became hegemonic in university
history departments, in both Europe and America. This focused
on pre-national spaces of production and trade; on the peasantry
in seigneurial society; on urbanization, industrialization, and
sometimes the formation of social classes along with the conflicts
this generated. It began to understand, at this stage, that the
'objectivist' historical writing inherited from the nineteenth
century no longer offered a very credible model of pure scientific
thought. And yet, in order to justify its 'scientific' label, and in
competition with the prestige capital accumulated in sociology,
anthropology and economics departments, a far from negligible
fringe of historians, particularly in France and the United States,
turned towards quantitative history. In the second chapter of this
book, I showed how, in the 1950s and 1960s, writers for *Annales*
were gripped by a fever for diagrams, statistics, demographic data
and so on, with the aim of continuing to hold the envied 'scientific' label.

It is striking to note that, in the same years, there was not one
leading historian who cast a critical regard, theoretical or empirical, on the way in which modern history dealt with the formation of peoples and nations. In fact, a significant section of social
historiographies, Marxist included, were still marked with the
seal of the dominant national ideology. In representations of the
past, working classes were very distinct national entities, but
their specificities still appeared far more as occupational and
socioeconomic, rather than cultural and linguistic.[4]

When, with cultural globalization, new theses on the origins
of nationalism and the nation-state began to appear in the early

4   From the late nineteenth century, the socialist workers' movements in
Europe, despite directly expressing tensions between classes, were at the same time
cultural frameworks of integration in the process of nation formation.

1980s, these were formulated not by historians (with the exception of Eric Hobsbawm) but by sociologists, political scientists and even anthropologists. Historians were quite simply incapable of looking from outside at the pedagogical missions that their national profession served, and that had conferred on them an eminent status for so many years.[5]

Another shift slowly began in the early 1970s within the discipline of history itself, its main symptom being the questioning of certainties about its scientific character. From this time on, a majority of historians, including the desperate upholders of objectivism and realism, hesitated to define their profession as a science. In the late 1970s and the decade that followed, with the rising influence of cultural historiography, then its explosion into a thousand fragments of apolitical folklore and ahistorical remembrance, positivism came under attack from a new group of historians, and especially from academics in the departments of philosophy, language and literature, originally known as 'post-structuralist', then 'postmodernist'. For the most part, those who took an active part in this 'linguistic turn' found themselves accused of having never been true historians.

The retreat of national commitment and the process of decolonization are not sufficient to explain the shifts in the historical discipline, or those in the human and social sciences in general; there were clearly many other causes. I shall just introduce some of these, briefly and cautiously, in the guise of hypotheses. I already mentioned, in the second chapter of this book, the shift that took place in the world of production over the last quarter of the twentieth century, towards work on symbols and signs, the

---

5   Critical essays on the mythology of national history only began to appear in France in the early 1990s, and even so very slowly, from the margins rather than the centres of historiographical production. See S. Citron, *Le mythe national: L'histoire de France en question*, Paris: L'Atelier, 1991; A.-M. Thiesse, *La création des identités nationales*, Paris: Seuil, 1999; F. Reynaert, *Nos ancêtres les Gaulois et autres fadaises*, Paris: Fayard, 2010; J.-P. Demoule, *On a retrouvé l'histoire de France: Comment l'archéologie raconte notre passé*, Paris: Laffont, 2012.

new imbrication of the verbal and the visual in many channels of communication, and the accelerated revolutionizing of knowledge. All this helped to generate an awareness of the anachronistic and depreciated use of a certain vocabulary in the human 'sciences'. The relationship between the status of words and that of 'things', between signifier and signified, in the world of computerized production contributed to strengthening the doubts that weighed on the pseudo-scientific terms used for the reconstruction of 'things' in works of social research, particularly in the grand narratives about the past.

Changes under way in the world of production also led to the structure of social classes being challenged, a structure that was constituted at the same time as the formation of nations. The industrial working class experienced the beginnings of decline in the 1970s, as a result of automation and the transfer of sectors of industrial production outside the Western space. The rising influence of social history, in the wake of the Second World War, had been fuelled in part by the strengthening of the organized working class and the historical perspectives that then accompanied this phenomenon. The hope of seeing the consumer society evolve slowly or radically towards greater equality was a strong stimulus to the political imaginary, and underpinned for a time theories of historical progress born in the nineteenth century. The regression of the working class in the West, and the fall of Communist regimes transformed into capitalist societies, not only contributed to destroying the socialist vision (whether Communist or social-democratic), but also challenged one of the main metanarratives of critical social history, that deriving from Marxism. The loss of a promising future also had the effect of shaking certainties about the past.

Changes in gender relations, particularly in the universities, though initially still hesitant, began to influence the general culture and the 'masculine' status of language. Until the late 1970s, in fact, representations of the past were insensitive to the place of women in history, and to the subaltern status conceded them in the semantic structures of historical writing. The profusion of social history, Marxist and otherwise, was an integral part of a linguistic galaxy dominated by men, who knew themselves to be producers and writers of 'what really happened' – for men but not for women! Now, the new gender problematic drew in an increasing number of scholars in various fields, especially women but also men. In this way the discipline of history also experienced the vibrations of this conceptual earthquake, and became aware of the sexist subjectivity that had always characterized the narration of historical 'truth'.

Moreover, the relative decline of nationalism opened the way to a revaluing of cultural pluralism, which by the same token generated a positive view of multicultural historiography. Any trace of particularism that had not been flattened by the steamroller of national culture enjoyed a new springtime and attracted dedicated historians. Young historians immersed themselves in accounts of traditions that had remained marginal, yet whose shadows had persisted, to draw from them models that fuelled an identity politics of a new kind. 'Classic' historians had the sensation that writing about the past was shattering into a thousand pieces, losing any guiding thread, and falling into decline.

Before going into detail on these questions that generated fractures and doubts, I propose to examine the extent to which all this was a novelty, and where precisely its originality lay. With this objective, I shall go back in time to indicate earlier critiques of the supposed objectivity and realism of traditional historical narration. The history of doubt also has its importance, and could well aid us in deciphering contemporary characteristics.

From Nietzsche the Wicked to the Art of Croce

The cultural field in which national scientific historiography was born also saw its first bitter critique. This came, however, not from historians but from philosophers, more precisely from an atypical philosopher who has not ceased to trouble Western culture since his death. Friedrich Nietzsche can in fact be seen as the first critic of historiographical positivism, of a 'science of time'. True, his critique was typically incoherent, disordered and full of contradictions. His positions have invited changing and contrary interpretations – a fate that he shares with almost all major philosophers. However, his views unquestionably deserve mention.[6] Already in an early text 'On the Use and Abuse of History for Life', published in 1874 amid the triumphal march of national historiography, he launched a cry of alarm against the feverish excess of historical studies in German culture. It was true that consciousness and memory of the past differentiated man from the rest of the living world, but they also risked stifling him, oppressing his imagination and his creative faculties. Nietzsche clearly does not deny the necessity of historical awareness. But this should be content with an instrumental approach. In other words, how much historical awareness is useful to us, and what quantity of knowledge need we acquire in order not to sink into bestial amnesia?

Nietzsche deems ridiculous the historical discipline's claim to utter scientific truth. He compares it to 'medieval' theology, which, by the fear it inspired, sought to convince believers of the existence of a single truth. In pedagogic history what interested Nietzsche was not so much truth as such; he does not explicitly reject monumental history, in other words, the 'mythistory' that glorifies great men and exceptional events. Yet he very rapidly

---

6   Aside from Nietzsche, I shall not discuss other subsequent thinkers who, without being historians, published far-reaching criticism of historical writing. Some of the best known are Raymond Aron, *Introduction to the Philosophy of History: An Essay on the Limits of Historical Objectivity* [1938], Boston: Beacon Press, 1961; William H. Dray, *Laws and Explanations in History*, Oxford: Oxford University Press, 1957; Arthur C. Danto, *Analytical Philosophy of History*, Cambridge: Cambridge University Press, 1965; L. O. Mink, *Mind, History and Dialectic: The Philosophy of R. G. Collingwood*, Bloomington: Indiana University Press, 1969; Michel de Certeau, *The Writing of History*, New York: Columbia University Press, 1992; Paul Ricoeur, *Time and Narrative* (3 vols.), Chicago: Chicago University Press, 1990 and following.

reaches the conclusion that there are at least as many truths as there are historians.

In the same year of 1874, in parallel with this initial critique of positivism, Nietzsche had no hesitation in attacking head-on the Hegelian philosophy of history that, according to him, was the inspiration of German historians. This determinist philosophy, which saw the culmination of the dialectical process precisely in Hegel's own time in Berlin and sanctified the omnipotence of history, 'practically turns every moment into a sheer gaping at success, into an idolatry of the actual'.[7]

The bitter tone in which Nietzsche attacked historians in the mid-1870s is very likely explained by the criticisms these had levelled at *The Birth of Tragedy*, deemed insufficiently professional, and he also targets the dispassionate and pseudo-scientific aridity of their writings. Above all, however, he expresses disgust at their obsequious submission to the Prussian state. Their political future, according to him, was in line with their very German taste for proofs, along with their self-assured notion of a necessary historical process, whether Hegelian or positivist: 'But the man who has once learnt to crook the knee and bow the head before the "power of history", nods "yes" at last, like a Chinese doll, to every power, whether it be a government or a public opinion or a numerical majority; and his limbs move correctly as the "power" pulls the string.'[8]

Nietzsche was himself of Prussian birth and the son of a pastor, like a good number of the historians he despised, but unlike them he did not replace theology with politicized national history; he decided to leave Germany for Basle, and even renounced Prussian citizenship. His critical gaze on history and historians was closely linked to his situation as an a-national and even anti-national thinker. He detested German nationalism,

---

7   Friedrich Nietzsche, 'On the Use and Abuse of History for Life', at wikisource.org (trans. Adrian Collins).
8   Ibid.

which he included in his general disgust for mediocrity, stupidity, crowds, politics, and above all hypocrisy. He saw German bourgeois provincialism as a source of abominations, similar to the consolatory ideologies that, in a conformist symbiosis, had been substituted for belief in God. In *Beyond Good and Evil*, published in 1886, he wrote,

> If a people suffers, *wants* to suffer from national nervous fever and political ambition, it must be expected that various clouds and disturbances will pass across its spirit, little attacks of acquired stupidity, in short. With today's Germans, for example, it is now the anti-French stupidity, now the anti-Jewish, now the anti-Polish, now the Christian-Romantic, now the Wagnerian, now the Teutonic, now the Prussian (just think of those pitiful historians, those Sybels and Treitschkes with their heavily bandaged heads), and whatever else they are called, these little becloudings of the German spirit and conscience.[9]

The same essay makes clear the source of Nietzsche's critical stance towards historians. Where these, with their major responsibility for the construction of the nation, had always believed in their imagination and remained totally captive to the product of their historiographical work, Nietzsche showed himself more lucid and free from illusions. A hundred years before any significant abandonment of old-established notions about peoples and nationalism, he maintained unambiguously, 'What we in Europe today call a "nation" and what is actually more of a *res facta* [man-made] than *nata* [born] (sometimes even easily confounded with a *res ficta et picta*) [something invented and painted] is certainly something evolving, young, easily displaced.'[10]

---

9   Friedrich Nietzsche, *Beyond Good and Evil: Prelude to a Philosophy of the Future*, Oxford: Oxford University Press, 2008, 141; original italics.
10   Ibid., 142.

In these striking intuitions, Nietzsche revealed what he considered conventional lies, deeply implanted in the historiographical discourse of his day. At the same time, it is evident that his marked aversion to the use of force in German politics prevented him from really grasping the weight and vigour of the historians' edifying mythologies, in other words their pedagogical role in favour of muscular egoism, collective rallying, territorial conquest and imperial power. The philosopher who showed so much interest in ancient myths did not perceive that the national ideologies that were rampant around him and swamped non-political universalism were in fact mythologies of a new kind. These escaped him on account of the scientific nimbus with which they surrounded themselves – synonymous for Nietzsche with such hypocrisy that they did not even merit being criticized or heeded. Their claim to objectivity only reinforced the contempt he felt towards them, and prevented him from detecting the power of triumphant conviction that their factitious realism precisely bore.

For this restless rebel thinker there could be no reality other than from a relative viewpoint, and the fact that historians did not understand that only attested to the pitiful character of their profession:

> *Facta!* Yes, *facta ficta!* – The historian need not concern himself with events which have actually happened, but only those which are supposed to have happened; for none but the latter have produced an effect . . . All historians record things which have never existed, except in imagination.[11]

To imagine that the historical past could be understood objectively by way of such a metaphorical and unscientific chain of words betokened a ridiculous pretension. According to Nietzsche,

---

11 Friedrich Nietzsche, *The Dawn of Day*, CreateSpace 2013, 80. Nietzsche also expresses contempt for Ranke: 'one Leopold Ranke, this born classical *advocatus* of every *causa fortior*, this most prudent of all prudent "realists" ' (*On the Genealogy of Morality*, Oxford: Oxford University Press, 2008, 'Third Essay', para 19, 103).

historical truths were in the last analysis no more than illusions, whose fictional character had been forgotten or always ignored.

All this does not mean that Nietzsche was an ahistorical thinker. As a rigorous philologist he certainly attacked the dominant historiography, but not history as such. He constantly reflected on the past and interpreted it, starting from the principle that without an understanding of the past, understanding of the present is impossible, as likewise the slightest idea about the future. He emphasized that any philosophy worthy of its name had to be always well anchored in its time, and understood that his own philosophy would be judged by the same standard.

Nietzsche expressed his admiration for the apolitical cultural historiography of Jacob Burckhardt, his colleague and friend at the University of Basle, but what is most surprising is his good opinion of Hippolyte Taine, the representative par excellence of historiographical determinism. The fact that Taine was French excused all his positivist faults, and Nietzsche, who even kept up a brief correspondence with Taine, did not hesitate to describe him as 'the first living historian',[12] though that did not prevent him from also proclaiming that even he was too contaminated by the sirens of German philosophy.

Nietzsche was perhaps the first insurgent against history's claim to assert itself as a science, but he was certainly not the last. In 1893, still during Nietzsche's lifetime, Benedetto Croce published a famous lecture entitled 'History Brought under the General Concept of Art',[13] an impressive work for a young dilettante. Croce was not a professional philosopher and even lacked

---

12   Nietzsche, *Beyond Good and Evil*, aphorism 254, 142. See also Thomas H. Brobjer, 'Nietzsche's View of the Value of Historical Studies and Methods', *Journal of the History of Ideas*, 65/1, 2004, 301–32; also by this author, 'The Late Nietzsche's Fundamental Critique of Historical Scholarship', in M. Dries (ed.), *Nietzsche on Time and History*, Berlin: Walter de Gruyter, 2008, 51–60.

13   Benedetto Croce, *La Storia ridotta sotto il concetto generale dell'arte*, Naples: F. Giannini, 1893. An English translation is accessible at academia.edu.

a university degree. He never obtained academic employment as a historian. He was fortunate to receive a generous legacy that enabled him throughout his life to write and produce in complete independence of institutions.

Croce's exceptional analytic talent and his great clarity of expression were evident from his earliest writings on history. The question that he sought to answer was apparently very simple: is history a science or an art? Droysen's famous *Historik*, along with the stubborn insistence on the part of German historians to see their work as a particular science, was the driving motor of his reflection. Croce refused to embark in their wake, and rejected the traditional division between natural and human sciences. He was clearly not fully aware of the political-ideological role that the widespread use of the term 'science' played, but he categorically opposed the confusion between different domains with the shared aim of understanding and deciphering the world in which we live.

For Croce, as opposed to the champions of positivism, not every knowledge that aims to formulate a truth of some kind is a science. Science is an investigation that deals with generality, and with this objective it creates conceptual mechanisms that seek to clarify the relationship between parts and integrate them into a whole. History was not a science and would never be one, since, as Schopenhauer had explained, science always deals with typical objects, whereas history is interested in human details and concrete facts. Where science is based on logical abstractions, history sticks to concrete representations. Science subjects the particular to the general, something that history refrains from doing. That is why science enables laws to be brought to light and formulated, whereas in history any attempt of this kind is doomed to failure from the start.[14]

This in no way means that history is superfluous or must be considered minor in relation to science. But to properly understand its nature and functions, it has to be situated in a different

---

14   Ibid., 10–13.

field of mental and intellectual creation; in other words, it must be integrated in its true family, that of art. To best grasp the classification proposed by Croce, therefore, let us start by examining the definition that he gives.

For the young Croce, art is not the creation of the beautiful. Beauty is fugitive and thus hard to define. Art is neither a pleasure nor the representation of a sensitivity or of the good, and no more is it the expression of an ideal. The beauty of a landscape can be admired without its being a work of art, and clearly a pleasure is not defined as an art. In the last analysis, art must be perceived as a certain human representation of a reality, but not a scientific one. This representation does not question the reality but describes it and seeks to give it expression. 'Whenever the particular is subsumed under the general, the result is science; whenever the particular is represented as such, it is art'.[15]

It would thus be wrong to say that history was a 'science of development', as it is actually a representation of development, of human activity inscribed in time. All art is definitively a kind of intuitive representation of a reality. From this starting point, the question arises whether everything pertains to art. According to Croce, this depends on the content, and only a content that arouses human interest falls within art. If an aesthetic work includes irritating elements it will not be seen as art, whatever its formal qualities. In this respect, history is indeed a category of art, dealing with what actually interests us. However, as distinct from other arts, history expresses not what could have happened but only what we think did happen; in other words, the real and not the imaginary.

---

15   Ibid., 15. One of the reasons why Croce does not classify history as literature is, he says, the existence of a history that transcribes the past by figurative and plastic means. The cinema was not yet born when Croce wrote this first lecture. But if we consider the place held by cinema and television in the formation and distribution of historical narratives, and consequently in the shaping of the consciousness of the majority of human beings in the twentieth century, there can be no doubt that Croce was correct in his preference to speak of history as art rather than literature.

History is a precise creation, founded on investigation, the collection of data, critique and interpretation. These preliminaries of the historian's work, however, do not yet amount to an artistic realization. The writing of history becomes an art only when the phase of research is completed and the historian structures a narrative. The historian's ideal, only rarely achieved, consists in creating an exhaustive account. Every historian knows that this is impossible, but the ideal is needed to guide their work. The fact that this narrative is a work of art that expresses a reality, and not a science that explains it, in no way detracts from its value as an important segment of human culture.

In this lecture, the strength of the young Croce lies in his refusal to follow the excessively wide and elastic definition of science given by German historians and philosophers. He succeeded, far better than these, in freeing himself from the naturalism and determinism that continued to characterize them. Yet his article suffers from an inability to clarify the concept of art in a satisfactory way. Besides, if we accept the idea that art is essentially based on the intuition of reality and not on its conceptualization, it is hard to include history in this. When, at the end of their work, historians weld into a narrative unity all the pieces they have collected, they do indeed need a good dose of intuition, but it is also true that when it comes to conceptualization they are almost always trapped by the rhetoric of the documentation on which they have drawn. Despite this, the construction of historical narrative escapes the definition of art understood as representation of a reality, rather than as seeking to analyse the real. Croce would recognize this later and seek to correct his initial point of view, while continuing to maintain that the writing of history was more akin to art than to science. His own historical work, moreover, attests to the fact that he was more of an artist than a dry historian, and it has to be recognized that his historical essays are distinguished far more by their literary qualities than by their historiographical virtues. They are also far less national and more European than are other Italian historical writings of their time.

Not long after the publication of this essay on history, Croce began a flirtation with contemporary Marxists, publishing in their journals and undertaking an assiduous reading of Marx.[16] This convergence was initially in the direction of the anti-determinism of the philosopher Antonio Labriola, rather than towards the orthodox current of Marx's heirs. In the great controversy of the late 1890s within the Marxist camp, bearing both on the political path for the workers' movement to take and on the conception of history, Croce rallied to the 'revisionists', who also included both Eduard Bernstein and Georges Sorel. The young Italian philosopher immediately joined the lively critique against the naive and pseudo-scientific determinism characteristic of socialist thought at this time.

Croce's attention was particularly drawn at this stage by Sorel's original attempt to rescue historical materialism from the hands of Engels and his epigones, drawing in his case on Vico. Croce also began an enduring correspondence with the French thinker. His many expressions of praise for Sorel include the following appreciation, which attests to their common position – a similar version of which would later be found in Max Weber:

> But Sorel now advances to precisely this conclusion, borrowing a happy phrase from his first article: that Marx's work is not intended to explain by means of law analogous to physical laws, but only to throw partial and indirect light on economic reality. The method which Marx employs in his inquiry, says Sorel, is a metaphysical instrument; he makes a metaphysics of economics . . . Marx builds an ideal construction which helps him to explain the conditions of labour in capitalist society.[17]

---

16   See his stimulating collection of articles, *Historical Materialism and the Economics of Karl Marx*, Whitefish, MT: Kessinger, 2004.

17   Ibid., 77.

Sorel's position, which sought to know historical reality not by scientific laws but by the intermediary of an 'ideal construction', agreed at this point with the anti-positivist views of the Neapolitan thinker. This 'constructivist' conception would distance both men from classical Marxism, leading Sorel towards a pragmatic position, and maturing in Croce a kind of pure idealist perspective on history. Contrary to Sorel, Croce would abandon any interest in Marx, accusing him of scientific romanticism,[18] and he came to see socialism in general as a harmful utopia. Croce's later writings on historical theories were developments of his first essay, and continued to resonate with a number of Italian scholars, as well as with the famous British historian R. G. Collingwood.

In his book *The Concept of History*, Collingwood gives a stimulating presentation of Croce's philosophy of history, recognizing its influence on his own conceptions.[19] Whether this British historian succeeded in formulating an original problematic, however, is another question. While *The Concept of History* contains a brilliant and limpid summary of various interpretations of history up to the 1930s, and develops a particularly convincing idealist separation between biological evolution and human history, in other words between nature and culture, the book's theoretical conclusion scarcely makes any new contribution.[20]

Carl Becker, or History as Societal Memory

Another anglophone writer, on the other hand, aroused general unease in the early 1930s. If Nietzsche, Croce and even Collingwood were philosophers more than historical writers,

---

18   See, for example, Benedetto Croce, *Theory and History of Historiography* [1916], London: Harrap, 1921, 267.

19   R. G. Collingwood, *The Idea of History* [1946], New York: Oxford University Press, 1994.

20   The chapter 'The Social Sciences and History' in Peter Winch's, *The Idea of a Social Science and Its Relation to Philosophy* (London: Routledge, 2007) gives an exhaustive critical summary of Collingwood's approach.

Carl L. Becker was a professional researcher, who wrote more than a dozen 'empirical' books. Coming from the ranks of the American guild of historians, he marked his difference from them in that, contrary to many of his colleagues whose exclusive concern was with their own national history, he also worked on the European past. His best-known book was *The Heavenly City of the Eighteenth-Century Philosophers* (1932), an impressive work on the European Enlightenment. Becker was a man of transatlantic culture, more at ease with Pascal and Diderot, Nietzsche and Croce, than among such positivist American historians as Albert J. Beveridge or George B. Adams.

In 1931, Becker was invited to deliver a lecture at the annual congress of the American Historical Association, of which he was that year's president. His chosen title was 'Everyman His Own Historian'. The surprise was general, and Becker's expression aroused sharp disagreement.[21] Instead of celebrating the qualities of his profession and paying homage to the discipline's scientific character, as was customary at this kind of event, this atypical scholar chose to cast doubt on the objectivity and neutrality of historians in their reconstruction of the past. Both form and substance of his speech diverged from 'proper' practice. With great simplicity, but in a language rich with images, Becker laid out his conception of historical writing, and more particularly of its limits. It is hardly likely that an accredited European historian would have presented a similar position at this time.

History, in its initial meaning, is the memory of things that have been done or said. As a consequence, every human being is their own historian, as everyone remembers things that happened to them, what they said or what was said to them. They use this memory to organize their world, and without it they would be unable to attain their objective. They cannot remember everything, which gives rise to a process of selection, particularly on

---

21   *American Historical Review*, 37, December 1931, 221–36, available at historians.org.

grounds of utility; it is needs that dictate the inscription of memory in the brain. There are certainly things that are remembered without having any immediate utility. People are infused with an accumulated general culture and a wide knowledge acquired at different moments of their education, and these form an integral part of their memory. The core of personal memory, however, remains pragmatic. Human beings, accordingly, even if guided by egoistic interest, are good historians of themselves. Carl Becker summed up the consciousness of the past in each human being in the following words: 'It is rather an imaginative creation, a personal possession which each one of us, Mr Everyman, fashions out of his individual experience, adapts to his practical or emotional needs, and adorns as well as may be to suit his aesthetic tastes.'[22]

With this declaration we find ourselves at the heart of Becker's theoretical problematic: to what degree does personal memory resemble general history? Is the latter so different from the psychological mechanisms that underpin human action? Becker's response is quite unambiguous: the discipline of history is organized and functions according to the needs of the society that its mission is to serve. Not every individual needs to remember everything in order to act; in the same way, history proceeds to a selection of things that are pertinent to it. In the modern world, this is the responsibility of the professional historian, who has replaced the tribal sorcerer, the troubadour or the priest of agricultural societies. It is the historian who preserves tradition, who expands personal experience, and who creates a continuous and collective present linked to the past. Each generation is persuaded that its narrative is richer than that of the previous generation, inasmuch as it contains more facts. Written history thus presents itself as a narrative aiming to embody the truth: 'but to suppose that the facts, once established in all their fullness, will "speak for themselves" is an illusion. It was perhaps peculiarly the illusion

---

22   Ibid., 228.

of those historians of the last century who found some special magic in the word "scientific". The scientific historian, it seems, was one who set forth the facts without injecting any extraneous meaning into them.'[23]

Becker explicitly draws on the scepticism of Nietzsche, and does not hold back from an ironic comment on Fustel de Coulanges, the 'scientific' historian who maintained that he did not recount history but let history speak through his voice (even when, for motives of a national order, he sought to show that France had no German roots). Not only do facts not speak for themselves; they do not even exist unless someone comes to assert them. Only the historian, who selects facts, gives them a meaning by integrating them into a constructed literary discourse. Facts have no form; they cannot be equated with bricks of a standard format that need only be heaped up:

> Since history is not part of the external material world, but an imaginative reconstruction of vanished events, its form and substance are inseparable: in the realm of literary discourse substance, being an idea, *is* form; and form, conveying the idea, *is* substance. It is thus not the undiscriminated fact, but the perceiving mind of the historian that speaks: the special meaning which the facts are made to convey emerges from the substance-form which the historian employs to recreate imaginatively a series of events not present to perception.[24]

All this does not, in Becker's view, invalidate the cultural need for historiography. Just as every human being needs a memory, so humanity requires a written history in order to continue to learn, but historians should show themselves more modest and effective in their works. They should understand the meaning of the functions of memory they perform, and acquit these in the most

---

23   Ibid., 232.
24   Ibid., 233–34; original italics.

useful way possible, in the interest of the public whom their mission is to serve.

Becker's historiographical relativism fitted very well into the American pragmatic tradition, which William James had laid the foundations of in the early twentieth century. The quest for truth, or more exactly for authenticity, was not rejected, as a more adequate knowledge of reality made it possible to perform more appropriate action. However, the discovery of effective truth is not made by abstract observation relayed by pure logic, but rather by way of human practice. The alliance between the consciousness that inspires and the action applied contributes to the accumulation of experience. Intelligent historians are aware that their work does not proceed from a scientific heuristic but from a functional approach, responding to the needs, tastes and objectives of the society for which they work, and to the limits of which they are subject.

Carl Becker's 1931 address was no different in spirit from his previous writings. This relativism and pragmatism were already present in his earlier essays, if less coherently, and would again be found in his many later works.[25] It is interesting to note, moreover, that Becker was not completely isolated in such theoretical views. The tendency to relativism, if circumspect, was already present among his well-known teachers, especially Frederick J. Turner and James H. Robinson. The former had particularly declared that the present, instead of being the victim of the past, should explicitly make use of it as a function of its own interest. And Robinson, for his part, recognized that history was in fact the self-awareness of humanity and that facts assume importance in this only if they contribute to resolving the enigmas of human existence.[26] In the same vein, Charles A. Beard, a celebrated

---

25   See, for example, his article of 1910, 'Detachment and the Writing of History', in P. L. Snyder (ed.), *Detachment and the Writing of History: Essays and Letters of Carl L. Becker*, Ithaca: Cornell University Press, 1958, 3–28.

26   See on this subject the interesting article by Milton M. Klein, 'Everyman, His Own Historian: Carl Becker as Historiographer', *History Teacher*, 19/1, 1985, 103–4.

colleague of Becker, hesitated for a long time between relativism and objectivism, without a definite decision.[27] It would be hard to find similar questioning and doubt about the very purposes of their profession among major German or French historians of the first half of the twentieth century. This 'balance of forces' between past and present, in historiography as in nationalism, was very specific in the United States, right from an early phase in the country's development.

In 1961, at a time when the leading *Annales* historians were unhesitatingly seeking to imitate the structuralist scientism of their anthropologist and sociologist colleagues, the British historian E. H. Carr was invited to speak at Cambridge University in the context of the Trevelyan Lectures. Carr, considered at this time a major specialist in the field of international relations, and a leading one on the history of the USSR, chose to present a synthesis of his positions on the 'science' of history. These lectures were later collected into a successful book under the title *What Is History?*[28]

Such a brilliant summary of the purposes and merits of the historical discipline had not been produced by a professional historian since Marc Bloch's *The Historian's Craft*, published just after the war. Despite a few contradictions and a lack of coherence in certain parts, we can apply to Carr himself the verdict that he delivered on Isaiah Berlin: 'Even when he talks nonsense, he earns our indulgence by talking it in an engaging and attractive way.'[29]

The status of facts, causality, objectivity and subjectivity, values, and the relationship between past and future are successively treated with clarity, but also with surprising theoretical

27   See his presidential speech at the congress of the American Historical Association, 'Written History as an Act of Faith', *American Historical Review*, 39/2, 1934, 219–31; also Jack W. Meiland, 'The Historical Relativism of Charles A. Beard', *History and Theory*, 12/4, 1973, 405–13.
28   E. H. Carr, *What Is History?*, New York: Vintage, 1967.
29   Ibid., 121.

twists. Carr's lectures stand more or less halfway between a cautious positivism and a certain relativism, with the result that at the end of the lecture it is hard to say whether Carr is a convinced realist disguised as a sceptical pragmatist, or vice versa. He takes visible pleasure in adopting an indeterminate position, leaving it to his listeners and readers to extend his logic according to their preferences and personal tastes.

The conventional approach to Carr's acrobatic presentation is to interpret him, in the wake of Marc Bloch (though Carr was probably unfamiliar with *The Historian's Craft*), as seeing history as a science, and basing himself on the same arguments as the French historian. But this is not a return to the naive beliefs of Buckle or Taine, who sought solid natural laws in history. Science had also evolved a good deal from the time of Galileo and Newton, freeing itself along the way from determinism to base itself on new principles of indeterminacy. As Carr himself emphasizes, 'Modern theories in physics, we are told, deal only with the probabilities of events taking place . . . Science now prefers to treat its pronouncements as general rules or guides, the validity of which can be tested only in specific action.'[30]

From Aristotle to Collingwood, by way of Descartes, all those who claimed that history was not a science because it dealt with particulars were mistaken. Scientists and historians worked in the same manner, and in fact both of them dealt with the particular: 'no two geological formations, no two animals of the same species, and no two atoms, are identical. Similarly, no two historical events are identical.'[31] But this prevents neither the historian nor the modern physicist from proceeding to generalizations, or from recourse to abstract terms (war, revolution and so on). Besides, in contrast to its predecessors, modern science does not advance by the discovery of new laws, but confines itself to

30   Ibid., 87.
31   Ibid., 79.

proposing hypotheses. The scientist's historian colleague proceeds in the same fashion. Neither of the two can put forward definitive predictions: 'The status of the hypotheses used by the historian in the process of his enquiry seems remarkably similar to that of the hypotheses used by the scientist.'[32]

Just like Bloch before him, Carr was deeply marked by the changes that had taken place in scientific theories in the early twentieth century, without, however, completely understanding these. He did not hesitate to declare that his own conceptions were based both on the famous essay *Science and Hypothesis* by the mathematician Henri Poincaré, one of the founders of chaos theory, and on Georges Sorel, who had proposed the idea that social research and history always depend on the isolation of parts of a totality and the construction of an independent model. According to Poincaré and Sorel, any scientific procedure remains always at the level of a partial and probable hypothesis, which sticks to temporary results and remains open to improvement.[33]

All the examples Carr adduces to present his doctrine depend on day-to-day prediction and an appeal to common sense, ignoring the fact that science is not reducible to this. The concept of 'law', for example, despite being a human invention, is not just a verbal assertion, but a hypothesis confirmed and reconfirmed by nature, even if in conditions that may be circumscribed and not absolutely universal. Human experience, which acts and creates its physical environment in nature, consolidates laws step by step as the result of predictions and tests. The historical hypothesis, on the other hand, creates nothing more than books, whether stimulating or boring. These books clearly make up an important part of culture, able to arouse intelligence and bring illumination, but this is something that good novels may also do, without being equated with science.

---

32   Ibid., 77.
33   Ibid., 73, 77.

Carr, however, constantly surprises his readers. His whole earlier analysis on the historiographical use of facts contradicts his 'scientific' conclusions. As a reflective and deliberately ironic historian, he perceives the limits of his work, and knows perfectly well that he is no longer in the century opened by Ranke, that of the domination and worship of facts. Facts do not speak for themselves, and are not like fish that can be bought on the market and made into a tasty dish:

> The facts speak only when the historian calls on them: it is he who decides to which facts to give the floor, and in what order or context . . . a fact is like a sack – it won't stand up until you've put something in it . . . The belief in a hard core of historical facts existing objectively and independently of the interpretation of the historian is a preposterous fallacy, but one which it is very hard to eradicate.[34]

The collection and arrangement of facts is a selective work, depending on the ideological preferences and agenda of the person who assembles them and places them in contexts elaborated by their imagination and according to their particular logic. But Carr is not content with this; as against the tradition from Ranke to Bloch, for whom documents are sacrosanct, he goes on to raise incisive questions as to the supposedly 'historical' nature of facts. For example, a document (an order, a regulation, a contract or treaty, an exchange of letters, a personal diary and so on) cannot tell more than its author had in their mind. The fact is not a natural given; it takes form, and already changes form, in the mind of the person manufacturing the document.

The history of classical 'Antiquity', for example, particularly excites us by the illusion that we have access to all its events. On the one hand, however, documentation on 'Antiquity' is

---

34   Ibid., 9–10.

very thin and fragmentary, while, on the other hand, it was almost entirely produced in its time by a very restricted group of Athenian citizens, who were neither slaves, nor Spartiates, nor Thebans, nor, of course, from the Persian Empire. In the same way, our whole knowledge of the Middle Ages derives from the chronicles of professional clergy, inspired by faith and desirous for their readers to be likewise true believers. A countless number of items from other persons, perhaps different ones, have definitively disappeared, and thus do not share in the feast organized by later historiographical narration. As Carr maintains, 'Generations of historians, scribes and chroniclers have determined beyond the possibility of appeal the face of the past.'[35] This is why there had never been factual history and never would be.

Benedetto Croce was right to maintain that all history is contemporary; there is also truth in the forceful assertion of Carl Becker that the historian participates in the creation of facts. And if Collingwood was correct in advancing the idea that historians reformulate in their minds the motivations of the protagonists in the accounts that they piece together, we have therefore to study who the historian is before familiarizing ourselves with his or her relation to the facts: 'It follows that when we take up a work of history, we should not consider in first place the facts it contains, but rather the author who relates them.'[36]

It is this approach, then, according to which there is no absolute historical objectivity, that should guide us in the study of history. And yet this should not lead to the mistaken conclusion that commentaries cannot be ranked, or that all historical interpretations are equivalent. Carr does not accept the extreme conclusions that might be drawn from Croce's logical scepticism or Becker's pragmatism. History should not be placed in the service of a utilitarian objective, nor be a 'catch-all' subjective

---

35   Ibid., 13.
36   Ibid., 23.

interpretation. It is true that facts do not speak, and that they are always subjective, but in no case can we ignore them, constrain them or falsify them. In the face of facts, the historian's status is like that of the individual in society, dependent on them and at the same time acting on them as an autonomous subject, both submitting to the environment and controlling it. 'The historian is neither the humble slave, nor the tyrannical master, of his facts. The relation between the historian and his facts is one of equality, give-and-take'; history is thus 'a perpetual dialogue between present and past'.[37]

Historians conduct a dialogue not only with the past, but also with their social and political environment. Every historian is part of history, being the product of currents of ideas in which they bathe and with which they are therefore infused; and the processes of change that take place in the course of their life may also lead them to evolve. This is why, in his final pages, Carr emphasizes that history is actually not a dialogue between individuals and the past, but rather a constant exchange between the society of today and that of yesterday.

If we apply this historical logic to Carr's book, we might cautiously propose that 'early 1960s Carr' perfectly displays advance signals of the destabilization of his discipline, which would accelerate during the following decade. The British historian bent all his strength to gluing together and filling the first cracks that his intellectual honesty had compelled him to display. That the venue for this should have been a prestigious lecture series at Cambridge University, and not on the margins of his profession, was a sure sign of the path on which historiography would either 'advance' or 'get bogged down' in the years to come.[38]

---

37   Ibid., 34.

38   For a postmodern appreciation of Carr's contribution and his limits, see Keith Jenkins, *On 'What Is History?': From Carr and Elton to Rorty and White*, London: Routledge, 1995, 43–63.

Discourse of Power, Plot and True Novel

In all Carr's discussion there is no hint of the place and time he is
speaking from. Very clearly, following his own logic, what his voice
utters is not empirical facts; the content of his work is rather
provided by the era in which he lived and wrote. From his point of
view, historians are above all the general and abstract expression of
the zeitgeist. They are not the spokespeople of a definite social
class, not dependent on a government institution or a network of
power positions, nor are they in the service of a specific national
culture. The fact that Carr's subject was international relations, the
Bolshevik Revolution and the Soviet regime enabled him to offer
stimulating viewpoints, something that was generally not the case
with his colleagues, who remained tightly moored throughout
their lives to their British historiography. The results obtained by
the social history that became hegemonic in Cambridge in the
1960s, however, set limits to his bold critique.

The same year of 1961 in which Carr's lectures were published
saw the appearance in France of a series of texts by Michel
Foucault. Despite the latter not being an accredited historian,
the whole of his work may be seen as critical history, off the
beaten track and seeking to divide human knowledge into pieces
that could be looked at from outside. Foucault's approach to
history was opposed from the start to the idea that scientific
consciousness or knowledge express or represent the spirit of the
time and social advances. Life, work or language are not objects
of knowledge but inherent to it. Foucault's distance from Sartre's
quasi-Marxist *praxis*, quite similar to Carr's approach to history,
soon became his ideological calling card.

It is important here to stress Foucault's contribution to a new
awareness, one that recognizes that every discourse of knowledge
is also a discourse of power, produced by an authority – in which
respect historiography is no different from other fields of knowledge. The historical discipline, like any other field of learning,
establishes a 'dispositive' of power that frames the production of

discourse and sets its limits. The collegium of academic specialists is authorized to utter the truth about the past, and to block
any outside element susceptible of challenging this authority.
This certainly does not mean rejecting historiography, or decree-
ing whether it is false or true; it is simply that the nature of what
it produces would be incomprehensible without acknowledging
this context. It is also necessary to keep in mind that discourses
are not simply presentations, but also constitute practices of
power, as they play an active part in the formation of the social
objects that they speak about.[39]

In parallel with Foucault's new ideas, conventional historiography would experience another assault from an unexpected
direction. In 1967, the semiologist Roland Barthes published
a critical article entitled 'The Discourse of History'.[40] Drawing
on criteria established by the linguist Roman Jakobson, Barthes
proposed a re-examination of the status of narratives about the
past and the way in which we read them. In contrast to other
literary critics, he had read many historical works and was
himself the author of a book on Jules Michelet. A deep analysis
of texts by Herodotus, Machiavelli and also Augustin Thierry
had led him to the conclusion that, despite its traditionally
accepted appearance of objectivity, the writing of history was
not so different from literary fiction: historians also use literary stratagems and metaphorical techniques. Even without
being always aware of it, they resort to metonymy, the lyrical
or symbolic style, or else the epic and dramatic. They remarkably resemble the realist writers of the nineteenth century,
sincerely and naively persuaded that by banishing from their

---

39   Foucault's ideas about history are scattered throughout his writings, and
vary from one text to another. An important and specific reference to the discipline
can be found, for example, in Chapter 7 of *The Order of Things: An Archaeology of the
Human Sciences*, New York: Vintage, 1994; and in the Introduction to *The Archaeology
of Knowledge*, New York: Vintage, 1982.

40   Roland Barthes, 'The Discourse of History', *Social Science Information*, 6/4,
1967, 63–75. The same year, the American philosopher Richard Rorty published *The
Linguistic Turn*, which would later give its name to a 'heretical' tendency.

stories the first-person pronoun, they precisely reflected an objective reality.

The historian may, for example, reduce a decade to a few sentences, yet devote several whole chapters to a single year. Are we then really dealing with the objective embodiment of a historical reality? Historians introduce a wealth of detail and enliven their text with references and footnotes in order to give an image of authenticity; in this way, they think they are demonstrating the scientific purity of their work. The writing of past history, however, is actually a procession of signifiers disguised as a collection of facts and seeking to expunge the traces of the process that created them. Finally, the historical narrative is a product of the imagination and not of science. Nietzsche was right to maintain that there is no fact in itself, and that a meaning always has to be injected for something to become a fact. Barthes's essay ends quite unambiguously:

> In the historical discourse of our civilization, the process of signification is always aimed at 'filling out' the meaning of History. The historian is not so much a collector of facts as a collector and relater of signifiers; that is to say, he organizes them with the purpose of establishing positive meaning and filling the vacuum of pure, meaningless series. As we can see, simply from looking at its structure and without having to invoke the substance of its content, historical discourse is essentially ideological elaboration, or to put it more precisely, an *imaginary* elaboration.[41]

It is hard to assess the impact of this essay on the French intellectual world. What is certain, however, is that Barthes's writings, along with those of other contemporary philosophers, sceptics and critics of objectivism, such as Michel Foucault, Jacques Derrida, Jean-François Lyotard, Jean Baudrillard, and later Paul

---

41   Ibid. [Translation modified.]

Ricoeur and Michel de Certeau, signal the beginning of cracks that appeared at the very heart of the guild of historians, some of which would underlie the historiographical controversies of the late twentieth century.

Two books by professional historians illustrate these developments: Paul Veyne, a specialist in the world of 'Antiquity', published *Writing History* in 1971,[42] followed two years later by the American medievalist Hayden White's *Metahistory*.[43] Whereas White's work has continued to arouse waves of reaction, discussion and original and productive comment in the English-speaking world, Veyne's book has remained almost ignored in the French historiographical field.

This might seem quite paradoxical. French philosophy and literary criticism, sometimes described as 'post-structuralist' or 'postmodernist', has enjoyed substantial resonance with a whole generation of British, American, Dutch and German historians, whereas in France, investigators of the past seem to have been immune to the rising tide of scepticism in the fields of philosophy, literature and language. This phenomenon is hard to fully decipher. If the hypothesis formulated in the previous chapter proves even partially correct, in other words that there is an immanent connection between positivism and nationalism, then the strong persistence of 'national identity' in France, compared with its more rapid retreat in other Western countries, might offer an approach to explaining the stubborn adherence of French historians (the *Annales* school and others) to the idea of historical certainty.

This working hypothesis can perhaps find support in an older document. The year 1954 saw the publication of a striking book by Henri-Irénée Marrou, *De la connaissance historique*.[44] A

42   Paul Veyne, *Writing History: Essay on Epistemology*, Manchester: Manchester University Press, 1984.

43   Hayden White, *Metahistory: The Historical Imagination in Nineteenth-Century Europe*, Baltimore: Johns Hopkins University Press, 1973.

44   Henri-Irénée Marrou, *De la connaissance historique*, Paris: Seuil, 1975.

professor at the Sorbonne, a brilliant historian of Christianity and an existentialist in philosophy, Marrou opted for a rather sceptical approach towards both the writing of history and current French politics (he was perhaps the only eminent historian to take a courageous stand when the Algerian insurrection broke out in 1956). His explicit critique of positivism was close to that of Carr. Even if Marrou still deemed it legitimate to apply to history the label 'science', he rejected the claim that any kind of law could be discovered, and constantly stressed that facts, no matter what their importance, depended on the subjective point of view of the historian who arranges them. He also cast doubt on the historians' pseudo-realist conceptual ability, preferring Max Weber's notion of the ideal type.[45] Moreover, Marrou always believed that every historian possesses an ideological agenda, which precisely confers on them a great moral responsibility in the reconstruction of the past.

Marrou's championing of a universal Christian idealism, very far from the *Annales* school, enabled him already in the 1950s to distance himself from historiographical objectivism (this religious humanist dimension was also an aspect of Paul Ricoeur and Michel de Certeau). Paul Veyne, on the other hand, had no need of religious belief to break with the positivist national heritage in the early 1970s. Raymond Aron was able to say of Veyne in 1971 that he came from outside; in other words, that he stood at a clear remove from the milieu of *Annales* and the Sorbonne, and at a still greater distance from their 'scientistic' self-sufficiency. Veyne, a professor at Aix-en-Provence, seemed oblivious to the politics of the day and the controversies in the capital.[46] He did, however, display impressive erudition in the field of classical 'Antiquity', being particularly familiar with ancient texts dealing to some degree with the narration of history.

---

45   Ibid., 153–59.

46   Raymond Aron, 'Comment l'historien écrit l'épistemologie: à propos du livre de Paul Veyne', *Annales: Économies, sociétés, civilisations*, 26/2, 1971, 1319–54.

Paul Veyne would subsequently become an unconditional admirer of Michel Foucault, but apart from a fleeting allusion, *Writing History* contains no reference to Foucault's writing, and likewise ignored Roland Barthes and other semiologists and philosophers of the day. Three figures, Max Weber, Raymond Aron and Henri-Irénée Marrou, form the starting point of Veyne's epistemological approach, which is vigorous to say the least. A hundred and fifty years of the discipline's scientific arrogance spurred him to reveal the methodological and theoretical contradictions of the prevailing historiography, which he did in sharp, clear and intransigent language.

Historians had always made out that the controversy as to the scientific status of their discipline was pointless; their role, they said, was to write historical accounts, not to weigh themselves down with theoretical ratiocinations. At the very start of his book, Veyne gives a stinging response to this argument:

> No, it is not useless to know if history is a science, for 'science' is not a lofty word, but a precise term; and experience proves that indifference to the debate about words is usually the accompaniment of a confusion of ideas on the matter . . . History is not a science, and has little to expect from sciences; it does not explain and has no method. Better still, history, about which much has been said for two centuries, does not exist. Then what is history? . . . the answer to the question has not changed over the 2,200 years since the successors of Aristotle found it – historians tell of true events in which man is the actor; history is a true novel.[47]

Veyne's book gives the impression that the child of Hans Christian Andersen's story 'The Emperor's New Clothes' has been reborn in the features of a rebel historian, infuriated by the scientific

---

47   Paul Veyne, *Writing History: Essay on Epistemology*, Manchester: Manchester University Press, 1984, ix–x.

pseudo-costume worn by a sovereign who is actually naked, but whose marvellous raiment the whole world extols. With Paul Veyne, we take leave not only of Ranke, but also of Droysen and Dilthey, not only of Seignobos and Langlois, but also of Marc Bloch and E. H. Carr.

Veyne pursued his logic 'almost' to its end. He had written little on history before producing this penetrating critical essay, but would go on to write much more. Contrary to the majority of his fellow historians, he was determined to know just what he was doing, in order to avoid encumbering himself with illusions or becoming mired in the rhetorical swamp of comfortable generalizations. And indeed, his clear-sightedness actually favoured his narrative talent, as well as the liberated and fertile imagination that is displayed in his subsequent work. With the enthusiastic support of Raymond Aron he was appointed to the Collège de France – a golden closet that ultimately served to restrain a bit this rebel from the provinces.

As can be seen in the above quotation, for Veyne history was not scientific and never could be. Despite its recourse to abstract generalizations, history always has to come to terms with the specific and concrete; it is a nominalist discipline even if it uses general terms. When it chooses to resort to universal conceptualizations, it unconsciously continues nonetheless attempting to describe the unique. Historians commit a cardinal error in believing that the universal concepts that appear in their text are adequate, and coincide with a reality that actually happened. The universal concept is in fact a kind of ideal type that we construct, and with whose aid we combine, accumulate and classify facts, proceed to comparisons and produce narratives.

There is nothing reprehensible, Veyne argues, in developing a comparative history, on condition that we are able to wield it with empirical precaution, and particularly that we know its limits. However, recourse to general concepts without awareness of the anachronism that these almost always conceal is a familiar procedure of historians. We can never repeat often enough that no war is like another, and no revolution triggered by the same causes. Likewise, that there are no 'productive forces', simply men who produce in various circumstances. Patriotism, a concept created in the nineteenth century, can in no way be applied to the ancient world – though this mistake is made by certain historians, who are even unaware of the problem. And finally, it will never be possible to identify the whole set of factors that underlie any particular historical phenomenon, which is, moreover, one of the main reasons for our permanent inability to predict these in advance.

We must realize, at all events, that the habitual concepts of historiography in no way resemble those used in the natural sciences, where abstractions are an inherent part of a system of laws that have no validity for human history. Historical explanation, therefore, is never normative, but only causal and hypothetical. In history, as against the natural sciences, explanation takes the form of a logical account that contains a series of causes and results which we are able to arrange and understand. Make no mistake, 'Between the historical explanation and the scientific explanation there is not a nuance but an abyss, because a leap is needed to pass from one to the other, because science demands a conversion, and because a scientific law is not drawn from an everyday maxim.'[48]

This is why replacing the term 'explanation' with that of 'understanding', as Droysen and Dilthey both proposed, with a view to preserving the coveted title 'science', takes us no further forward. Clearly, none of this negates the value of history, nor does it in any way lead to the conclusion that we should stop writing it. But instead of defining it as a science, it should be viewed as a specific kind of art that requires competence and experience. It could also be seen as a kind of literature; in other words, a specific narration of events, which Paul Veyne chooses to call a 'plot'. The plot in question is a scarcely scientific mixture

---

48   Ibid., 164–5.

or arrangements of facts mixed in with material factors, ascribed purposes, and, of course, accidents. The writing of the plot organizes a series of brief and segmented episodes, to end up with a coherent and logical account. Historiography, whether structuralist, quantitative or comparative, almost always contains a share of plot; and what is dismissed as a non-event is simply what has not yet been recognized as an event. It would quite clearly be foolish not to admit the existence of facts; that is, circumscribed events that happen independently of the investigator-subject. However, these facts possess no meaning in themselves, being no more than empty chronological series. There is no difference in principle between historical facts and physical ones, but they are radically distinguished by our ability to describe their interrelations. Reconstruction of the causes of a historical event always forms an integral part of the plot.

Such basic historiographical concepts as 'process', 'mutation', 'structure', 'society' or 'economy', however, are abstract constructions of historians. There is no law or obligatory role for producing syntheses, and it is impossible, therefore, to speak of tried and tested methods. Nor is there any determinism in acceptable historical explanations, only possibilities. This is why the most important historian of the modern age was precisely seen as a sociologist: Max Weber, whom Paul Veyne considers the thinker most aware of the techniques of his research and the limits of his work. It is true that the Weberian principle of the ideal type does not bring a solution to all the problems of representing the past and the present, but it is productive, and more trustworthy, in that it does not claim to reflect a given reality.

Paul Veyne would subsequently prefer Michel Foucault, a 'pure historian', to Max Weber, which is why, in the second edition of his book, his specific analysis of the Weberian ideal type is replaced by a more ample description of Foucault's contribution. In both cases, however, for this rebel historian, narration of the past remains a purely intellectual activity, inspired by curiosity, or by the thirst and passion for knowledge. Veyne holds not only that the technique of writing narratives presenting the past has scarcely changed since Thucycides (in other words, for nearly 2,400 years), but also that the motivations that lead people to produce historiography have remained similar, if not identical. He has no hesitation in declaring,

> History is one of the most harmless products ever elaborated by the chemistry of the intellect; it devalues, takes away passion, not because it re-establishes truth against partisan errors, but because its truth is always deceptive and because the history of our land rapidly appears as boring as that of foreign nations . . . The theatre of history makes the audience feel passions that, being lived in an intellectual mode, undergo a kind of purification; their gratuitousness makes every sentiment vain that is not apolitical.[49]

Strange as it may seem, these words of Paul Veyne carry no suggestion of irony. French historiography had come a long way from the early nineteenth century, when Augustin Thierry clearly presented the national-political functions of the new profession. Besides, it is hard to imagine the great total wars of the twentieth century, or the wars of national liberation that followed, without the important role played by history as educator of the masses.

The fact that a historian such as Veyne could have turned his back on all this leads us to think that, by the late twentieth century, the initial functions of the profession had been blurred and were on the retreat, perhaps even that their term of validity was expiring. Like the child in Andersen's tale, Veyne seems to have seen that the emperor was naked, but he still did not ask what purpose this majestic sovereign served, or where the source of his royal–scientific power lay.

The explanation may perhaps lie in the fact that Veyne wrote this book in 1969–70, in a very particular context. As a

---

49   Ibid., 83–4.

communist, he seems to have suffered in his daily life the fren-
zied politicization of his students, so characteristic of this time.
Ironically enough, the naive depoliticization of the historical
discipline that he sought to achieve may have actually been help-
ful to him. It undeniably agreed with the antipolitical atmosphere that the *Annales* team continued to maintain, particularly
in the 1970s. And so it is not very surprising that, despite his
assault on the 'truth' that 'accredited' historians had supposedly
attained, Veyne was invited to participate with full honours in
the writing of *Faire de l'histoire*, a high point of French historiography in the mid-1970s.[50]

Paul Veyne's book met with a mixed reception. On the one
hand, several prominent thinkers such as Raymond Aron, Paul
Ricoeur and Michel de Certeau paid it great attention, if without
sharing all Veyne's positions;[51] on the other hand, with one or
two exceptions, there was no reaction on the part of historians.
This hesitant silence was striking, and is well illustrated by the
case of Roger Chartier. Coming as he did from the *Annales* circle,
and soon to be appointed to the Collège de France, Chartier
published in the 1990s a wide-ranging article on the relation of
philosophy and history.[52] It was impossible for Chartier to
ignore Veyne's book in this article, but he 'dispatched' it in a
categorical rejection of his colleague's theoretical approach.
Moreover, Chartier surprisingly announced to his readers that

50   See Paul Veyne, 'L'histoire conceptualisante', in Jacques Le Goff and Pierre
Nora (eds), *Faire de l'histoire*, vol. 1, Paris: Gallimard, 1971, 62–92. This article
shows a more moderate Veyne: history is not always a science, 'it contains kernels of
scientificity' (62). He remains for all that faithful to Max Weber, stressing that
'conceptualization is no more than another name for the Weberian ideal type' (69).

51   I mentioned above Raymond Aron's review article. See also Michel de
Certeau, 'Une épistémologie de transition: Paul Veyne', *Annales: Économies, sociétés,
civilisations*, 27/6, 1972, 1317–27; Ricoeur, *Time and Narrative*, vol. 1, 170–6.
Henri-Irénée Marrou, in the second edition of *De la connaissance historique*, also
referred to Veyne's work as a 'fine book' (163).

52   Roger Chartier, 'Philosophie et histoire: Un dialogue', in F. Bédarida (ed.),
L'histoire ou le métier d'historien en France 1945–1995, Paris: Éditions de la Maison
des sciences de l'homme, 1995, 149–69.

Writing History had been published in 1974. This might have passed as a slip of the pen, if this epitome of French historians had not returned to the charge: 'A year earlier, in 1973, Hayden White defended a comparable, if not identical, position.'[53]

Veyne, however, had preceded Hayden White by two years and was quite unfamiliar with this American historian, who for his part knew nothing of Veyne despite his own essay appearing after that of his French colleague. It seems in any case that the analogy (though not an exact similarity) between the two works can be largely put down to the 'spirit of the time'.

Is Historical Narrative Merely Fiction?

White's first book met with a warm welcome (which was less the case with its successors), though criticisms were expressed. His work was translated into German, Italian, Spanish, Russian, Japanese and so on, but it is significant that none of his books has yet been published in France.[54] Hundreds of articles, and even whole books, have been devoted to White in many languages. His recognition is particularly marked in the English-speaking world, but in continental Europe, too, his mark is felt on doctoral theses and in academic conferences. Hayden White has come to be seen as the 'postmodern' starting point of historiography's linguistic turn, and in large measure also of the defences raised against it.[55] Many other historians quickly came round to the new paradigm, including Frank Ankersmit, Robert F. Berkhofer, Alun Munslow, Keith Jenkins, David Harlan, Marc

---

53   Ibid., 162. Oddly enough, Veyne is also unmentioned in François Hartog's major theoretical works on historiography. See *Évidence de l'histoire*, Paris: Éditions de l'EHESS, 2005; and *Croire en l'histoire*, Paris: Flammarion, 2013.

54   All I have been able to find is a single article in French in a purely literary periodical: Hayden White, 'La rhétorique de l'interprétation', *Littérature*, 71, 1988, 5–23. Paul Ricoeur is exceptional in his reference to White; see *Time and Narrative*, 142–79.

55   On White's influence on historians and literary critics, see Richard T. Vann, 'The Reception of Hayden White', *History and Theory*, 37/2, 1998, 143–61.

Poster, Robert Rosenstone and Sande Cohen. A more restrained adoption can be seen also with Dominick LaCapra, Joan Scott, Gabrielle Spiegel and several others from a range of backgrounds. In the wake of this turn, several historians set out to demonstrate a new critical spirit either in the rhetoric of their narratives or in their procedure in empirical work. Many would now better perceive the limits of their profession.

The explorer who discovers a new land always has a forerunner. In several respects, for example, Marrou preceded Veyne, and Becker likewise anticipated White on some key points. And if, in my view, Roland Barthes's essay of 1967 was the real springboard for the linguistic leap as far as historical writing in general is concerned, an article by the philosopher and literary critic Louis O. Mink, dating from 1966, marks the hesitant beginning of a previously unknown state of mind even in the United States.[56] Mink had done pioneering work by drawing attention to the literary tools present in the historian's backpack, but it was Hayden White, a historian specializing in the European past, who first proceeded to a broad deconstruction of the entire historiographical corpus. This American historian had already published a number of theoretical articles, but it was only in his book *Metahistory* that he managed a broader presentation of his positions.

Carl Becker had already established the premise that form and substance constitute an inseparable whole in the narration of the past. Such narration would be incomprehensible if the poetry and narrative modes specific to each historian were not preserved intact. To illustrate this thesis, White drew on the historical writings of Michelet, Ranke, Tocqueville and Burckhardt, to which he added a detailed and brilliant analysis of the philosophies of history of Marx, Nietzsche and Croce – the last two serving as signposts on the path of the historiographical saga. White used five categories to judge texts dealing with the past: chronicle,

---

56   Louis O. Mink, 'The Autonomy of Historical Understanding', *History and Theory*, 26/1, 1987, 1–14.

story, emplotment, mode of argument and mode of ideological implication.[57]

Events do happen, of course, and it would be foolish to deny it; but the nub of the problem is what to make of them. In other words, how to relate them? The historian's constructive imagination intervenes to bring order to the mixture of evidence, with a view to giving all this a meaning. Imagination is always needed in order to reach the real. Historians use chronicles that they transform into logical and coherent stories, with a beginning, a middle and an end. They proceed to a selection on the basis of their collection of facts, including some of these and excluding others, emphasizing a certain number and casting into oblivion those that are not pertinent. They integrate into their story various types of explanation: ideographic, holistic, mechanical and contextual. Up to this point, White has not gone far beyond Croce, Becker or Barthes, simply spelling out in more detail the theoretical principles that guide the writing up of research.

White's specific contribution lies in his particular use of the concept of 'emplotment', and in his deciphering of the codes that underlie narrative strategies. According to him, there are four main types of plot: romance, such as pervades the writings of Michelet, for example; comedy, particularly used by Ranke in his austere explanations; tragedy, for which Tocqueville showed a marked inclination; and satire, which gives Burckhardt's writing its particular character. Alongside these familiar literary forms there are four rhetorical tools that White, following Vico, calls 'tropes', and which he sees particularly as a kind of borrowing: the trope gives a word a different sense from that of ordinary language.[58]

---

57   White, *Metahistory*, 5. In a later article, White posited 'annals' as different and prior to chronicles, given their total absence of narrative. See 'The Value of Narrativity in the Representation of Reality', *Critical Inquiry*, 7/1, 1980, 5–27.

58   On the origin of this term and its avatars, see White's preface to his collection of articles *Tropics of Discourse: Essays in Cultural Criticism*, Baltimore: Johns Hopkins University Press, 1985, 2.

According to White, the most significant 'meta-tropes' in the elaboration of writing are metaphor, which is a shift in the customary use of a word and its application in a different rhetorical space; metonymy, which consists in substituting the name of a concrete thing for an abstract term, or vice versa; synecdoche, the use of a word referring to a part to signify the whole, or else the whole to signify a part; and irony, a form of deliberate devaluing or self-denigration as to the ability to correctly describe a reality.

Historians constantly resort to these linguistic tools in order to imbue their narratives with vitality, power and meaning. The romantic Michelet uses a profusion of metaphors. Ranke's comic spirit incites him to frequent synecdoche. Burckhardt's satiric spirit, like that of Voltaire and Gibbon before him, fills his plots with irony. Recourse to these linguistic forms, however, is not always conscious for historians, who borrow them from the literature of their time and slip them into their writings without thinking too much of it.

But this is not quite exact. As Roman Jakobson has shown, historians, just like other writers, communicate with their future readers in the spontaneous deciphering of the rhetorical codes inserted in their narratives. In any given culture there is a collaboration, or an imperceptible dialogue, between an author and those he or she addresses. Literary norms make it possible to understand the writer, who makes use of them in turn to organize facts, explain them and construct a narrative with them. Collingwood had already emphasized the impossibility of explaining what a tragedy is to someone who has never previously experienced a tragic situation. The literary object is therefore the end product of conventions and a transmission that combines the production of the narrative and its reception. In other words, everyone shares certain common prejudices that make possible the attribution of meaning and the transformation of ignorance into knowledge.

A year after the appearance of this essay, and in response to initial criticisms, White published a brilliant article entitled 'The

Historical Text as Literary Artefact'. Here he expressed the point of view that the opposition of historians to his book came chiefly from their general 'reluctance to consider historical narratives as what they most manifestly are: verbal fictions, the contents of which are as much *invented* as *found* and the forms of which have more in common with their counterparts in literature than they have with those in the sciences'.[59]

White does not explain at all the relationship between 'found' and 'invented', but, according to him, if historical work depends on the discovery of evidence, it remains all the same that a same series of events is susceptible to being conveyed in various forms of plot. White does not tell us what is the weight of evidence and events vis-à-vis the thinking subject who organizes them. There is certainly no immutable formula in his work to describe the reciprocal dependence and balance of forces between words and 'things'. We are faced all the same with a disturbing set of questions: does the organizing of material in a comic or tragic expression depend completely on what is actually 'found'? Is a set of events – which we call, for example, 'extermination of the Indians', 'African slave trade', 'mass murders in Europe' (Nazi or Stalinist) – devoid of any inherent meaning, so that we might indifferently relate it ironically or as a pleasant satire? Does certain evidence not impose itself more than any other, right from the phase of collection and research? Given the complexity of these problems, there can be no unambiguous response – hence the many arguments and the growing unease that followed.

Historiographical objectivism was clearly under threat, and the relativism that White openly proclaimed became manifest. Plots depend on the affinities of the narrator, and are imposed from outside on the chronological course of events. But what are the historian's affinities that lead him to opt for one narrative

---

59   Hayden White, 'The Historical Text as Literary Artefact', in *Tropics of Discourse*, 82; original italics.

strategy and reject another? Is it purely a question of aesthetic tastes or state of mind? Or does the historian's *Weltanschauung* intervene already in the phase of research and the necessary selection of evidence, as well as in the process of writing?

In contrast to Paul Veyne, who seemed to ignore the politics embedded in historiography (though he revised his views somewhat in the wake of his encounter with Foucault), Hayden White showed greater ingenuity. Alongside the division into genres, tropes and other literary conventions, and obsessed as he was with four-way divisions, he offered a simplistic division into four ideological categories. Following from Karl Mannheim, who had indicated five categories in the twentieth century's political consciousness, White reduced these to four for the nineteenth century: anarchism, conservatism, radicalism and liberalism. This was not a matter of precise political currents, rather of ideological sensibilities as bearers of specific historical forms.

White's categorization was essentially based on a single criterion, that of social change. The conservative clearly fears change and prefers the existing order, presenting himself as a champion of the rhythm of nature. Ranke, for example, whose writings sacralize the Prussian regime and nation, corresponds perfectly to this definition.[60] The liberal, for his part, supports change as long as this remains moderate and cautious, presenting it as unavoidable, especially if it is only partial and does not affect the system as a whole. The liberal also views favourably the sociopolitical rhythm expressed in the action of parliaments. Tocqueville, even if he was a liberal of a particular kind (a tragic realist), fits more or less into this category.[61] Burckhardt was disillusioned with liberalism, while Croce was always a somewhat versatile liberal. The radical and the anarchist, on the other hand, aspire to a global transformation of the human community, which they

---

60   White, *Metahistory*, 173–5.
61   Ibid., 205.

desire to render more harmonious. For White, accordingly, Michelet's positions may be described as anarchist.[62]

These distinctions, which are problematic even in Mannheim, become clumsy and even ridiculous with the American historian, in comparison with his brilliant poetic analyses. The actors he chooses to embody the leading roles in this demonstration of historiography or philosophy of history are hard to fit into his systematic ideological classification. Thus Burckhardt was more of a conservative than a liberal, while Michelet was far from being an anarchist. And White has to utter this important warning:

> I should also stress that a given historian's emplotment of the historical process or way of explaining it in a formal argument need not be regarded as a function of his consciously held ideological position. Rather, the form that he gives to his historical accounts can be said to have ideological implications consonant with one or another of the four positions differentiated above. Just as every ideology is attended by a specific idea of history and its processes, so too, I maintain, is every idea of history attended by specifically determinable ideological implications.[63]

In other words, despite the weight of politics, it is aesthetics that largely determines ideology in the writing of the past. Do structural necessities of narration, then, play a greater part than the values conveyed by a view of the world? White, when he analysed the dominant ideologies, already tended to classify these in a personalized way, according to their conscious relation to processes of historical change. The ideas of the Enlightenment, such as equality and liberty, scarcely appear in this classification,

---

62   Ibid., 163.
63   Ibid., 24. The insufficiently deep relation to politics and modern ideology, in both Hayden White and Paul Veyne, may be explained by the fact that the former was a medievalist and the latter a historian of antiquity.

while among the factors that determine the modes of production of plot, aesthetic values, despite being taken into consideration, occupy a completely secondary place. In the same way, relations between social classes, the internal contradictions of a society and the structures of power do not really appear as pertinent in the ideological and political formation of historical writers. In the end, White is quite close to Veyne in his ingenuity, and thus far removed from the political and critical lucidity of Barthes.

Aside from this question, White's book has further surprises in terms of what it does not contain. To deal with the writing of history in the nineteenth century without mentioning its profes-sionalization and academic institutionalization is problematic to say the least. Tocqueville, for example, was a politician and in no way an academic; his writings were little read by other historians. Moreover, historical production in French universities lagged significantly behind that in the Teutonic world. It is also inap-propriate to choose as examples these particular French- and German-language authors, given that Burckhardt was a rather un-German historian who taught in Switzerland (and not by chance).

To isolate a few celebrities, even given their scintillating styles, as representative of nineteenth-century historiography is both deceptive and, as a procedure, not very fitting for a historian. We may respect the aesthetic of the four-way division dear to White, but to choose Tocqueville rather than Droysen, and Burckhardt instead of Treitschke, without verifying their actual impact on those reading and studying history in the nineteenth century, amounts to not taking seriously the significance and nature of the imaginary dialogue between author and readers. The major-ity of nineteenth-century historians had 'something in common' with their readers: they shared not only widespread literary 'tropes' but also the hegemonic ideology. White is clearly aware that the dominant ideas were fundamentally those of the bour-geoisie, but he does not spell out to his readers that in the nine-teenth century there could not be in Germany a single professional scholar of Nietzsche's type, nor, a fortiori, an accredited academic historian who was anything like Marx. The ideological apparatus of the nation-state, to use Louis Althusser's terminology, did not tolerate any deviance, and certainly not in the prestigious professional field of teaching about the past.[64]

In the extreme case, it would be possible to ignore the little interest that White displays in the institutionalization of his profession, as well as his clumsy approach to ideology, but it is hard to understand how the most important meta-ideology of the era could have escaped his attention: construction of the national past, the very raison d'être of historical writing, is kept completely marginal. It is true that White makes some commonplace observations on the nationalism of Ranke and Michelet, but a reading of his book suggests that these historians aspired above all to give their writings a stylized literary expression, rather than to please their readers from an ideological point of view, and equally the academic establishment that accorded them fame and security. Were nation-state functions not a determinant element among the various factors involved in the rise of historiographical production? And was its ideological and political character oriented in this direction? By taking Tocqueville and Burckhardt as representative figures of nineteenth-century history writing, rather than, for example, Thierry, Droysen, Sybel or Treitschke, White manages to ignore the political dimension, and particularly the national question that is central to this in historical writing, and even more so in its pedagogic function.

Even the strong point of White's argument, on the poetics of historical writing, displays certain fault lines. Modern historiography was born at the same time as the narrative strategies developed in the realist novel. The novel itself, however, was shaped by the new modes of publication that arose in the long nineteenth century. We do not know how many historians took the time to

---

64   Louis Althusser, 'Ideology and Ideological State Apparatuses', in *Lenin and Philosophy and Other Essays*, London: Verso, 2001, 11–43.

read novels published in book form. Many certainly did read these, however, in the form of instalments published in periodicals, as was the practice at this time both in Europe and in America. This publication in daily or weekly episodes gave rise to specific modes of expression that were not without resonance in historical narration. As in television serials today, tragedy or romance unfold in a rhythm marked by episodes, to which the reader is forced to adapt. Political articles published in the press inspired historiographical writing, just as did works of fiction; many books also assumed the aspect of a long article, particularly by the lightness of their contents.

These lacunas do not cancel out White's achievements. His later writings would mark a development from his initial positions, showing greater interaction between rhetorical expression and ideological weight. In this way he came to a more significant conclusion, in an important article entitled 'The Politics of Historical Interpretation', published in 1982:

> The social function of a properly disciplined study of history and the political interests it served at its inception in the early nineteenth century, the period of the consolidation of the (bourgeois) nation-state, are well-known and hardly in need of documentation. We do not have to impute dark ideological motives to those who endowed history with the authority of a discipline in order to recognize the ideological benefits to new social classes and political constituencies that professional, academic historiography served and, *mutatis mutandis*, continues to serve down to our own time.[65]

As with Paul Veyne, it may be the confrontation with Michel Foucault that contributed to this development, even if Hayden

---

65   Hayden White, 'The Politics of Historical Interpretation: Discipline and De-sublimation [1982]', in *The Content of the Form*, Baltimore: Johns Hopkins University Press, 1987, 60–1.

White would maintain that he never felt comfortable with Foucault's theory of power.[66] His poetic classifications became more flexible, while the rigid catalogue of meta-tropes disappeared in the wake of criticisms. One thing in White's work, however, remained unchanged throughout: the idea that historical narratives are verbal fictions that have nothing in common with scientific representations. The difference between history and literature is equally clear: contrary to the novelist, the historian is not entitled to present events and characters that did not appear in past reality. The historian does not invent new facts, he is always obliged to use the evidence he has noted and the discoveries he has made. Fiction 'only' appears in the fashioning, the arrangement, the attribution of meaning.

History as Crime Scene and the Negation of the Shoah

Those who followed the path opened by Hayden White simply reinforced the ambient scepticism, and continued to pose a serious challenge to historiography. Thus a study of the writings of Frank Ankersmit or Robert F. Berkhofer, two of the most familiar critics of 'normal' history, helps to understand the nature of the crisis that spread throughout the discipline on the question of narration. In parallel with this, the writings of other authors show the impossibility of bringing together under a common denominator the whole range of suspicions weighing on historical writing.

Berkhofer, the critical historian of the myth of the American 'new frontier' and of white racism, sharpened and complemented White's intuitions in a fundamental book published in 1995, *Beyond the Great Story*.[67] After an extensive career as a 'normal' sociocultural historian, Berkhofer decided to stop echoing a pseudoscientific official voice that was deemed to

---

66   Interview with Hayden White in E. Domanska, *Encounters: Philosophy of History after Postmodernism*, Charlottesville: University Press of Virginia, 1998, 32.

67   Robert F. Berkhofer, *Beyond the Great Story: History as Text and Discourse*, Cambridge, MA: Harvard University Press, 1997.

represent past reality. He systematically undertook to show the limits of traditional history, which was oblivious to these. For him, the authority of evidence that confers legitimacy on the discipline is actually an arbitrary codification and pure convention, which imposes on the reader a 'great story' of a continuous past. The traditional historian always seeks to convince the reader that the elaboration of his commentary corresponds to an exhaustive collection of the facts; and by doing so, armed with the voice of competence, he seeks to give his narration a convincing aspect of realism.

For Berkhofer, the plurality of voices that had not previously managed to get themselves heard, and the multiplicity of fluctuating and fragmentary stories, had to strip the profession of its mysterious halo of truth and neutrality. By revealing their systems of writing, historians would gain both in honesty and in realism. The reader had to be aware of the politics that hide behind historical representations, and be clear that all historical writing was ideological. The best history would be that which not only disclosed the balance of forces that exists in every society, but also refused to ignore that the multiple voices that can transcribe the past are never on a footing of equality.[68]

Ankersmit, a specialist in intellectual history at the University of Groningen in the Netherlands, agreed with White on the decisive weight given to the narrative. He believes that in history the narrative functions almost as the formula does in the natural sciences, but with a completely different creative imagination. Ankersmit, however, constantly maintains that at the level of sentences – that is, the simple mentioning of isolated events – it is possible to speak the 'truth'. Historical research collects facts, which narration goes on to interpret by integrating them into a series of arguments. In the writing of history, what is important and meaningful is located precisely at the level of the story, where

---

68   See the excellent chapter 'Politics and Paradigms', in ibid., 202–42, in particular Berkhofer's analysis of Howard Zinn's positions at 216–17.

literary construction and political–ideological partiality are an unavoidable transition.

It should not be deduced from all this that narrative commentary is necessarily arbitrary. With the help of facts, it is possible to confirm or refute theses about the past; and it is up to a more 'credible' interpretation, one that rejects a priori definitions, to contradict its predecessor. However, it is only in dry chronicles that it is possible to remain 'modern and objective'. If the choice is made of sincerity in narrative construction, this is a condemnation to 'postmodern' confusion, or else to producing a very fragile history. The relationship between language and reality suffers from a systematic instability, in that the argument is always over a metaphor. And Ankersmit ends up with a conclusion that is not found with White: 'The ethical dimension must therefore be ubiquitous in historiography. Modern historiography is based on a political decision.'[69]

It is uncertain whether all followers of White's deconstruction would approve this last declaration. For many, in fact, aesthetics and narrative expression form the quintessence of historical writing. There is therefore no necessary coincidence between critical historians and postmodern ones, or again between expressly political researchers and others with no interest at all in politics. Postmodernism has not created a coherent historiographical profession of faith. In fact, deconstructivism (to use the terminology sometimes employed) has been unable to replace positivist modernism as a complete uniform narrative, given that it did not propose new systemic theoretical fields.

Opponents of the new approaches to the writing of history displayed a conservative reflex in defending the boundaries of their discipline. After a hundred and fifty years of absolute hegemony over the production of 'scientific' knowledge about the past,

---

69   Frank Ankersmit, 'Six Theses on Narrativist Philosophy of History' (5.4.1.), in *History and Tropology: The Rise and Fall of Metaphor*, Oakland: University of California Press, 1994, 42.

they would not accept abandoning this without a fight. Arnaldo Momigliano was one of the first to react to Hayden White's book, followed in particular by Richard Evans, Gertrude Himmelfarb, Roger Chartier, Carlo Ginzburg and other historians. They rose up against the new barbarians who were invading the empire of their truths. This splendid realm of erudition, which was founded by Prussian historians in the nineteenth century and which, in the rising age of nations, had known better days than the late twentieth century, also began to unravel from within. The disquiet of conservatives would grow, now that the banner of revolt against historiographical objectivism was no longer raised just by lone philosophers such as Nietzsche and Croce, or by such atypical historians as Collingwood and Carl Becker. The scepticism was now shared by many members of the guild itself.

The majority of historians of a postmodern bent foreswore narrative strategies in their writing, in other words, the role of rhetoric in the written representation of the past. They abandoned techniques of collection of sources, criteria for classifying these and clarifying their nature, while the staunch opponents of these new concepts, like guardians of their profession's temple, remained attached to the discipline's investigative dimension. Truth for them lay particularly in the footnotes; in other words, in sources, this being the only way that the reality of the past could be known. The historian's role was above all to examine the facts; the historian was their guardian, as well as the virtually neutral instrument of their distribution.

In their counteroffensive, 'responsible' historians resorted to various weapons: from generalizing accusations, sometimes no more than personal insult, through to scholarly debates, in which the capacity of language to express past reality was examined by methodological reflection and serious argument. In broad terms, two key issues that historians evoked in defending themselves against the threat of postmodernism deserve closer scrutiny.

The first of these is the analogy of the crime scene. In the attempt to gather evidence with a view to verifying the facts, the historian was said to be much like a detective or an examining magistrate.[70] The crime scene is characterized by the same elements that define the field of historical research. The detective, like the historian, seeks to transcribe what has happened. Step by step, each of them collects fragmentary indications that enable them to piece together the plot. Detectives cannot start from the assumption that, given the impossibility of reaching absolute truth, they should either give free rein to their creative imagination or abandon the investigation. Which is why there is neither a detective nor a serious historian who is postmodern. If society were to abandon its claim to discover the truth about a crime, it would lose all morality, and by the same token its ability to exist as a civilized body; this applies equally to its capacity to piece together its own past. If it did not make studies of its origins, the chain of factors and processes that have formed it, it would drift into a destructive nihilism. Society rewards its policemen and detectives, and also its historians, for revealing the truth about what happened.

The comparison between detective and historian seems quite logical, even if the former has inspired more stories than the latter. However, those who see a resemblance between the two are mistaken on at least one point. This does not bear on the contrast between the police officer's report or interview, concise and sober, and the historian's narrative, prolix and overflowing with abstract concepts. Nor is it uniquely due to the difference between the number of indications and the nature of the evidence, which for the detective is mainly physical or based on direct testimony, while the historian has to rely on literary, written and often very ancient documents. Another more problematic dimension complicates the comparison: detectives do not initially seek to reach the truth about the past. Their

---

70   See Arnaldo Momigliano, 'The Rhetoric of History and the History of Rhetoric: On Hayden White's Tropes', in E. S. Shaffer (ed.), *Comparative Criticism: A Yearbook*, 3, Cambridge: Cambridge University Press, 1981, 266–7.

investigations aim at finding the person guilty of a crime. Discovery of the truth is only a corollary of this investigation, even if, clearly enough, identification of the guilty party depends on a truthful reconstruction of what happened: the boundaries and limits of the crime scene are subject to this specific purpose that is defined at the start.

Should we see the comparison between detective and historian as pertinent despite such differences? It could be, if we start from the postulate that historians do not embark on a research project in order to discover the truth about the past, but interrogate history about a specific problem that interests and preoccupies them. The question to which they seek a response dictates the orientation of their investigation, and the type and amount of evidence necessary, and it defines a spatial and temporal boundary. Historians' questions may be guided by various motivations, but these always depend on the ideologies they are steeped in, and the established conventions of the discipline at this particular time. Their view of the world, therefore, is not simply expressed in the literary work they produce at the end of the process, but is a factor that orients them right from the start along the paths they select in the course of their research. Even for those historians who show intellectual honesty and do not arbitrarily arrange their discoveries, the collection of facts responds to an ultimate objective that is not simply abstract. And so, as with the detective, the truth is surrounded by interests and needs that are partly external to it, although in principle they are supposed not to contradict it.

The measured and critical postmodernist may claim that, as the overburdened scene of the past is different from the limited scene of a crime, the historian will always be a failed detective. Historians will never be able to locate all pertinent discoveries (too poor, in the case of antiquity, and too abundant, in the case of modern times); the result will always be uncertainty and doubt. If we are dealing with a political postmodernist, he or she will point out not only the dependence of the scholar on the codes of their discipline, but also the connections that this has with state bodies or private establishments. It is true that the historical discipline possesses a wide autonomy in the liberal democratic world, but this is variable according to place and time; independence is never absolute. History always lies close to the bosom of political and cultural elites; the few sharpshooters outside the conventions are simply exceptions who confirm the rule.

The painful debate about the Shoah has been a second difficulty for postmodernists. In fact, by uttering doubts about the possibility of presenting the reality of the past, do the new historians provide weapons for those who deny the existence of the Shoah? And is it just accidental that the two phenomena – postmodernism and negationism – should have appeared simultaneously in Europe, and even in North America? Almost all historians hostile to historical relativism have brought up the memory of the Shoah as an inhibitory argument against sceptical theories.

A number of points need spelling out, if we are to make headway in this debate. First of all, the term 'Shoah', taken from biblical Hebrew and applied to the mass extermination of Jews and their descendants during the Second World War, is a fairly late entry into contemporary language.[71] In Israel, the general custom was to refer to the great tragedy as 'the destruction of European Jews'. This was also the title given by Raul Hilberg to his pioneering book published in 1961.[72] The term 'Shoah' was not widespread in Israel until the early 1970s, reaching Europe in the following decade. It entered the French

---

71   I use the expression 'descendants of Jews', since many victims of Jewish origin, contrary to the stubborn insistence of their murderers, did not identify as Jews or keep up any Jewish religious practice. In my view, this is not simply a question of proper terminology, but one of respect for the identity of the victims.

72   In the early 1960s, Hilberg offered this fundamental work to the university presses of Columbia and Princeton, who both declined it. His book was finally published by a small press in England. It was translated into German by a far left publishing house, and did not appear in French until 1988.

language through Claude Lanzmann's eponymous film, and the word would now rival 'Holocaust', taken from the ancient Greek (thanks, it seems, to the writer Elie Wiesel) and popularized by a television series. Both terms, in fact, have misleading connotations: *shoah* in Hebrew means a natural catastrophe, while *holocaust* was originally a sacrifice by fire. The murder of millions of Jews was neither a natural phenomenon nor an act of sacrifice. We have to recognize that it was a documentary film and a television series that brought this relatively new concept into the field of academic research. Dozens of books, and hundreds of scholarly articles, would subsequently use these two 'scientific' terms to denote the extermination of Jews and their descendants.

Aside from terminology there is a further problem to clarify. Until the late 1960s, the Nazi genocide was not included in Israeli history textbooks, while in Europe and the United States it was mentioned only marginally in relation to the Second World War. Very little specific historical work had been undertaken on this subject. The Nazis were indeed perceived by the broad public as criminals, but the particularity of the 'final solution of the Jewish question', just like the extermination of the Roma, was very little known. It was rather the heroism of the Resistance throughout Europe, and the battles of Stalingrad and El Alamein, that held pride of place in historical narratives. As I explained in the previous chapter, it was only when the members of political, intellectual and economic elites that had collaborated with the Nazis, both in Germany and in other parts of Europe, had begun to disappear that European civilization could be defined as 'Judaeo-Christian' and begin to recognize its unconscionable crimes.

Research specifically devoted to the killing of Jews and their descendants, as something completely distinct from the murder of other victims (the Roma, the mentally ill, homosexuals), experienced an upsurge in the 1980s, in parallel with the emergence of negationism. Yet it is important to emphasize that the challenge to the reality of extermination came in no way from any academic historiographical school. One academic, Robert Faurisson, did indeed figure among the avatars of Holocaust denial, but he was a professor of literature rather than of history, and was rapidly forced to resign his post. In Britain, David Irving was an amateur historian with no professional status or intellectual ability to present a proper argument. Ernst Zündel, a Canadian of German origin and head of a publishing house, expressed neo-Nazi ideas. The other Holocaust deniers were still less 'erudite'; their paltry books lack any value, and clearly betray an ideological background of anti-Semitism.[73] For obvious political motives, Holocaust denial found a louder voice in the Islamic and Arab world, for example with the former Iranian president Mahmoud Ahmedinejad, well known for his caricature-like utterances.

To sum up, there was not a single professional historian among those who denied the reality of the extermination of the Jews. This fact, however, did not dissuade a number of scholars from seeing denial of the Shoah both as a new anti-Semitic danger on a world scale, and as a threat to the very existence of the discipline of history. The immediate reaction to the new negationist lies was quite understandable, particularly on the part of those who had directly suffered Nazi persecution and crime;[74] all the same, it was a quite disproportionate exaggeration to attribute the denial of the Shoah to any kind of 'historiographical school'. Government legislative measures, in both Israel and various European countries, only gave greater importance to certain pseudo-scholars and marginal figures, only too happy with the attention paid to them.

---

73   If denial of the Shoah did not give rise to any academic debate, the same was not the case with its relativizing, or with the comparisons made by German historians such as Andreas Hillgruber between the extermination perpetrated by the Nazis and the destruction of the German army by 'Bolshevism' at the end of the war.

74   I have particularly in mind here my friend Pierre Vidal-Naquet, and his important book *Assassins of Memory*, New York: Columbia University Press, 1993.

In 1992, the Israeli historian Saul Friedländer edited a collection of articles under the title *Probing the Limits of Representation*.[75] The majority of its contributors were not specialists in the historical field in question, but well known in intellectual history or philosophy of history. They included Hayden White, Sande Cohen and Dominick LaCapra, invited as heretics in relation to conventional historiography. Ranged against them as staunch opponents were the irreducible champions of objectivism. White's contribution raised particular interest, as he made a surprising retreat from his previous positions. Fearful of providing an alibi for deniers of the Shoah, he abandoned the logic of his own doctrine and explained himself as follows: 'In the case of an emplotment of the events of the Third Reich in a "comic" or "pastoral" mode, we would be eminently justified in appealing to "the facts" in order to dismiss it from the lists of "competing narratives" of the Third Reich.'[76]

White's weak points, in other words his complete neutralization of any moral aspect in the facts, and the absence of implication in relation to ideological positions, now appeared in broad daylight. He did not retract his critique of realist representation in traditional historiography; this was fundamentally plausible and justified. However, he now insisted, certain series of events, regarding mass murder, deadly pandemics, the brutal trade in women and other horrors, even if transcribed in stories, risk being set aside or even expunged from history books; they cannot provide the object of a plot, whether comic or bucolic. In some extreme cases, at least for the civilizations we are familiar with, there are singular facts that already 'speak' to us, arousing suffering, distress or great unease. Even the Nazis, in their mass butcheries, were often embarrassed at their own actions, and sought before carrying out executions to conceal these in various ways

75   Saul Friedländer (ed.), *Probing the Limits of Representation: Nazism and the 'Final Solution'*, Cambridge, MA: Harvard University Press, 1992.

76   Hayden White, 'Historical Emplotment and the Story of Truth', in *Proving the Limits of Representation*, 40.

from their families, and even from their own direct gaze. The petty-bourgeois morality of many of them, with the exception of a few madmen, forced them to brush certain 'facts' under the carpet, to avoid their giving rise to a written narration.

This rule does not just apply to the factual formulations of 'scientific' historiographical narration. It is not possible in literary or cinematic fiction, and still less so in authentic accounts, to present large-scale massacres, or the massive trade in slaves, in a comic or idyllic mode. Anyone who seeks to do so, despite this repulsion, is forced to resort to a tragi-comic form, or one of compassionate irony.

We have seen how, in the field of concepts, the debate between moderns and postmodernists on the subject of the 'final solution' and Nazism reveals its limits. It clearly requires a more precise approach.

Inventing a Myth and Constructing an Ideal Type

The nub of the polemic with deniers of the Shoah bore not on its particular circumstances nor on the coining of the concept, but on factual data: some denied the existence of gas chambers, while others claimed that the Jewish victims were 'only' a few tens of thousands rather than millions. Others again, still more extreme, declared that there was no intention to kill the Jews, and that if some of them perished it was due to disease. As far as the 'bare' series of facts is concerned, the problem is relatively simple: either the evidence collected is all a lie, or it is exact and coherent; and in fact it was not hard to refute the arguments of the negationists – as Pierre Vidal-Naquet elegantly did. Even if no written order from Hitler to exterminate Jews and others has been found, and even if traces of Zyklon B have not been collected from the walls of the gas chambers, there is not the slightest ambiguity as to the testimonies of victims, bystanders and some of the executioners themselves, added to which are the physical remains of the camps, and the demographic data on the people exterminated.[77] The figure of six million may be inexact, but it is clear that more than five million Jews and their descendants did not survive beyond 1945; they were murdered either in the camps or elsewhere.

The most serious question concerns the circumstances in which the new concept was formulated, the features of the political and ideological context in which it appeared, and the modes of its reception. The terms 'Shoah' and 'Holocaust' that are current today, as we saw, were integrated into research and writing not from the actual events, but from cinema and television. As in any conceptualization, these terms separate series of events, introduce differences between groups of people, and effect a distinction between times and places. Thus the Nazis murdered, in the camps and other killing fields, close to eleven million human beings, of whom around half were, in their eyes, Jews. This number can be viewed as a series of events containing a minimal narrative construction.

It is clearly possible, and necessary, to expand from these basic 'facts' to the context of an increasingly complex project of persecution. The Nazi conception of national purification saw the Jews as a threat to the German 'race-people'; they were not alone in posing such a threat, but held pride of place among victims. 'Bolsheviks', Roma, the mentally ill, homosexuals, and even non-'Aryan' Slavs were considered to belong to an inferior race that besieged and stifled the German '*ethnos*'. Extermination, however, has been an inherent element of modern nationalism, and its radical perversion. The dehumanizing of the nation's enemies is present in all nationalism; in National Socialism it simply came to a paroxysm. Yet we should be wary of seeing this ethnocentric conception of the other as the exclusive cause of mass extermination. Several circumstances, including the total

---

77   The opening of the Moscow archives in the 1990s, and particularly the Osoby (special archive), made possible a definite improvement in our knowledge of Nazi massacres.

war embarked on and waged by Germany, need also to be seen as factors that triggered the growing radicalization of the bureaucratic apparatus of crime.

The problem is that 'Shoah' and 'Holocaust' are terms applied only to those whom the Nazis viewed as Jews. The Roma, for example, are excluded from it, despite being included in the Nazi extermination project and murdered en masse. Likewise, Polish intellectuals, for whom the Auschwitz camp had initially been built, and who were its first victims, are left out of this tragic martyrdom. In the same order of ideas, we should remember that Raul Hilberg, the pioneer of Holocaust research and author of an enormous and fundamental work on the destruction of European Jews that is still unequalled, had to wait until 2012 to be translated into Hebrew. This was due, among other things, to the fact that his work focuses on the specific character of the executioners rather than on that of the victims. Besides, the fact that he harshly criticized Jewish collaboration with the organizers of the crime, and viewed the sporadic resistance of the victims as a negligible quantity, displeased the new historians of the Shoah.

The great majority of books, articles and films produced from the 1980s on, especially those designed for the general public (at this point some 123,000 titles), emphasize the Jewish particularity of the victims. They tend to make the 'Shoah-Holocaust' a kind of modern mythology, divorced from its historical context and absolutely different from any other historical conceptualization. Thus the Shoah is no longer a genocide, even one of the most terrible in terms of its scale, in a lineage of other genocides and mass murders; it is a specific ahistorical icon, whose ideological function is a problem in Western culture.[78]

This conceptualization of the extermination of the Jews, in isolation from the mass murders committed against all 'others' at

---

78   Even genuine postmodernists, such as Jean-François Lyotard, also see the Shoah as an act outside the human (an earthquake), which they have no tool for understanding. See Jean-François Lyotard, *The Differend: Phrases in Dispute*, Minneapolis: University of Minnesota Press, 1989, 109.

the same time, may appear legitimate, particularly in relation to its demographic dimension; on condition, however, that its limits are marked and the crime correctly defined. For example, when reference to the figure of six million victims contributes to ignoring that the total number was as high as eleven million, this falls into the trap of a negationism that is to my mind no less serious than that of denying the extermination of the Jews. Conceptualizing the specificity of the Shoah is only acceptable if there is an awareness that this means arranging a series of events into a story that, by being partial, does not fully correspond to the reality of the past. The French Revolution and the Second World War, for example, are also incomplete realizations of a past that is continuously extending. (As far as the French Revolution is concerned, there is still no consensus on the dates of its beginning or end; and the same holds for the start of the Second World War.) Any partitioning of time and space, and any creation of a great historical event, includes a share of ideological arbitrariness, which selects, sorts and organizes the detail of facts, thereby giving them each time a different meaning.

Moreover, the separation of Jews from other victims, and the emphasis on the terrible catastrophe that struck them, has various moral repercussions, which are absorbed into collective memories in different ways. Historical awareness of the extermination of the Jews, and the empathy for them that this aroused, have undeniably contributed to the decline of the strident anti-Judaism that had pervaded Western culture for many centuries; it can be seen as making a significant contribution to the normalization of the situation of Jews in the West. In Israel and among many of its sympathizers, on the other hand, the ideological function of the Shoah has always been quite different. It has had the effect of strengthening among Israelis and many other Jews the perception of being perpetual victims of history, and has equally aroused a deep suspicion towards anything defined as not Jewish. This has legitimized a form of ethnocentric isolationism, and an unrestrained behaviour towards anything perceived as a menace to Jewish identity, however imaginary this might be. Finally, it has also indirectly provided a justification for the hideous policy practised towards the Palestinians, and prevented an understanding that history is an arena in which the roles of victim and executioner are often exchanged.

In every case, if conceptualization and inclusion in the historic past are not presented as constructions issuing from research – in other words, as abstract expressions – they necessarily become mythological inventions in the service of ideological needs and specific policies, whether consciously or otherwise.

Once more it should be stressed that every conceptualization makes different plots possible, and that every narrative is ipso facto an interpretation that connects differently not only a beginning and an end, but also a cause and an effect. To situate the massive Nazi extermination against the background of modern imperialism, as for example Hannah Arendt did, is a different conceptualization from that which sees in the Shoah an immanent and determinist continuity of the traditional anti-Judaism of Christian Europe. To integrate the Shoah into the chain of mass crimes perpetrated from 1933 to 1945 in the space between the Volga and the Rhine, as Timothy Snyder does in his book *Bloodlands*,[79] gives a different sequencing, and accordingly a different version of the tragedy. This book has indeed aroused a certain unease among the majority of historians of the Shoah.

The use of the term 'myth' in relation to historical conceptualization, as I myself have done here, also deserves clarification, as it lies at the centre of a problematic that is troubling the guild of historians in the early twenty-first century. In the previous chapter, I put forward the argument that the best historical works published in the nineteenth and early twentieth centuries can be described as modern mythologies, which contributed to the building of various nations. Writers of history were persuaded

---

79 Timothy Snyder, *Bloodlands: Europe Between Hitler and Stalin*, New York: Basic Books, 2012.

that they told the truth about the past. They viewed their discipline as a science, their institutions as laboratories, and, carried away by overweening self-assurance, transmitted their 'realist' writings to whole generations of students at all levels.

All historical writing that is not aware that the actions and plots related do not coincide with past reality is potentially the bearer of a mythological dimension. It may well be a serious narrative full of references and quotations, distinguished by its 'exactness' and abstaining from any polemic, yet it remains nonetheless that this belief of the author, whether naive or not, associates him or her with many propagators of mythistory who continue to swell the ranks of the discipline today. A living myth is not a lie; it is a story about the past or the future whose veracity cannot be established in a rational manner, yet that no one can imagine rejecting. It remains valid, in the eyes of believers, until heretics succeed in refuting it. Even in this case, however, the belief is not necessarily shaken; myths, in fact, tend to preserve themselves as long as they are needed, or else until other myths come along to replace them. In history, all societies need myths to ensure their coherence and preserve their collective identity, in particular that of the elites that revolve around the sovereign power. Modernity has not changed this stubborn phenomenon; it has rather expanded it, by communicating it to greater masses.

In the late twentieth century, postmodern awareness of the illusion of any objectivity in the transcription of the past seriously shook the profession's conventions, just as the sharpshooter Nietzsche had dreamed of doing a century earlier. Yet however brilliant writers like Nietzsche and Barthes were, realizing that language is never in a position to indicate with certainty what is external to it, they could not propose, and clearly did not want to propose, a theoretical alternative to the traditional representation of the past. Later postmodernists also did not succeed in this, even if they formulated, as we have seen, a certain number of attractive and stimulating propositions. In fact, postmodernism is far more an expression of the crisis of the historiographical profession than it is its solution. The question it leaves in suspense is as follows: is it possible to seriously write a history that would not claim to be realistic and veridical? Can we think the past while escaping the mythological functions that have inspired the profession?

The postulates of Max Weber and Georges Sorel may help in finding the beginnings of a response. Both of these, in the wake of Nietzsche's sceptical work, were among the first to propose a change to the objectivist approach of professional historians. Contrary to the heretical philosopher, they did not reject the possibility of managing by way of words to say something about the profusion of reality, but they never believed in the ability to present this in its complex totality. Each element of boundless reality bears within it a totality impossible to decompose, which will never be transparent to the gaze of the observer. All research is a disentangling and a subjective sorting which leads to an abstract reconstruction.

Both of these thinkers, at almost the same time in the early twentieth century, arrived at similar, though not identical, conclusions. For Weber, history remained a science, but one that, in the best German hermeneutic tradition, was radically distinct from the natural sciences. According to Sorel, who was one of the very first critics of positivism in France, the 'human' disciplines lacked any scientific basis in the customary sense of the term. Weber subsumed his theoretical proposal under the notion of 'ideal type' (*Idealtypus*), while Sorel defined his approach by speaking of 'diremption' (which should be understood as 'break' or 'rift'). Weber reached his conclusions from a basis in the Kantian tradition, according to which 'the thing-in-itself' (*das Ding an sich*) cannot be identified by our cognitive faculties. Sorel, a qualified engineer from the École polytechnique, and inspired by his scientific meticulousness to describe the beliefs of the proletariat empathically as 'myths', perceived very well that conceptualization in the field of social research is totally different from scientific knowledge of the laws of nature.

Weber did not write any particular text on the 'ideal type'. This idea occurs scattered in several essays, from 1904 to the eve of his death, each time with new precisions. The following quotation marks one of the first times that Weber defined the process:

'An ideal type is formed by the one-sided *accentuation* of one or more points of view and by the synthesis of a great many diffuse, discrete, more or less present and occasionally absent *concrete individual* phenomena, which are arranged according to those one-sidedly emphasized viewpoints into a unified *analytical* construct [*Gedankenbild*].[80]

The ideal type, therefore, is not a moral construction but rather the intellectual abstraction of aspects of reality, which in no case coincides with anything concrete. This key concept is specific to social research, and applicable neither to the natural sciences nor to any other exact science. Weber introduced this conceptual tool for the first time in order to characterize and analyse histori-cal phenomena in the field of political economy. He explicitly says that he sees the laws proposed by Marx as a kind of ideal type par excellence.[81] He equally applied this method in his famous essay *The Protestant Ethic and the Spirit of Capitalism*, which is not a regular book of objectivist history, and does not claim to relate what happened. It offers a set of hypotheses about socioeconomic processes without always seeking to pin down the bonds of causality between them, or indicating every time their initial origin.[82]

---

80   Weber's first clarifications of this subject appear in *Die Objektivität sozialwissenschaftlicher und sozial politischer Erkenntnis* (1904). See Max Weber, '"Objectivity" in Social Science and Social Policy', *Methodology of Social Science*, Piscataway, NJ: Transaction, 2011, 90; original italics.

81   Ibid., 103.

82   A detailed explanation of Weber's methodology is given by Susan J. Hekman, *Weber: The Ideal Type and Contemporary Social Theory*, Notre Dame, IN: University of Notre Dame Press, 1983.

Sorel, who was unfamiliar with Weber's work, reached similar conclusions. In the vigorous controversy over Marxism at the turn of the century, he rejected the possibility of discovering laws in society parallel to the laws of nature, and maintained, before Weber, that Marx's political economy is actually a kind of ideal system. In *Reflections on Violence*, Sorel modified his terminology without changing his theoretical approach:

> Social philosophy is obliged, in order to study the most signif-icant phenomena of history, to proceed to a diremption, to examine certain parts without taking into account all of the ties which connect them to the whole, to determine in some manner the character of their activity by isolating them. When it has thus arrived at the most perfect understanding, it can no longer attempt to reconstitute the broken unity.[83]

Sorel would spell out this position more than once, maintaining that this analytic approach was characteristic of several writers who were not aware of proceeding in this way; even though awareness of it gives rise to a truer account when dealing with social research and history.[84] His essay *Reflections on Violence* may be seen as a productive application of this approach. In it Sorel depicts the conflict between social classes as fuelled by a mythical consciousness, leaving aside the legal and economic aspects of the phenomenon.

The paths taken by Weber and Sorel are not free of contradic-tion. They did not bequeath any vade mecum for applying their respective methods, which, aside from a general principle of orientation, require a certain originality each time they are actu-ally applied. In the fluid totality of reality, what are the

---

83   Georges Sorel, *Reflections on Violence*, Cambridge: Cambridge University Press, 1999, 259, also 262–4.

84   See, for example, 'Materials for a Theory of the Proletariat', in *From Georges Sorel: Essays in Socialism and Philosophy*, Oxford: Oxford University Press, 1976, 217–56.

significant elements to extract and pin down? How can we know what narrative technique to use, in order to distil an acceptable synthesis on the basis of the mass of discoveries? And, still more important, what is it that makes one particular construction better and more trustworthy than another?

Neither Weber's ideal type not Sorel's 'diremption' can be more than uncertain postulates to consider before embarking on a particular path of reflection, for those (including many post-modernists) who are not full-blown Nietzscheans. Certain models can spur us to make an effort to write a more 'humble' or less pretentious history. They can also help us produce a history conscious of the share of arbitrariness that it contains, and of the potential for mythology that it is susceptible to producing and spreading.

I tend to think that critical and reflexive accounts in a genre that is not widespread but has been proposed by Ankersmit and Berkhofer, accounts that dare to pass everything through a sieve of doubt, that are explicit about their own limitations right from the phase of revealing facts, and combine this with political transparency and a public declaration of ideological sensibilities, are the necessary condition for a more reliable history. This does not mean, however, that we shall ever succeed in writing the truth about the past. It is impossible to go on acting as if history were a science. Such pretention is totally incompatible with a serious epistemology of research.

Nonetheless, relative and partial truths, which give rise to new contradictions and will in their turn meet with challenge and supersession, genuinely find a place on the route map of the historian who breaks with tradition.

However, the question will still be posed: who really needs a historiography of this kind? In schools throughout the world, history is taught neither simply to satisfy an intellectual curiosity nor out of a pure love of research. It has never been confined simply to the field of academic erudition, increasing human knowledge quite impartially. It has always been, and is still, a pedagogical giant whose arms embrace every place of education in all the nation-states formed across the world over the last two hundred years. During this time, history has told almost all human beings, whose lives have been rudely shaken by modernity, where they come from, who they are, and where they are going. The relationship between history and the construction of imaginary collective identities appears the rationale for the birth and rising power of historiography, once this became a serious profession.

In the twenty-first century, does the state still need this kind of history, these super-narratives that enroll the past in order to build and stabilize a national present? It is more than probable that the transmission of a unifying national culture varies from one country to another. It is also very likely that it presents itself differently in the Western world than it does in other cultures that experienced a later nationalization of the masses. However, as I mentioned earlier in this chapter, the mobilizing charge of national pedagogic disciplines is on the decline in a growing number of places, and it does not look as if the breaches that have appeared in historic metanarratives can be filled. With the process of cultural and economic globalization restraining the capacity to imagine national (and even social) projects oriented to the future, will the past continue to fulfil the historical function that it has served until now? Will the past remain at all relevant in a world deprived of any impulse of utopian imagination?

It is hard to answer these questions with any degree of certainty. In the Talmudic tradition it is said that, after the destruction of the Second Temple, only fools still turn to prophecy. We are all now aware not only of the theoretical difficulties of the historical discipline, many of which have been presented in this book, but also of the pedagogic difficulties at different levels in the study of the past. The reasons for studying history in secondary education, rather than anthropology, economics or philosophy, for example, are in the process of losing their historical and political justification. We may even imagine a future situation in which history is stripped of its pedagogical role and becomes an academic discipline more like its colleagues in other fields of the humanities.

In parallel with this, we may suppose that popular history books will continue to be written, full of picturesque plots, fascinating characters or tragedies, as found in other fields of mass culture (the majority of historical novels already show signs of a development in this direction). In the same way, states, despite the relative weakening of their apparatus in the face of international corporate power, are not yet disposed to abandon the days of memory and commemorations that continue to glorify the logic of their existence; the decline in their real power has not affected their ostentatious national pose, which in no way needs a scholarly history. Religious traditions of the distant past are there to confirm this.

Clio, the ageing muse of history, seems today to be fading into the twilight. She may have tried to escape a long and painful death, yet she is well aware today that her future depends especially on her faculty to renew the boundaries between fields of research, as well as on the nature of the explanations and commentaries that this proposes. History's lack of ability to produce grand narratives, as theology and national historiography used to do, now serves it ill; but it cannot be ruled out that the future may bring new identity politics that need and solicit supra-narratives as yet unknown to us.

Even if her future is shrouded in mist, we may still hope that, despite her fatigue, Clio will continue to tell magnificent stories about human acts, without forgetting either to remind us that these are also accompanied by cruelty and terrible tragedy. And above all: she must persevere and try to explain to us, despite the insufficiencies of language, why on earth all this happened!

N.B.

In the late 1980s, when a 'post-Zionist' tendency arose in Israel, sociologists, political scientists, philosophers, geographers, linguists, writers and journalists all played their part, but there was not a single professional historian from a department of general history.[85] Along with my colleagues, 'non-national' historians, we remained spectators and witnessed the verbal battles without intervening. After all, the subjects of the polemic did not pertain to our fields of specialization, and such intervention would not have been professional. The 'scientific' division of labour proved its utility.

The Israeli media equated post-Zionism with postmodernism. The doubts about national aims, and the relativist scepticism about historical research itself, seemed to be closely imbricated. In fact, not all post-Zionists were postmodernists, and it is clear enough that not all postmodernists expressed critical post-Zionist ideas; but it is true that the two tendencies coincided in a number of linguists, literary critics, even political scientists.

The Israeli intellectual scene experienced this ferment for only a short period, before and a short while after the Oslo agreements, but then it calmed down and stepped back in line when the second Intifada broke out. The national bolts were screwed down, and the convoy of colonists stubbornly continued its eastward march, towards the rising sun. The myth of the land and its colonization proved stronger than any political rationality, let alone universal moral principles. Zionist historiography, which retrospectively invented a Jewish national ethnos, supposedly 'exiled' from its ancient homeland and 'returning' there after two thousand years, was no longer capable of modifying its supranarrative: the land of Israel (*Eretz Israel*) belongs to the Jewish people; Jerusalem, Bethlehem and Hebron are the country's

---

85   See the chapter 'Post-Zionism: A Historical or Intellectual Debate?', in my book *The Words and the Land*, 155–180..

heart, and not Tel Aviv, Haifa or Netanya. A section of left
Zionist historians felt a certain unease in the face of the repression of the indigenous population and the denial of its rights,
but they lacked the strength to start deconstructing the ideology
that they had themselves maintained for decades. The resistance
of the oppressed population and its violent uprisings only reinforced the pedagogical and mythological dogmas: professional
history remained an irreplaceable support for self-justification
and the preservation of a stable national consciousness.

There is a well-known Yiddish joke which tells how, in an East
European shtetl, a young genius was noted for his extraordinary
knowledge of the Talmud. He knew many pages by heart, and
did not omit a single comma when it was a matter of explaining
the law. People accordingly asked him if he was not preparing to
become a rabbi. The young man replied that he was indeed an
expert in all Jewish writings and could teach them perfectly well;
but there was one thing, he said, that he was unable to do: teach
the Torah and Talmud without constantly bursting out in
laughter.

I have long been aware that I am far from being a genius; that
is why I studied history, rather than philosophy or physics. I did,
however, dream at one point of teaching the Jewish, Zionist and
Israeli past in parallel with my lectures on European history.
However, I would never have been allowed to do so, for a very
simple reason: that given the conceptualizations, research works
and teaching methods of present-day Israel, I could not have
embarked on this without laughing out loud, and perhaps also
shedding a tear.

Index